To Constitute a Nation

A Cultural History of
Australia's Constitution

Helen Irving
University of Technology, Sydney

CAMBRIDGE UNIVERSITY PRESS
Cambridge, New York, Melbourne, Madrid, Cape Town,
Singapore, São Paulo, Delhi, Mexico City

Cambridge University Press
The Edinburgh Building, Cambridge CB2 8RU, UK

Published in the United States of America by Cambridge University Press, New York

www.cambridge.org
Information on this title: www.cambridge.org/9780521668972

© Helen Irving 1999

This publication is in copyright. Subject to statutory exception
and to the provisions of relevant collective licensing agreements,
no reproduction of any part may take place without the written
permission of Cambridge University Press.

First published 1997
First paperback edition 1999

A catalogue record for this book is available from the British Library

National Library of Australia Cataloguing in Publication Data
Irving, Helen.
To constitute a nation: a cultural history of Australia's
constitution.
Bibliography.
Includes index.
ISBN 0 521 66897 2 (pbk.).
1. Political culture – Australia – History. 2.
Constitutional history – Australia. 3. National
characteristics, Australian. 4. Australia – Politics and
government. I. Title.
306.20994

ISBN 978-0-521-58417-3 Hardback
ISBN 978-0-521-66897-2 Paperback

Cambridge University Press has no responsibility for the persistence or
accuracy of URLs for external or third-party internet websites referred to in
this publication, and does not guarantee that any content on such websites is,
or will remain, accurate or appropriate. Information regarding prices, travel
timetables, and other factual information given in this work is correct at
the time of first printing but Cambridge University Press does not guarantee
the accuracy of such information thereafter.

This book is dedicated to the memory of my brother,
Francis Irving, 1952–1973.

Contents

Preface	ix
Acknowledgements	xi
Chronology	xii
Introduction	1
1 Colonial Nuptials	6
2 The Imaginary Nation	25
3 Imagined Constitutions	46
4 Models For a Nation	62
5 Things Properly Federal	79
6 White Australians	100
7 Australian Natives	119
8 The People	134
9 Citizens	156
10 Half the Nation	171
11 The Federal Compact	196
Conclusion	212
Epilogue	216
Appendix: Key Sections of the Constitution	220
Notes	224
Select Bibliography	244
Index	253

Preface

This is a book which, among other things, talks about what was 'typical' in Australian life at the end of the nineteenth century, and about 'characteristic' Australian ways of doing things. These very terms, even before the claims they make are addressed, are bound to raise eyebrows. For many reasons, often entirely valid, historians and political scientists have for some time avoided any such generalisations about the features of Australian life. It has been felt by many that claims about what is typical privilege the (already privileged) dominant groups in society; that minority ways of doing things are marginalised and that difference is denied.

While I have tried to acknowledge, as far as possible, the range of responses and experiences of different groups in the decades leading up to Federation, I am none the less convinced that there was a shared political culture, one in which a typical way of doing things was both expressed and recognised. Political institutions do not arise from nowhere, and the fact that these are different from nation to nation is significant. The central thesis of this book is that the Australian Constitution was a product of a particularly Australian political culture. I have approached that culture as an anthropologist might, attempting to make sense of the whole, trying to see the forest in spite of the trees. I have depicted the Constitution as a 'vernacular' Constitution, as a local product, typical of a particular culture and region, an artefact of its time.

Studies of political culture in Australia have tended to concentrate on what is current, on the ideas and values of the existing population, gathering their data chiefly by asking people questions. A historical study demands a different approach and an alternative methodology, especially once all its subjects are beyond the interviewer's reach, as is now the case with Federation. What other sources are available, then; which are most useful for understanding the political culture of the past?

I have tried to cast my net as wide as possible, the guiding principle being the type of source in which the personal values of the participants are most likely to be expressed. It is rare for diaries to focus on political events, and there are indeed very few from the Federation period that do this, but individual political statements such as letters to the press and petitions are very revealing of the intersection between public issues and personal views. I have also leaned a lot on public speeches, on informal records of meetings and on newspaper commentary generally. And I have tried to integrate all this with the more formal records of debates, although focusing again on the exchange of views prior to a decision, more than the record of the concluded decision as such. Because this is an attempt to reconstruct the dominant political culture of the end of the nineteenth century, I have avoided lengthy discussion of existing secondary works, or detailed engagement with alternative interpretive models, and have worked as far as possible directly with primary sources.

This is also a book that treats Federation as a success story. That is not to say that I am uncritical of either the design or the results of the particular constitutional settlement Australians reached in 1901. It means, rather, that I have told the story of the Federalists more than that of their opponents, and of the positive hopes and expectations attached to Federation more than the fears, not only because by the end of the 1890s these were the majority, but because this is a history of what happened, rather than what might or should have happened. My aim is not for readers to close the last page having acquired a great fondness for the Constitution (although I hope they will have an enhanced appreciation of the immense difficulties involved in writing even an inadequate constitution); it is rather that they should have a greater understanding of what people, including ordinary people, believed they were doing in taking part in a movement to unite six mutually suspicious colonies into one nation.

When historians look back, as they will do, on the movement to create an Australian republic (perhaps also as its centenary approaches simultaneously with the twenty-second century), they will see many things, including many flaws in the way this was done. But it is to be hoped that they too will attempt to understand what Australians are trying to do in the 1990s, what it is they hope and imagine will come from a republic.

Although other external factors, particularly economic and technological ones, may in the last instance drive history forward, at each moment, nevertheless, the people who live through it are also trying to make history, if only in their imaginations. Australians cannot understand what they are trying to do now unless they understand what was imagined in the creation of the institutions they wish to reform. This is one 'naive' historian's attempt to contribute to that understanding.

This paperback reprint has given me the opportunity to add an Epilogue on the Constitution at the end of the twentieth century, and to make some corrections to the original text. I am very grateful to John Bannon for helping spot where these were needed.

Acknowledgements

I have accumulated many debts in writing this book. Among the people to whom I owe a great deal four deserve special mention: Michael Coper, whose wonderful and idiosyncratic work on the Australian Constitution inspired my interest in the first place; Ann Curthoys, who suggested that I should turn my interest into research and then supported that research in many ways; Tessa Milne, whose assistance and enthusiasm kept the whole thing going; and Donald Horne, who encouraged me to keep talking and who tirelessly offered advice and inspiration.

Rachel Grahame and Anna Cole also worked splendidly on the project at different stages and Dorothy Irving did some urgent research in Melbourne. I am enormously grateful for their support.

Enno Hermann and David Chang did the translations from the Australian German- and Chinese-language papers.

Many people have very generously shared their ideas with me: John Bannon, Sue Castrique, John Docker, Estelle Farrar, John Fisher, David Headon, Emma Grahame, Catriona Moore, Cheryl Saunders, and James Warden. Richard Phillipps and Narelle Bell advised me early on to speak with those who draft legislation, so that I would have some understanding of the task faced by the Constitution's framers. This led to an invaluable discussion with Michael Orpwood, New South Wales Deputy Parliamentary Counsel, and to my ongoing admiration for the skill and imagination involved in writing law.

I am also grateful to the anonymous readers at Cambridge University Press, who made many helpful suggestions which I have attempted to integrate into the final draft.

My husband, Stephen Gaukroger, and friends, in particular Lisa Lentini, Michael Shortland, and Janene Porter, have helped me in other, equally important ways. Cressida and Hugh Gaukroger have been, in every way, at the centre of it all.

This work was generously supported by Internal Research Grants from the University of Technology, Sydney, an Australian Research Council Large Grant, and a period as Research Affiliate in the Research School of Social Sciences at the Australian National University.

Chronology (1880–1903)

1881 Henry Parkes proposes Federal Council at Intercolonial Conference, Sydney.

1883 Queensland Government attempts to forestall German annexation of New Guinea by claiming the territory for Britain.
Colonial Premiers agree to establish Federal Council.
Sydney–Melbourne railway opened.

1885 Federal Council of Australasia Act passed by Imperial Parliament.

1887 Queen Victoria's Golden Jubilee.
First Colonial Conference, London.

1888 Intercolonial Chinese Conference, Sydney.

1889 Railway link from South Australia to Queensland completed.
Major-General James Bevan Edwards reports on the state of defence of the Australian colonies.
Henry Parkes's 'Tenterfield Oration'.

1890 Australasian Federation Conference (Federation Conference), Melbourne.
Western Australia gains self-government.

1891 National Australasian Convention (Federal Convention), Sydney. First draft Constitution completed.

1892 Depression hits.

1893 Australasian Federation League formed.
Corowa Conference.

1894 Women's suffrage in South Australia.

1895 Premiers' Conference, Hobart.
Federal Council of Australasia meeting, Hobart.

1896 Death of Henry Parkes.
Intercolonial Conference agrees to extend coloured immigration restriction.
Bathurst People's Federal Convention.

1897	First session, National Australasian Convention (Federal Convention), Adelaide, March–April.
	Queen Victoria's Diamond Jubilee.
	Second session, National Australasian Convention (Federal Convention), Sydney, September.
1898	Third session, National Australasian Convention (Federal Convention), Melbourne, January–March.
	First Sydney Women's Federal League formed.
	June: Referendum on Constitution Bill successful in Victoria, South Australia, Tasmania, defeated in New South Wales.
1899	January: 'Secret' Premiers' Conference.
	Women's Federal League formed in Hay and second Sydney Women's Federal League formed.
	Successful referendums on amended Constitution Bill held in all colonies except Western Australia.
	Women's suffrage in Western Australia.
1900	9 July: Constitution Bill signed by Queen Victoria.
	31 July: Successful West Australian referendum.
	17 September: Commonwealth of Australia proclaimed.
1901	1 January: Inauguration of Commonwealth.
	Death of Queen Victoria.
	March: First Federal election.
	9 May: Opening of first Commonwealth Parliament.
	Passage of 'White Australia' Immigration Restriction Act.
1902	Commonwealth Franchise Act.
1903	High Court of Australia opened.

Introduction

All stories can be told in different ways. This is no less true for history than it is for fiction. The making of the Australian Commonwealth through the Federation of the Australian colonies is a story rich with alternative versions and different perspectives. It could be told with a focus solely on the formal processes of writing the Constitution, or concentrate on the popular involvement in Federation. It could stress economic arrangements, or imperial relations, or ask which particular interests were served by Federation. Each of the states has its own story too, as well as sharing in a common national history.

There are cultural, social, economic, technological and political tales to tell. All of these alternatives have their own important history. But this book is written with the conviction that none operated in isolation, that there was not a single cause of Federation, that the tales must be told together. It tries to understand the way the processes worked together at a particular time, creating a unique matrix, a distinctive political culture at the end of the nineteenth century out of which the Commonwealth could be imagined as a reality and then shaped.

The cultural side of the story has scarcely been told. There are accounts of the Constitution's writing, of the Federation movement, of individual states and of different political groups.[1] There are, in addition, studies of other things that happened in the Federation decades: the emergence of the Labor Party; the evolution of Australian literature and art; the activities of women; and the culture of the imagination.[2] The challenge has been to locate Federation within these movements, to make it a living part of people's lives and the cultural forces that shaped them, to see it as having a meaning that is more than simply instrumental.

There are also several 'orthodox' historical accounts of the Federation story, most of which appear in larger general histories of Australia.[3] These histories are mostly written around the events whose record can be found in official publications, in the records of the constitutional Conventions, in minute books and in parliamentary debates. While it is the

2   To Constitute a Nation

central thesis of this book that such records do not tell the whole story, it is important nevertheless to be familiar with their history, to know the main, formal events and their progression.

The idea of joining the unwieldy Australian colonies together had been in the minds of officials for many decades before 1901 when Federation was achieved, even before the division of the colonies into the familiar areas of land that have since remained almost unchanged (with only the Northern Territory separating from South Australia in 1911) and which shaped the states of the Commonwealth after 1901. In the decade before the separation of Victoria (1851) and Queensland (1859) from New South Wales, which completed the colonial mapping of the nineteenth century, the federal 'idea was already in the air'.[4]

Earl Grey, Britain's Colonial Secretary, took the first formal initiative in this direction, sketching among other things, in 1847, the idea of a General Assembly to act as a central authority within Australia itself. In doing so, he made a list of what he considered to be the common concerns and interests of all the colonies over which the Assembly might have jurisdiction: customs duties, postal services, roads and railways. This might seem an unobjectionable, even modest undertaking, but the colonists themselves reacted with outrage at Grey's lack of consultation in devising his plan. Only a year later, however, William Wentworth, while still protesting, moved a motion in the New South Wales Parliament in which he commended the idea of a General Assembly. But this too led to dispute, this time over the dominance of New South Wales in any such scheme, and both Grey's and Wentworth's proposals came to nothing.

Over the following decades, federal schemes appeared with regularity. Those coming from the British authorities were particularly concerned with solving the problem caused by the regime of varying import tariffs in the colonies. Home-grown schemes (such as the Federal Assembly proposed by Edward Deas Thomson in New South Wales in 1856) tended to embrace a broader range of federal concerns, including land management, postal services, lighthouses, and intercolonial railways and telegraphs. Select committees were formed in several colonies on the question and conferences proposed.

At an Intercolonial Conference, in 1867, discussion indeed got so far as to resolve that there should be a Federal Council, with powers over ocean mail subsidies. Henry Parkes, at that stage Colonial Secretary in the New South Wales Government, characteristically saw the matter in visionary terms, and spoke prophetically of 'a new constellation in the heavens, and the footprints of six young giants [the colonies] in the morning dew'. But the young giants still preferred their own patches to the common plot of 'morning dew'.

While, as one federal scheme succeeded another, almost everyone agreed in principle that some sort of union was a good idea (and most accepted that tariffs, postal and telegraphic services, transport and immigration, if nothing else, were matters of common concern), each successive proposal failed. British schemes invariably came up against Australian protests over failure to consult; proposals from New South Wales (which produced the majority) irritated the other colonies because New South Wales always seemed to allocate itself the pre-eminent place in its scheme. Victorian schemes were rejected by New South Wales because these did not sufficiently recognise that colony's pre-eminence. And so it went on.

At yet another conference on the tariff question, in 1881, Henry Parkes, by then New South Wales Premier, repeated his trade-mark theme that 'the time is now come'. A federal authority, he argued, would be the preparation for a full Federation; a Federal Council, with limited powers to legislate on matters of common concern, would do the job. For many reasons, explored throughout this book, the 1880s would prove the turning point at which the 'federal idea' (found in all the schemes of the previous forty years) would be transformed into the Federation movement.

Two years later, with Henry Parkes out of office and out of the country, a further Intercolonial Conference actually committed itself to creating such a body: it would be called the Federal Council of Australasia. Its members were to include New Zealand and Fiji, as well as the six Australian colonies. The Victorian and New South Wales representatives at the Conference fought with each other and accused each other of wanting to dominate but, astonishingly, this time the proposal proceeded. It was, we may note in anticipation of later argument, the same year the railway line was joined (albeit on different gauges) all the way from Sydney to Melbourne, and Britain shrugged its shoulders at the Australians' alarm over German designs upon New Guinea.

The Federal Council of Australasia Act was passed by the Imperial (that is, the British) Parliament in August 1885, and thereafter a body existed which, in theory, would permit all the colonies to confer every two years and to 'legislate' on all those 'matters of common Australasian interest, in respect to which united action is desirable, as can be dealt with without unduly interfering with the management of the internal affairs of the several colonies by their respective legislatures'.[5]

Four years later, Premier again, Henry Parkes failed to support the Federal Council, but found once more that the time had come for Federation, when a British War Office examination of the Australian colonies' defence capability in 1889 concluded with a highly critical report. Parkes met with the New South Wales Governor, Lord Carrington,

4   *To Constitute a Nation*

and immediately took up his challenge to 'federate the colonies'. Returning from a Queensland meeting, Parkes spoke to a gathering in one of his former electorates, just across the New South Wales border. There, in what has become known as the 'Tenterfield Oration', Parkes pressed the urgency of the defence question and the desirability of holding a convention to devise a federal constitution. Then he wrote to the other Premiers and proposed such a meeting.

The meeting took place in Melbourne in 1890 and it was followed by a full National Australasian Convention in Sydney the following year. There, the first complete draft Bill for an Australian Constitution was written and adopted, and the Convention concluded with a commitment on the part of its representatives to put the Bill before their respective parliaments without delay.

Only Victoria, however, went any distance towards following the plan. As had happened many times before, with changes of government and in addition now with considerable change of fortune brought about by the severe Depression, inaction followed. The Bill was 'put by'.[6] It was six years before the second formal Convention would meet, this time over three sessions, in Adelaide and Sydney in 1897 and concluding in Melbourne in 1898.

But much had happened in the meantime. Federation Leagues had been established in the majority of colonies to promote the cause. In New South Wales, branches of these Leagues organised what were to become important meetings in the Federation story: one in Corowa in 1893, and a People's Federal Convention in Bathurst in 1896.

In between, while all the while the Federal Council continued to meet, a Premiers' Conference was held in Hobart in January 1895. There the procedure to set in train a new Convention was agreed to, leading to the popular election in early 1897 of ten delegates in each of four colonies (with the West Australian Parliament choosing its delegates, and Queensland remaining unrepresented). These fifty men then met on 22 March that year and, during sessions lasting several weeks at a time, up to 17 March 1898, they debated and conferred and drafted, and finally came up with a new Constitution for the Commonwealth of Australia.

In the form of a Bill for an Act of Parliament, the Constitution was then submitted to the voters in four colonies in mid-1898, where it received approval in all but New South Wales. Then, following what its critics called the 'Secret' Premiers' Conference, held in January 1899, certain modifications were made to the Bill, and it was put again to a referendum (this time with Queensland joining in) and passed.

The Australians had now completed their task of constitution writing, and the means of federating the colonies had been determined. It took one more step to activate the process. Unlike in America, where independence had been achieved by declaration, followed by war, the Australian colonies pursued the alternative means of parliamentary enactment. A small delegation of colonial politicians took the Constitution Bill, completed and approved, to London in early 1900, and there, after a struggle with the Colonial Secretary over several provisions, they saw the Bill pass through the Imperial Parliament, and receive the signature of the Head of State, Queen Victoria.

The West Australians acted at last, and held their referendum almost immediately, on 31 July. Its preparatory legal processes completed, the Commonwealth of Australia was proclaimed on 17 September, and inaugurated on 1 January 1901. But if good luck is best assured by 'breaking a leg', the Commonwealth was favoured in the weeks before, with a small hitch provided by its newly appointed Governor-General, Lord Hopetoun. It was Hopetoun's job to nominate the first prime minister, who would hold office, briefly, until the infrastructure existed for the first Commonwealth elections.

Hopetoun chose the wrong man. In what has become famous as the 'Hopetoun Blunder',[7] he picked William Lyne, the recently elected New South Wales Premier and prominent 'anti-Billite' (as opponents of Federation under the 1898/1899 Constitution Bill were called), thereby almost causing a mutiny among those colonial leaders who expected to serve in the interim Cabinet. But Lyne gave way and, acting this time on proper advice (one assumes), Hopetoun nominated the popular choice, Edmund Barton, the former New South Wales politician who had assumed the role of Federalist leader and acted as both spokesman and statesman of the movement for almost the entire preceding decade. With Barton in his rightful place, the Commonwealth Inauguration took place on the first day of the new year, the first day of the new century.

If the history of Federation seems thus to have progressed in a smooth, lineal direction, one process unfolding after another, it is because the processes are now finished and the story can be told that way. But it has to be borne in mind that a very great deal more than this happened and might have happened, that the processes were often complex and confused, that no one knew for certain at the conclusion of one meeting whether the following step to which they had committed themselves would in fact be taken.

These formal political steps are the skeleton of the larger, lived movement. In the chapters that follow, the flesh is put back, given shape, and ultimately clothed in—it is hoped—what comes as close as possible to the style of the day.

CHAPTER ONE

Colonial Nuptials

On 1 January 1901, in Sydney, New South Wales, an event which was both a beginning and an end took place. The Australian Commonwealth was inaugurated, launched like a great machine, with the flick of a switch. Australia's Constitution started up, turning slowly, indeed almost inaudibly at first, then whirring more efficiently as the months and the years went by. Shaping the relations of the political units of the nation, touching the very routines of daily lives (although most people, after a short while, no longer recognised this), it has continued in motion from that moment to the present where its noise has grown increasingly loud as its centenary of service approaches.

Technically, what the Inauguration of the Commonwealth did was join what had been the Australian colonies into a Federation. A Federation is a political entity with both a central parliament, which is able to exercise limited (and specified) powers across the whole nation, and individual regional (state) parliaments exercising the rest of the powers over their own territories. But the Inauguration was much more than this.

It was a rite of passage performed on that January day, a threshold moment where the usual and the habitual stand still, and the transition from one state of existence to another is marked. Rituals of separation and reincorporation, of symbolic death and rebirth take place on such occasions: baptisms, coming-of-age ceremonies, weddings, funerals. One historian, Gavin Souter, has described the events in Sydney on 1 January 1901 as an 'initiation', like the real tribal initiation that took place during the weeks between the Inauguration and the opening of the first Federal Parliament in Melbourne on 9 May 1901. The Aranda coming-of-age ceremony in Central Australia (witnessed in April that year by anthropologists, Walter Spencer and Francis Gillen) and the initiation of Australia were, Souter says, much like each other: 'a succession of shock-absorbing, status-confirming rites . . . associated with many totems'.[1] The analogy is a powerful reminder of the tribal nature of white society, of the existence of mutually uncomprehending worlds within the same territory, of the fragile links between them and of the power of social ritual.

But a different analogy works best to convey the atmosphere of the Inauguration and to capture its ambiguous nature. While the occasion was in many ways a coming-of-age, and the people at the time often spoke of Australia as the boy growing to manhood, or the daughter leaving her maternal home, this was not the main character of the ceremonial transformation on 1 January 1901. It was, in essence, a different type of ritual: more a marriage than an initiation.

A marriage, as distinct from a coming-of-age, is not a simple transformation, nor does it progress in a single, linear direction. Thus it was with the new nation. To begin with, there were several parties to the event, several 'sons' and 'daughters', already legally grown. Literally speaking, the colonies gained no greater legal independence, or adulthood, in federating than they would separately have achieved had they continued (as New Zealand did) with their own parliamentary systems. Full independence, or nation-statehood, came slowly to Australia, step by step (like real adulthood) over the decades to follow. But *nationhood*—the assumption of domestic independence, of cultural distinctiveness and of political and cultural 'destiny'—was achieved, if tentatively, and celebrated in the moment of federating. The six new states of the Commonwealth, legally but not yet socially mature, had decided to set up home together. On those ceremonial days throughout the first five months of the century, the decision was declared, reaffirmed and celebrated.

Federation was a matter of cementing alliances, 'entering the bonds of permanent matrimony', as future Prime Minister Alfred Deakin said in 1895.[2] Again and again, especially in the last years of the decade, the image of marriage was evoked, sometimes to reinforce the appeal of Federation, but just as often to warn that it was permanent and had to be entered into carefully. Anti-Billites also used the metaphor: New South Wales politician, George Dibbs, for example, said at a meeting during the first referendum campaign on the Constitution Bill, that this was not like an ordinary election, but more like 'a young man taking to himself a wife "for better or for worse"'. There were 'certain institutions', he added, implying that the same did not hold for Federation, 'which would allow a man to get rid of his wife if such a thing was expedient'. His audience laughed.[3]

But, whatever the anti-Billites thought, Federation was not entered into in haste. It had been a long and often stormy engagement. The colonies, said Victoria's Chief Justice five years before the event, 'were rather in the position of a young man and maiden. Each was anxious to have the other, but neither was anxious to begin'.[4] Western Australia in particular had to be wooed and cajoled before it was won, approval was sought from the family elders in Britain, the property settlement was written and rewritten several times, a decision had to be made about

8   *To Constitute a Nation*

which family home the newly-weds would occupy, temporarily, until a permanent home was built (Melbourne, it was agreed, because New South Wales would get the federal capital later).

When it came to concluding the federal union, inaugurating the Commonwealth, the affianced parties all publicly rejoiced. On the designated day, they dressed in their finest costumes, and travelled with their friends and family (even the hitherto grumpy old relatives, the anti-Billites) to the site of the formalities. A solemn and legally binding ceremony was performed by an official. Hymns were sung. And then the party began.

It was a party with something for everyone. If Federation involved property, as many historians insist,[5] it was celebrated as much more than a business merger. If it included a reaffirmation of Australia's British heritage, it was all the more a declaration of Australianness. If the celebrations were military and jingoistic,[6] they were also, even overwhelmingly, about popular culture, creative potential and the preservation of peace.

Less than four years earlier, Queen Victoria's Diamond Jubilee had set the pattern for an Australian *fin de siècle* celebration on a national scale. As much as the 'Record Reign' itself, the Jubilee was an opportunity for celebrating the vastness and power of the Empire and also, in particular, the pace of progress. Banquets, carnivals, concerts, church services, fireworks and, above all, illuminations: these were the signs of modernity. People 'flocked' into the city centres by train and bus, to look at the night-time lights. 'Those who witness the illuminations in Sydney tonight', said the *Sydney Morning Herald*, would be reminded of the Coronation sixty years before, in the age of oil lamps: 'Now the streets every night are brilliant with gas . . . When one thinks of these dingy illuminants . . . it helps to make real the advances of modern progress'.[7] The radical nationalist *Bulletin*, a recent convert to Federation, published a poem that ended: 'God Save the Queen/Who booms the gas consumption'.[8]

In London, Australia's Premiers (five of them 'on leave' between sessions of the 1897–98 Federal Convention) joined colonial leaders from around the Empire to watch the great Jubilee procession of royalty and Imperial troops (including 'the tallest man in the British army', standing at six feet, five inches[9]) as it wound its way from Buckingham Palace to St Paul's Cathedral. The symbols of this celebration spoke of imperial unity and might, of family and muscular Christian virtue, all captured in the small, stout figure of Victoria, by now almost nothing more than a totem held up by a far-flung tribe for veneration and worship. It was, essentially, a massive, military parade, something of a novelty in those days, the sort of thing the world would grow tired of over the next fifty years.

In some respects the Commonwealth celebrations three and a half years later were modelled on the Jubilee. The great parade of Imperial

Colonial Nuptials   9

troops was repeated, and images of the Queen were abundant. Although by 1901 gas was no longer a novelty and electric lighting had begun to take its place, the illuminations were still a central feature, with the visiting English journalist E. K. Knight finding Melbourne's lights so brilliant as to attract 'the attention of the Martians' and startle them.[10]

But the Inauguration was different from the Jubilee. As an act of union, a 'marriage' of the six Australian colonies, it involved a transformation, the performance of a ritual, a moment around which all the other festivities revolved. The people who would celebrate had personally given their consent to the act. It was not a matter of recognising the simple passage of years, of applauding what the *Bulletin* in 1897 called 'much continuous sitting'. The difference lay in the focus of the ritual, in the popular investment in the event. And in the arches.

Nations once built arches to celebrate their military triumphs. Drawing together a victorious returning army, the triumphal arch framed the marching troops, lifting up the eye and the heart to symbolise and celebrate the nation's transcendence. In Sydney, on 1 January 1901 many thousands of Imperial troops marched through the streets and beneath a series of massive arches. The new nation had crowned itself with triumph. The victors, it might have seemed, marched in triumphant return. But, looked at closely, these structures tell a different story from the European arches of marble and stone. They were built by citizens' committees, not emperors. They shared something of the growing fascination with arches found in the 'City Beautiful' movement.[11] But they were assembled out of everyday materials, most were decorative and picturesque, rather than stern and classical, and none was permanent.

Reporting the Sydney procession the day after, Melbourne's *Argus* told of a little girl, hatless, shoeless, and stockingless, standing under a tree in the Domain where the waiting troops were marshalled (and supposedly out of bounds to the public). In the sentimental, allegorical style of the period, it related how the child, with her 'frank, open brow and fair curls . . . laughed and waved her hands towards the troops and called to the soldiers'. She seemed 'like the embodiment of young Australia welcoming the armies of the Empire'.[12]

Young Australia was not stiff and military. It was self-consciously informal, hatless and shoeless. Australian statesmen did not display their Imperial honours. Those who became pompous and official or took themselves too seriously were laughed at. Just before the Inauguration, Australia's French newspaper found this typical irreverence a matter for comment, worrying that the New South Wales Government was insufficiently concerned with the need for gravity and solemnity on the occasion. It warned that Australian crowds, while not violent, were not respectful of officials. Their tendency to ungovernability might lead to a disorderly

10   *To Constitute a Nation*

ceremony, thought the editor. It would be reported all over the world, and would damage the dignity of the new nation.[13]

In the event, his fears proved unfounded. Although the odd hitch and one or two disputes did occur behind the scenes, the public itself was orderly and responsible, and no incident marred the nation's dignity. The *Argus* noted this as 'remarkable', since 'the police would take no instructions from the military, and the military would listen to no suggestions of the police'. The crowd amused itself while waiting, the newspaper recorded, 'making facetious remarks to stray individuals who broke out of line . . . Any important looking person who sought to cross [the road] by waving some coloured ticket was especially teased and the delight of the crowd knew no bounds when such a one was turned back'.[14]

The military parade on the day of the Inauguration (as well as for the opening of Parliament in May) included much that was formal and regimented. Along the streets marched the highly colourful spectacle of the Royal Horse Artillery, Lancers, Huzzars, Yeomanry and Royal Field Artillery, the Coldstream Guards, Royal Fusiliers, the Indian Mixed Contingent, members of the Soudan Force of 1885, Australasian Lancers, cadets, infantry, rangers and others. The Indians, especially, bore themselves with lofty detachment, some noted, while others thought that even they could not resist a smile.[15] The Australians freshly returned from the Boer War were greeted with immense enthusiasm. But it was not a display of weapons or closely serried ranks. Military and other bands played along the route. In Melbourne, where the parade was repeated, it was 'perhaps significant that more than one of the bands played the inspiriting strains of There'll be a High Time in the Old Town Tonight'.[16]

The troops were greatly admired but the audience was not in awe. Australian soldiers were greeted with affection, all the more because they were simple and unadorned, their uniforms plain, unostentatious and 'workmanlike'. In fact, commented the *Sydney Mail*, the brilliance of the Imperial outfits 'rather decreased than increased when massed, while the effect of the khaki in the mass . . . was to throw up the men rather than the uniform'.[17] Ahead of them, the many dignitaries in the procession looked, so the *Courrier Australien* disapprovingly thought, as though they were mingling amiably at the end of a race-meeting.[18]

Travelling with the tour of the Duke and Duchess of York for the first Federal Parliament, Mr Knight found the decorations so splendid as to make the British 'attempts at the adornment of London on great occasions look sordid in comparison'. Even the Diamond Jubilee did not compare. Knight noted the stands for spectators built along the procession route, two or three storeys high against shop fronts: 'Most decidedly they do these things well in Australia'.[19] And he lauded those other ingenious structures, the arches. While arches had featured in various Australian parades and royal welcomes over the years before

Colonial Nuptials   11

Federation, none exceeded, before or after, the number and scale and inventiveness of those built for the Inauguration and the opening of Parliament.

In Sydney there were ten arches between the Domain and the entrance to Centennial Park. They stood on average around fourteen metres high and spanned the road at more than seven and a half metres. Three further arches—of Progress, Empire and Flora and Fauna—had been planned and designed, but were found too costly to build. The survivors were a military arch, a floral arch to welcome the new Governor-General, an American, a French and a German community Arch, a Citizens' Commonwealth Arch, a Melbourne Arch, and one each for wool, wheat and coal. In Melbourne, to welcome the Yorks, were a King's Arch, a Duke's Arch, a Queen's Arch, a Municipal Arch, and German, Chinese, and Butter Arches. In Brisbane for the royal visit (in addition to three arches for the Inauguration), an Aboriginal Arch was erected, covered with native foliage, native animal skins, boomerangs and native weapons, and sixty Aboriginal men, women and children. A second, topped by a crown, was dotted with samples of Queensland's primary products: wool, heads and horns of oxen, wheat and corn cobs, pineapples, sugar cane, pearl shells, gold and precious stones. Perth had a Triumphant Arch: 'One People, One Destiny'. Hobart had an Apple Arch. Some large country towns, like Albury and Ballarat, had their own arches. Sydney had another set for the visit of the Yorks. They were all the result of ingenuity, makeshift, raw materials and new techniques in plaster finishes.

The Wool Arch, for example, was made of wire netting on a wooden frame with scoured wool sticking through to give the effect of solid wool bales. Earlier designs, including for a 'colossal' sheep with real skin wool, its feet resting on piers about six and a half metres high, had been rejected because of the fear (well grounded, as it turned out) of rain soaking the wool. The Wheat Arch solved the rain problem with hollow glass piers filled with sheafs of real wheat. The Citizens' Commonwealth Arch, the largest and most classically styled of them, was constructed using a new plaster technique that imitated marble. The Coal Arch was made of forty tonnes of real coal blocks.

In Sydney a subcommittee of the Decorations and Illuminations Committee (chaired by President of the New South Wales Art Gallery, Edward Du Faur), itself a subcommittee of the central Organising Committee (chaired by John Portus, Secretary of the Public Works Department), had set out to commission arches that were 'representative of some phase or other of Australian life'.[20] It was the motivating idea all around the country. What we see now are the national icons of the era, representing self-government, imperial community, affection for royalty, and primary industry: citizens, soldiers, royals, and agriculture.

But where do we place the 'ethnic' community arches? These represented the non-British 'citizens' in Australia: American, Chinese, German, French and, if we include the 'allegorical cars' (as floats were known then) in the processions, Canadian, Japanese, and Italian. With flags and banners, Pitt Street in Sydney was turned into a 'French Avenue' and Park Street became the 'Avenue of Nations'. 'The decorations', commented the press, 'like the crowds, are also cosmopolitan. German, French and American arches tower above one another in dazzling masses of colour. We are all one today, even to our arts and our methods of showing our unity'.[21]

The Scandinavian community, uncomfortable with the idea of a temporary, decorative contribution, added only a flag to the street decorations, and donated £500 to the Camperdown Children's Hospital, to endow a bed 'as a token towards the country which has held out a hand of liberty and friendship'.[22] Their newspaper, *Nordern*, expressed concern about the élitism of official functions: 'those who are best paid for their work . . . get everything free, whereas the core of the population . . . stay [home], since there is no free pass for them, but they still have to pay for all the fun by the sweat of their brow'. They also deplored the waste: 'Numerous grandiose festivities . . . have already gone and what· is left of the whole glitter, are a few triumphal arches, a multitude of tired people and an immense number of urine bottles and empty beer barrels'.[23] But it was not all frivolous: food parcels were handed out to the poor, and, among other things, children from the Camperdown Hospital were transported around the city one evening so that they could view the decorations.

The *Australische Zeitung* announced preparations for the construction of the German Arch (with an appeal for assistance by the committee involved) and, in addition to speculating upon the likely effect of £6000 worth of alcohol on the party, noted that both South Australia and Germany were supplying potatoes to Sydney to meet the expected extra demand. The celebrations would be, the paper concluded, 'a unique and magnificent event for Australia, that will not be repeated for generations'.[24]

Along with its scepticism about the level of gravity and public order likely on the day, the French *Courrier Australien* recorded its community's preparations. The *Chinese Australian Herald* noted the events and the preparations, including measures taken in Sydney to prevent crowds climbing on shop roofs. It remarked upon the inclusion of associations and societies in the Inauguration procession, pointing out to the reader that, although these were similar to societies found in China, the 'difference is that they are friendly to the government, but in China, people's organisations always fight against the government'.[25]

Colonial Nuptials   13

In the eyes of these non-British residents, Australians were typically, it seems, a little too casual about formalities, rather frivolous and hedonistic, rather more democratic in their politics than their economics. These themes reappeared more than once, as we shall see, in the many observations of Australia made by outsiders during the years leading up to the Inauguration.

The organisers of the 'ethnic' contributions to the Inauguration did so, in the majority of cases, with the support of their relevant consul in Australia; it is likely that they were members of the professional or business communities in the cities. The Chinese procession and dragon in Melbourne, its 'mouth as wide and comprehensive as the Common-wealth Constitution',[26] were almost certainly the work of the business community around Little Bourke Street, but we know little about the identity of the unhappy Chinese participants in Rockhampton who came close to destroying their decorations because they believed themselves excluded from the local football ground at the end of the day's parade,[27] and those who built the Japanese 'Man of War' float in the street march at Kalgoorlie.

What such people had in common, it seems, was the desire to demonstrate loyalty, civic involvement and membership of the Australian community, what at the time was described as citizenship. They expressed both pride in their original cultural identity and in its new cultural setting. They declared the contribution they had made to the latter. The members of that 2 per cent of the population in 1901 who did not have a British background did not seek to represent themselves as typical, or even as Australian. Like those who wrote 'Welcome from the Chinese Citizens' on their beautiful, silk-draped, musical arch in Swanston Street, Melbourne, at the very height of a movement to restrict the membership of Australia's national community, they identified themselves as citizens.

What, then, was a 'typical' Australian on that day? If it did not take in members of such communities, neither did it include the large majority of those present at the celebrations: urban Australians. The thirty stockmen from Queensland, all members of the Australian Workers' Union, who rode in the Sydney procession, and the two hundred more (some even, it was commented, from Paterson's Snowy River itself) in Melbourne four months later were treated by the press as 'typical Australians' and 'a typical Australian display'. The 'citizens were anxious to know, in many cases, what a real Australian stockman is like', said the Melbourne *Age*, and they recognised them by 'their easy-going Australian style', their skill with the horses, their 'easy grace' and their tough, resilient spirit.[28]

Statistically, the image of Australia as rural, and the typical Australian as the outback rider or bushman, was far from the truth. But Australians

14   *To Constitute a Nation*

then (as now) were engaged in a romance with the bush. A romance is never truthful; the feelings it expresses are always out of proportion to the qualities of its object. Australians knew that the vastness of unpopulated territory distinguished their country more clearly than anything else from the British 'mother' country. They knew that it gave them an imaginary escape as well as the right to be 'easy-going', even if they never left the city. They knew also that Australia depended on its rural industries, even though they imagined the bushman not so much as a farmer, but more often as the pioneer in the untamed environment. But at that stage in Australia's history, when rural industries made up the bulk of the country's wealth, the myth of the countryman was more substantial than it could later claim to be.

And country people had played a key role in the accomplishment of Federation, especially in strategically important regions. In the Riverina along the Murray River border, in Bathurst, 'City of Plains', in the West Australian goldfields, in Queensland's north, and Tasmanian coastal towns, the vicissitudes of life away from urban centres had especially generated federal enthusiasm. Many country people, rejoicing in particular at the success of their cause, came to the cities for the celebrations of 1901, taking advantage of reduced rail fares, and of the appeal made to city people to provide accommodation. Indeed, towns within easy travelling distance of Sydney, and some (like Wagga Wagga) much further away, were recorded as very quiet, even 'empty' on 1 January 1901. In Broken Hill a huge crowd at the Municipal Council heard certain aldermen condemn the Mayor for his 'objectionable' response to the central Organising Committee when invited to represent his town at the Sydney celebrations, and the Mayor's claim in reply that he had wanted 'to protest against everything being dragged to Sydney'.[29]

Around the new nation, other country towns were not so quiet. Some few did little more than raise a flag (there being no official Australian flag it could have been one of a number), but many others had parades and carnivals and sporting competitions, and most commonly a 'monster picnic' at the local show grounds or oval, to which the town's children marched to receive a medal and be 'regaled with dainties'. In Geraldton, in the pouring rain, they were told by the town's priest that, like all Australian children, 'they had come from parents of other nations . . . but their parents' nationality, nor their religion need never, and should never interfere with their good citizenship'.[30] We do not know now what impression this day left on the children, whether the exhortation to good citizenship or the 'dainties' impressed them most, but it is not to be deplored if what remained was the memory of an unusual day on which they had cake, and after which they returned to the business of growing up.[31]

Country policemen, brought in to supplement the urban forces in dealing with the crowds and the immensely swollen city population, played their part as well. In addition came lots of gum trees and wattles, cut off at the stump and tied to poles and along verandah posts—street decorations in the city (where, three months earlier, the Mayor had used his casting vote against an alderman's motion to spend £250 on the most 'elevating, beautiful and lasting' tribute to the Commonwealth: the planting of street trees).[32] Taken together, the contribution of rural Australia was disproportionately greater than its numerical size. Perhaps, in this sense, they had a right to have their members treated as typical in the celebratory processions. It is curious, however, that something 'typical', like the stockmen on their horses, should appear as such a novelty and be greeted with such wonder.

But myths must not be measured against reality. They should not be tested for falsehood. Exercised through rituals such as this, they play a central social function of identifying and binding a community, of expressing and affirming its dominant or shared values, and in that respect they capture a reality. The Australian bush myth expressed a type of commitment to the values associated with the rural pioneer: resourcefulness, pragmatism, rough egalitarianism and romanticism. These values, growing out of both dream and experience, shaped what had now emerged as the white Australian 'type'. Australian Federation and Australia's Constitution itself were products of that type.

Where, then, we must ask, were the other representatives of the bush, those with even greater claim to be real or true, those for whom another set of myths constituted both community and land? The absence of Aboriginal Australians from the nation-making processes, the redefinition of 'natives' as white men and the literal exclusion of the original natives from the community described in the Constitution are discussed in later chapters. Aborigines as a class were not to be citizens of the new nation either by legal means or by claiming the title for themselves, as women and non-British Australians did. What did the Aborigines who took part in the Commonwealth celebrations represent? In Brisbane they were placed among the native flora and fauna, decorations rather than participants. But miners, too, wielding picks, stood on the walls of the Coal Arch in Sydney, miming their daily work as the Inauguration procession went by. Whether the Aborigines who stood on the arch built to welcome the Duke and Duchess of York chose to do so, like the miners, or found amusement in the curiosity of the crowd, whether they cared about Federation or recognised the British royal family, we do not know.

Other Aborigines were given at least a more active role and recognition. 'Not only are the Fijians and the local residents from the South Sea Islands, but the Australian aboriginals are to be represented on

16   *To Constitute a Nation*

Commonwealth Day', commented one journal. 'From northern Queensland and Western Australia, where the finest specimens of a fast vanishing race still roam the boundless plains free as the air . . . are to come the once proud possessors of the Australian soil, with spear and boomerang.'[33] Twenty-five Aborigines from Queensland, organised by the Aboriginal Protector, Archibald Meston, and his son, came to Sydney, where they acted both themselves, in a display of weapons and dancing, and their ancestors, in a reconstruction of Captain Cook's landing at Kurnell in Botany Bay. The press treated the display of skills as a marvel and a wonder, in the manner of tourists watching the rituals of another country. The idea of the *tableau vivant* at Kurnell had been rejected at first by the New South Wales Premier 'as verging on the burlesque'. But whatever he thought beforehand, William Lyne ended up among the dignitaries at the scene, and enjoyed (one hopes) the picnic in a tent that followed the performance.

Many of these picnickers had been in the carriages of colonial dignitaries, moving along the decorated city streets on the first of January. Ahead of them marched two hundred policemen, followed by the labour section of the procession. Led by the Railway Band, it consisted of ten men from each trade, amounting to more than two hundred men in all. Silver-miners wearing lamps and carrying picks, coal-miners, gold-miners and tin-miners, all in white with sashes, timber-cutters, dockers, house-painters with a painted banner, journeymen, seamen, butchers, and engineers bearing a model steamer christened *Federation*, bakers wearing cooks' hats, furniture-makers with miniature pieces of furniture on wands over their shoulders, stonemasons, iron-moulders, gas-stokers, one with a plain, black gas pipe bound into a bouquet of flowers, ten tailors with fig-leaves in their lapels (to indicate the origin of their profession) and more. Behind them travelled two carriages with presidents and secretaries of the Labour League, the major unions, and the New South Wales Labour Council. And, after these, came members of lodges and friendly societies. And, with many more labour representatives, allegorical cars and banners, they rode again in a second procession, whose 'intrinsic grandeur added to the glory of the historic occasion', on 5 January.[34] A section of fire-fighters with equipment separated the labour representatives from Church leaders, and the Italian and Canadian allegorical cars preceded the politicians, mayors, judges, senior academics (even those, like Lyne and Sydney University's Chancellor, Dr Normand MacLaurin, not so long ago ardent anti-Billites). And then came the troops, along the streets and under the ten 'triumphal' arches where a momentary relief from the January sun might have been experienced.

It was an exceedingly hot day, but it might have been worse. Indeed it had begun much worse, with heavy showers and strong winds

Colonial Nuptials 17

throughout the preceding night and into the early morning, leaving in their wake much rapid work cleaning up and mending decorations and arches. Had the storm come later, the procession, instead of a dazzling triumph, might well have become a soggy challenge. This reminder that the best laid plans of men may suddenly be defeated by nature gives rise to curiosity about the planning for other natural challenges. How were essential human needs and functions met on a mass scale on that day? Even the most glorious celebrations must provide for the body as well as the spirit.

The Danish reference to abandoned 'urine bottles' suggests one way the male members of the crowd at least may have provisioned themselves. A likely additional method is suggested, indirectly, by the campaigns waged by women around this time for legislation prohibiting men from urinating in lanes. But, although the extreme heat of the day may well have helped, the Organising Committee could not rely on such measures alone, and commissioned a Mr Bromley to construct eighteen 'temporary sanitary conveniences' (at a cost of £115).[35]

The thousands of troops were garrisoned in Sydney's Domain, where the New South Wales Government provided 'food and shelter in camp or quarters' and, one assumes, further 'sanitary conveniences'. As they marched in the heat, one person in the crowd took it upon himself to hold out cups of water, 'seldom refused by the sweating Tommies', the press noted, except for a single soldier who waved the cup away, in spite of 'parched lips'. Some of the ambulance stations along the route were useful, it turned out, not just for the crowds but also for the sixteen soldiers who succumbed to the heat: 'several of these', noted the same paper, Australians.[36]

How did the journalists know that the 'Tommy's' lips were parched, that there were Australians among the heat-struck soldiers? Why were certain events noted or recorded for posterity, and not others? In the very language of reports and communications, in the events singled out for special measures or attention, the overriding imperatives of distance and climate, pride in the myth of toughness and resilience, are coupled with an irresistible irony. A distinctive sense of Australianness was sought and conveyed, both self-consciously and unreflectively on that day above all. Both 'natives' and visitors made special efforts to notice and comment on the unique and the typical around them.

The furnishing of public facilities had also been closely regulated before the event and although many owners of buildings on the procession route had applied to construct viewing platforms on their property, a limited number only were approved, each being inspected by authorities in the days before. Contrary to the *Courier*'s view, the organisers clearly experienced considerable anxiety in anticipation of accidents or

18   *To Constitute a Nation*

public disturbances.[37] But, despite the familiar disregard for authority in person, the crowds on the day accepted a significant degree of control. From the evidence of photos of the procession, it seems that only a few attempted to disregard police instructions, including a ban on climbing fences and street structures (one man, we observe, found an ingenious alternative, standing on stilts at the back of the crowd).

The *Bulletin* had condemned the arches (as well as the numerous flag poles) on the grounds that they blocked the traffic and would probably lead to loss of life.[38] Nothing of this nature happened, although some accidents, perhaps inevitably, did occur. A policeman was killed by a runaway horse; two elderly people died in the crowd; and several horses were burned to death, ironically, in a city fire station, when decorative Chinese lanterns set the building alight. Only days after the end of the celebrations did something of the kind predicted by the *Bulletin* occur and then for a special reason. The Coal Arch, built out of real coal by the residents of Newcastle (and considered by the *Courrier Australien* to be a '*succès du jour*') began to crumble as its pieces of coal were pilfered, collapsing soon after the celebrations were completed and injuring a man and a child. But, throughout the ten days of festivities, public order was maintained. At the end of it all, a special 'Smoke Concert' was held in the Sydney Town Hall 'in recognition of the excellent work done by the police during the celebrations'.[39]

Similar measures were repeated in Melbourne four months later, and on varying scales in cities around the new nation in both January and May. In Sydney alone, the decorations, the banquets, the carnivals and concerts, the military reviews and regattas, not to mention the fireworks (£2500 worth—'excluding customs duty'—commissioned from Pain & Sons of London, and stored in the Ordnance Store), plus much more that followed for ten days after the Inauguration all add up to a feat of immense organisation. The extraordinary thing (from our perspective almost one hundred years later) is that organisation did not begin until five months before. It was at that point that invitations went to Britain for the Imperial troops to be sent. And it was only two months before that the various committees and subcommittees were set up.

In Sydney the central Organising Committee consisted of a mélange of ex officio members of government, senior bureaucrats, business men, the Mayor of Sydney, the Chancellor of the University, insurance and friendly society representatives, newspaper men, the Inspector-General of Police, a member of the Fire Brigades Board, the Government Architect, a member of the Labour Council, and representatives from each of the subcommittees. A Reception and Entertainment Committee (over one hundred members), a Citizens' Committee, Decorations and Illuminations Committee, Processions and Demonstrations Committee, and

Theatrical, Athletic, Aquatic, Cycling, and Musical Committees were formed. In addition the 'Feeding the Poor' and 'Treating the Poor' Committees met a commitment to provide free entertainment and services to the poor, which they completed by distributing more than five thousand coupons for groceries and two thousand tickets for meals.

These committees, with their many subcommittees, and much interlocking membership, drew together both ordinary citizens and leading lights (including all the Heads of Churches and Synagogue) and some whose names are, for other reasons, still known to us today: William Lister Lister, Sidney Long, J. F. Archibald, Walter Vernon. There were, in addition, the various 'ethnic' community committees, and numerous municipal organisations outside the city centre. 'In fact', said the *Review of Reviews*, 'almost everyone you met either already belonged, or was on the point of belonging, to some organised body whose sole object in life for the time being was to make the festivities a brilliant success'.[40]

Co-ordinating the committees alone (if indeed this was achieved) must have proved a trial in itself. The effect of this complex, dispersed and unwieldy democratic committee structure and wide membership, along with the small amount of time available to bring it all together, made participation less orchestrated than our modern standards might allow, and made the events and decorations themselves, outside the grand official parade and swearing-in, more homely and popular, even spontaneous. The *Town and Country Journal* even found it all a little too popular, complaining after the event that there was only one 'Commonwealth entertainment which [could] be accurately described as a social function'.[41] The ten-day timetable in Sydney contained indeed endless sporting, musical and carnival activities. A simple event like the illuminated and decorated bicycle competition brought participation as close to the popular as possible (Miss Perryman, with her 'Japanese' bicycle, won first prize of £10).

How much did this all cost? There was, of course, a range of estimates and some criticism levelled at waste. For the day of the Inauguration, the New South Wales Government had set aside £20 000 and, although this sum was probably exceeded, John Portus kept a tight purse (ruling out the three extra arches, for example). Committees also raised considerable sums privately for their arches, decorations and festivities. Over the whole ten days, costs built up, and the government felt constrained some three months later to announce publicly, in 'view of the many extravagant statements which have been made as to the cost of the Commonwealth celebrations', that 'accounts, minus deductions' (for increased customs and railway receipts, among other things) gave a nett cost of £53 518.[42] Announced with such confidence, it was clearly an acceptable sum for the time. Despite its editor's presence on the Reception and

20   *To Constitute a Nation*

Entertainment Committee, however, the *Bulletin* thought the celebrations too lavish and expensive, that the Commonwealth did not need 'tawdry' ceremonies to demonstrate its greatness. It satirised the passion for arches with a cartoon, 'The Arch of the Unemployed', in which the ragged bodies of hungry men are piled on top of each other to form a pathetic arch.

Some individuals among the miserable, and perhaps also the unfortunate, members of the population did get something out of the day. In honour of the Inauguration, leniency was granted to around seventy prisoners, including a Mr Joyce, awaiting execution for the murder of his wife, who found his sentence commuted to life imprisonment. Others were released, or had their sentence reduced by up to three years.[43] We can assume that the day lived on in their memories at least.

On the eleventh day of the New Year, removal of the decorations began: 'Faded ropes of foliage were handed down and coiled up for removal, and discoloured drapings were rudely torn away', masts and illuminations were put away in storage for the royal visit in May, and all the arches except the Citizens' Arch (which survived a little longer while unsuccessful appeals to make it permanent were under review) were being dismantled.[44]

The solidity and grandeur of the arches and pavilions are all the more remarkable because they were not only temporary, but some, like the Melbourne Arch, were erected (albeit in something of a panic) in a matter of days. If the arches all got built, and public safety was preserved, and the decorations held up to the relief of all those concerned, a couple of human problems did occur to mar the enjoyment of certain others. The most serious was a dispute over the order of precedence in the Sydney procession and it flared up so close to the day that a resolution could not be reached in time. The procession had been organised in reverse order of importance, partly to keep the crowds in their place waiting for the best, rather than dispersing at random. This meant, unequivocally, that the new Governor-General must come last, but what about the others? It was a particular problem when it came to the Church leaders, given Australia's parallel histories of official non-sectarianism and Catholic–Anglican tensions. The final order decided on placed Cardinal Moran in front of, that is to say, in order of precedence, behind, the Anglican Archbishop of Sydney. Moran (whose case the British Government, it seems, supported) was unable to persuade the organisers that a Cardinal is always senior to an Archbishop—'even at the Court of St James'—and was so offended that he withdrew from the procession and the swearing-in, choosing to appear instead alongside the choir of two thousand Catholic schoolchildren on the steps of St Mary's Cathedral. His boycott also meant a change in the order of prayers at Centennial Park (and led, no doubt, to the decision to have the Governor-General rather than a priest read the prayer at the opening of Parliament). The organisers insisted that their choice was not sectarian, but simply gave priority to the Head of the Church with the greatest number of adherents in Australia, while Premier Lyne claimed he was only following the list provided by Hopetoun's Secretary, Captain Wallington.[45]

But neither the Irish nor the French communities were persuaded, and the dispute might have been a serious setback to the symbolic unity of the celebrations save that it did not, perhaps fortunately, only concern the Catholic representative. Wesleyan, Presbyterian, and Methodist leaders also boycotted the procession over the order of precedence. The *Courrier Australien* tempered its outrage at what the editors thought was almost a deliberate affront, and called it instead a silly mistake. Apart from the Archbishop, a sufficient number of other religious leaders, both Christian and Jewish, did appear in the procession, so that the separation of Church and State in the new Constitution was not too literally represented in its celebration. The Sydney *Hebrew Standard*, observing this dispute, commented politely that quarrels over religious precedence 'cannot seriously be entertained' in a Commonwealth 'which gives equal liberty to all its people'.[46]

Church leaders were not the only ones offended by the place they were allocated in the procession. Foreign consuls failed to be treated as the equivalent of military officers in spite of, it was claimed, promises from the incoming Governor-General, and they too withdrew, although unlike Cardinal Moran they did almost all go to Centennial Park for the swearing-in. The French Consul alone missed out and, no doubt aware that his absence could be open to misinterpretation, took pains to have it announced in the press that this was due to his carriage having been blocked by traffic near (of all places) St Mary's Cathedral.

In Centennial Park the marriage took place. Under a temporary canopy (one thinks of a *chuppah*) made of wood and delicate plasterwork, the Archbishop recited the Lord's Prayer, a prayer for the Commonwealth and a prayer for the Governor-General. Then the Clerk of the South Australian Parliament, Mr Edwin Blackmore (who had been Clerk at the 1897–98 Federal Convention), read the Declaration of the Commonwealth and the Letters-Patent of the Governor-General. Lord Hopetoun, who had to be sworn in before he could perform his vice-regal functions, then received the civil imprimatur from the Deputy Governor of New South Wales, Chief Justice Sir Frederick Darley. Kissing the Bible twice, he turned to watch as the oath of office was administered to the new Prime Minister and his Cabinet. Some stepped up confidently, although Deakin, while speaking firmly, visibly shook with emotion.

22   *To Constitute a Nation*

Every state was represented in person in the nuptial act. From New South Wales, Barton was Prime Minister and Minister for External Affairs and Lyne had Home Affairs; Deakin and Turner from Victoria were Attorney-General and Treasurer; Kingston from South Australia, Minister for Trade and Customs; Forrest from Western Australia, Postmaster-General; Dickson from Queensland, Minister for Defence. Tasmania (included at the last minute) had Neil Lewis as Minister without Portfolio. As the hot wind blew, papers flew off the ritual table, the very same table upon which Queen Victoria had signed the Commonwealth Act six months before, and while officials scurried around to collect them, the new Governor-General smiled in amusement. Deakin trembled and Hopetoun smiled. Since symbolism reigned that day, this scene might readily be imagined as capturing the different levels of investment in the occasion by the Australian and British parties. Certainly the contrast seems symbolically apt, as we proceed in the following chapters through the years leading up to this moment and ask as we go: who desired its consummation most ardently?

The now-united partners, emerging from the pavilion, heard a mass choir rendition of 'God Save the Queen', the 'Hallelujah Chorus' and 'the stirring strains of a Federal anthem'. Afterwards, among other things, ten thousand children sang 'Advance Australia Fair' and 'Rule Britannia', 'pieces in which they always prove at home'.[47] 'And now the deed august is done/And all Australia knit in one/In witness of the glorious sun', declaimed 'Lyon Harvey' in an extraordinary twelve-page 'Metrical Souvenir' of the celebrations. For a moment, deeply solemn, they remembered that they had created a nation, but that the nation-building lay before them: that 'glory but inserts the tendril root/And then her office truly is discharged/The rich reward for all our toils and pains/"One People and One Destiny" remains'.[48]

And then the party. Relaxed, and in the absence of the Governor-General who by the evening was too ill to attend, the Australians allowed their habitual disregard for authority to manifest itself again at the official banquet. It was enhanced no doubt (the *Courrier Australien* certainly thought so) by the liberal allowance of champagne, and perhaps also by the sense of carnival in the release that follows a commanding, highly controlled ritual ceremony. In the pre-microphone days, speech-makers had no other recourse but to shout above a noisy audience. Even after appeals for silence, with Sir Samuel Griffith apologising for 'his voice not being so strong as it used to be', the great oratorical efforts were talked over by the audience in the Sydney Town Hall, and 'scores' left before the new Prime Minister, Edmund Barton, began his speech. Those who remained continued their conversations. Only former New South Wales Premier, George Reid (who had three years earlier

Colonial Nuptials   23

earned the nickname of 'Yes-No' Reid for advising the people of New South Wales that he supported the Constitution, but they should oppose it), ever popular as an orator, received an ovation, which must have compensated him, one newspaper thought, for not being chosen as first Prime Minister.[49]

Eight hundred men (including consuls of seventeen nations) sat at the banquet tables in the hall, with four hundred women seated separately in the upstairs galleries (despite many vacant seats among the men below). They toasted the Commonwealth, they toasted themselves and their efforts, they toasted the Queen. But like more than one member of the party on that day, Victoria did not live to see the fruits of the federal union. A very old, frail woman (whose faculties Alfred Deakin had found six months beforehand to be failing, although 'it was the fashion everywhere to speak as if [they] were absolutely unimpaired'[50]), she died twenty-one days later. It cannot have been a surprise, and although the borders on the papers were ruled in black, and mourning dress was expected for the official engagements that followed ('correct' fashions in 'semi-mourning toilette' were advertised), this did not prevent the opening of Parliament on 9 May from embracing a similar range of festivities.

The honeymoon was not altogether a smooth one. The Queensland member of Cabinet, Sir James Dickson, Minister for Defence (and the only member of the ministry born outside Australia), preceded Victoria in death only ten days after he had taken his vow of office in the plaster pavilion. Lord Hopetoun, unhappy with his salary, petitioned London to relieve him of his Governor-Generalship before his second year of office was out.

But the marriage, if not without conflict, has endured. Perhaps like all marriages, it was partly a matter of love, partly of convenience, partly of proximity. Even Western Australia, the most reluctant member of the union, and soon to seek 'divorce', celebrated generously on the day (patriotic mottoes, illuminations, flags, decorated trams offering free rides to children, a children's procession and carnivals, and a Father Christmas with a snow-covered bicycle!).

By the time of the Inauguration, Federation was a popular movement. That is not to say it was a mass movement. It was popular by being in the air, and even if it was more often believed to be inevitable than actively promoted, it achieved ultimate legitimacy. No movement in history can claim to have had, numerically, an absolute majority of its actors in the vanguard. The marriage of the Australian colonies, which created an indissoluble union, was—perhaps uniquely for nations—not an arranged one. It was, for all its inevitable flaws, a marriage of consent, and the popular party to celebrate its consummation underlined its closeness to, rather than its remoteness from the people. History, one newspaper said,

> knows no other instance where a proclamation of free nationhood was read and the oaths of government administered in the open day, in a broad-bound common part of the people, and under the eyes of more than one hundred thousand of the men, women and children citizens of the building nation.[51]

What does it take to constitute a nation in the absence of external pressure? Imagining a community, defining the outsider, identifying a national 'type', engaging the aspirations of emerging sectors of society, structuring an agreement to which the parties are prepared to adhere.

'Regarded on the whole', said Alfred Deakin, 'it is safe to say that if ever anything ought to be styled providential it is the extraordinary combination of circumstances, persons and their most intricate interrelations' that culminated in Federation.[52] For Deakin, who stood trembling at the ritual moment of transition from one state of existence to another, this was perhaps his finest hour. If the crowd was not too bothered with transcendence and spiritual greatness, those who witnessed and described the event were keen to note this very attitude as yet another affirmation of Australianness.

A thing called Australia had been created. It was looked upon with affection, pride and curiosity. What did it mean to be Australian, people asked themselves. In the act of answering their own question they began to sketch what they had imagined now for years, and the rituals they performed to confirm their response affirmed, as social rituals do, the transcendent power of the very thing that had been created.

CHAPTER TWO

The Imaginary Nation

> We ought not lightly to disregard all the
> powers which the imagination can call forth,
> in picturing the future of these great colonies.[1]

The Inauguration was not the real beginning. For Australia to become a nation, Australians had first to imagine a nation. Before a nation can be formed, a group of separate populations must imagine themselves part of a larger national community. Then they must imagine it as natural and inevitable that such a community should exist. By the time a constitution is written, the process is almost at its end.

But to write a constitution is no simple matter. There is much more to it than just imagining a national community.[2] Nations may remain in the imagination, as many have done in history. They may be imposed from without or formed as the result of conflict rather than dreams of kinship. For a nation to be made, that is, *crafted*, where one previously did not exist, political will must be generated alongside the imagination. When the political will is engaged, a specific constitution can be imagined. This must describe not only the powers and jurisdictions of the new nation, but also its membership, including a guide to how the members are to co-exist thereafter.

And, finally, if the political and legal skill is available, a viable real constitution may be written and pass into law. ' "The Australian Nation" of which we speak and hear so much', wrote Robert Garran, who six years later was to become the great public servant of the new Commonwealth, 'has never yet existed. Our nationality has hitherto been nothing but a sentiment, an idea. Nationality can have no real meaning, no real efficacy, unless it embodies the relations of a national citizenship'.[3] It was the attempt to bring the imaginary and the real together that drove the Federation movement of the last two decades of the century.

The Australian Constitution was the product of this process. The fact that it still functions, whether smoothly or not, is a remarkable achievement on the scale of things. But that achievement is another story. This is the story of the writing of Australia's Constitution, and how it reflected the will to create a nation.

The nation that came into existence on 1 January 1901 was a nation just out of its chrysalis, still soft and fragile, fully formed but not quite recognisable. The sense of cultural community, the infrastructure of domestic sovereignty, the will for future complete independence all existed at that time, making Australia distinctively a nation. But full international sovereignty had not yet been achieved, nor was it sought.

A nation, but not yet a nation-state. A nation-state is a fully sovereign body in international relations and law; it may ratify treaties, engage in diplomacy, even invade another territory, without the risk that its actions might be legally overturned by an external body. A nation-state can perform what is called an Act of State for which there is no appeal outside its own parliaments or tribunals, 'for which there might be a remedy by diplomatic representation, but not by litigation. The capacity to perform such an act belong[s] to the Sovereign alone'.[4]

In 1901, and for many years after, both the British Parliament (in theory the British Sovereign) and the British Privy Council had the power to alter decisions made in Australia in so far as these affected external affairs. But the new Australian nation was sovereign in all domestic matters and this, combined with the overwhelming sense at the time that Australians had a distinctive, specifically Australian identity, made Australia a nation.

In the processes of being formed, the nation was imagined as a community. In most of the references to community, the boundaries stopped at the borders of the territory we now know as Australia. But there was also a wider sense of community, sometimes including just England and Australia together, sometimes embracing the whole British Empire. Membership of this larger community did not rule out or diminish the sense of membership of the national community. Australia's was both a post-colonial nation and a peculiarly Australian nation, domestically sovereign, culturally distinctive, but still tied in community, language and law to the nation from which it had sprung. At the time, this complex web of affinities seemed very satisfactory to almost everyone, and was nothing like the puzzle it would later appear to be.

The Australian Constitution captured in law the multiple identities of Australia's population. Alfred Deakin, new Attorney-General in the new Commonwealth of Australia, pointed out in early 1902 that the Constitution, 'large and elastic as it is, is necessarily limited by the ideas and circumstances which obtained in the year 1900'; it stands 'and will stand on the Statute-book just as in the hour in which it was assented to. But the nation lives, grows and expands'.[5]

But one hundred years later, while the nation has indeed evolved, grown and expanded (although nowhere near as much as imagined back then), the genesis of the Constitution in 'the ideas and circumstances' of its time has largely been forgotten. For many people, the Constitution seems always to have existed: to have been found fully formed, as if written on tablets of stone, or delivered in the mail-bag of the British Colonial Office. Nothing could be further from the truth.

The Australian Constitution was written by human mortals, in Australia itself. It was written through a long and complex process, with many drafts, over many meetings, by many hands. A constitution is not a dog licence, as Edmund Barton himself declared.[6] It cannot be written as a simple, transparent and technical act, where a single purpose is matched directly to a policy. Whatever we think now of the Constitution's framers, those members of the various constitutional conventions of the 1890s, the idea that they could write a constitution just as they chose, effectively to suit their own interests, and in isolation from the wider political culture, is unconvincing.

Not only did the framers have to produce a legally viable document, they had also to satisfy the inconsistent demands of each of the states, the interests of Britain, and the scrutiny of the Australian press. Ultimately, their constitution had to attract a majority of votes in a referendum where the Australian electorate was effectively the final judge. It had to work.

The framers had to write a constitution that expressed the values and standards of their period, at least sufficiently for their product to acquire general legitimacy. They were humans, not prophets and, needing to work collectively, they could not be hermits. They drew therefore upon the values, meanings, ideas and sources of inspiration available to them. Their document did not please everybody. Nor did it reflect everyone's values. But it did attain sufficient legitimacy to establish a nation.

The Australian Constitution still stands, almost unchanged, as a reflection of the prevailing values of the 1890s. It is an artefact of that time, with all the hidden richness of a plain, colourless piece of flint, dug up by an archeologist who knows that in it is captured a whole cultural system.

Well before the Constitution was shaped, the community it would represent had to be imagined. It had to be imagined as a community distinct from, even separable from Britain. London had long been the imaginative centre for the majority of Australia's white population, and England was 'Home'. Long after Federation was achieved, England would still be called Home by some, perhaps even by many, but at some crucial point this had to become a metaphor, a reference to the past (as in childhood), rather than to a place to which the speaker seeks literally to return or retire. Another Home had to be acknowledged. 'Make yourself a united people', said Henry Parkes, Premier of New South Wales, at the first Federation Conference in 1890: 'appear before the world as one, and the dream of going "home" would die away. We should create an Australian home . . . We should have "home" within our own shores'.[7]

28   *To Constitute a Nation*

White Australians were imagining themselves grown up. The desire to have a home of their own was growing. Around the end of the 1880s, the idea of an alternative community began to find expression in many forms. The metaphor of kinship among all white Australians was seized upon and employed so frequently that it seems to have been taken as literally true. Telling the 1890 Conference not to forget that 'in this country, we are separated only by imaginary lines, and that we are a people one in blood, race, religion and aspiration', Alfred Deakin accused South Australian Thomas Playford of speaking of his fellow Australians as if they belonged to 'a different race, language, creed'.[8] 'No, no', responded Playford.

Deakin was echoing Henry Parkes, whose famous assertion that 'the crimson thread of kinship runs through us all' became a catch-cry for Federalists. Again and again throughout the 1890s, Australians were reminded of what Australians had begun to articulate a decade before: that they were part of a community, related to each other, bound by common ancestry, bound to cement their kinship in a common nation. They were, most importantly, a separate community, not just the overseas relations of the British. If Rose Scott, an ardent New South Wales anti-Billite, deplored the appeal to community, and warned against attempting a union between people 'whose interests are naturally as far apart as their geographical boundaries and who will in time develop racial distinctions such as even now mark the difference between an Englishman and an American',[9] her argument only served to underline the strength of the opposite sentiment.

In contrast to an inevitable 'racial' separation, the union of the separate parts into one nation was, many thought, inevitable. It was part of the forward march of progress: 'One People, One Destiny', said Parkes. The Bathurst People's Federal Convention in 1896 adopted the motto, 'By our Union we are made equal to our Destiny'. On the Citizens' Arch for the Commonwealth Inauguration one of the slogans spoke of 'the Union which Nature has ordained and patriotism has accomplished'. It is, writes Benedict Anderson, 'the magic of nationalism to turn chance into destiny'.[10] Although Australian nation-building lacked the religious fervour of much European nationalism, it did not lack this magic.

The last decades of the nineteenth century were dominated by teleological thinking, by the idea that history unfolded according to an inevitable process, that it moved forward and onward through the working of inherent and immutable laws. In the Western world, evolution and progress were key words of this age and Australians applied them to the Federation movement.

The old view that small communities were 'best calculated to promote human happiness' was passing away before 'the law which is massing modern communities into large aggregations', wrote the Melbourne *Age* in 1895; it is now 'the day of great nationalities, and Australians are but following the bent of the time'.[11] That same year, Chief Justice of Queensland Sir Samuel Griffith (who was in 1891 Queensland Premier and the leading draftsman of the first Constitution Bill) also described Federation in such terms:

> If Australia has any destiny as a country, if there are to be Australian patriots, Australia must submit to the common law of humanity as declared by universal experience . . . Every lesson of history teaches that the manifest destiny of Australia is to be one people . . . Those who oppose union are opposing an irresistible force, which, however strenuous the opposition, must ultimately prevail.[12]

National sentiment, said Tasmania's Attorney-General, Andrew Inglis Clark, 'will go on and grow in the several colonies whether we now assist or not in giving it that political independence or autonomy which it craves for, and which it deserves'.[13]

But destiny and kinship can take many directions. The Australian colonies had several 'sisters' around the Empire, the products too of British colonisation: English-speaking countries with common strengths and weaknesses, common problems dealing with their native populations, vast, seemingly unpopulated territories, weak defence forces, emerging nationalist communities. If the ties of blood and common origin had alone been the source of community, kinship with Canada and South Africa should have been felt more keenly. Imperial Federation should have had greater success.

The Imperial Federation movement was at its most intense in those same transitional years, between the mid-1880s and the early 1890s, during which time its rival, Australian Federation, was successfully emerging.[14] The aim of the Imperial Federationists was to unite Australia as one state among others in a great and permanent Federation of the English-speaking Empire, with its centre in London. But faced with the choice between Imperial and Australian Federation, most Australians opted for the latter. Radical nationalists thought Imperial Federation 'a conspiracy of Australian plutocrats, British aristocrats and Queensland reactionaries'.[15] The *Bulletin* believed it would assist Britain's commercial interests at the expense of Australia's;[16] moderate nationalists could see no appeal in constructing a federation of nations, without first creating an Australian nation through the federation of its colonies.

But there was more to this than timing. In writing a constitution for a nation, rather than for a state within an Imperial Federation, the Australians took pains to measure themselves, as we shall see, against their

30   *To Constitute a Nation*

sisters. They sought a clear distinction between the colonies they believed similar—those which in the imagined future could belong to the national community—and those they decided were dissimilar, and could not. They disavowed in particular a common community with the most recently federated English-speaking nation, the one with perhaps greatest claim to similarity and affinity: Canada.

New Zealand, on the other hand, was so very similar (in the Australian mind) to the six Australian colonies that the choice of belonging to the federal community or remaining apart was effectively left to the New Zealanders themselves. Western Australia, like New Zealand, also belonged naturally, or so the Easterners thought. That colony itself remained uncertain of its place in the community for so long that it decided to join only after the Australian Constitution had been passed as an Act of British Parliament and its name is therefore not to be found in the Constitution's Preamble, but 'pencilled in' under a separate section below it, in the hope that the colony would before long come to the party.

Anti-Federalists attempted at times to stem the tide against this sense of separate Australian identity. In the campaign to keep Western Australia out of the Federation, one local Member of the Legislative Council told his audience that the sentiment of being a British subject was 'a little bit higher' than that of being Australian. In an anecdotal age, he told an anecdote of finding himself on a railway platform in Paris, and wondering what would happen if he said he was Australian: would the French officials have said to each other, 'keep your eye on it, till I get a stick' or asked him 'what ship his father was sent out in'? He was greeted with 'uproar' and laughter, and cries that Australians were British subjects.[17] In his somewhat tasteless attempt at humour, Mr Haynes, MLC, had demonstrated his failure to appreciate the subtle and by then almost universal sentiment that white Australians could be distinctive and separate (and be proud of being so) yet still remain firmly British.

There was a period this century when it seemed to Australian historians puzzling, even improbable, that Australians could genuinely feel themselves both British and authentically Australian at the same time. It is now more or less accepted that a person may have simultaneously and authentically more than one cultural identity. But it is also known that, however much immigrants cling to their old cultural identity, they are inexorably changed by the experience of living elsewhere. Their identity draws on the new landscape. And the landscape, being viewed through new cultural eyes, is itself changed.

So it was in nineteenth-century Australia. If Alfred Deakin called himself an 'independent Australian Briton', he did not really believe he lived or thought just as the Englishman did in Britain. Deakin, indeed, scorned

The Imaginary Nation 31

much he found in England, in particular the 'class-feeling' and 'snobbishness' that 'pervades English society from top to bottom'.[18] The 'Australian Briton' did not share in this English culture, but had a new type of identity, its shape already emerging the moment white people began to occupy Australian soil. It was this identity that was articulated one hundred years later in the processes of forming a nation.

'In many ways the people of the various Australian colonies had the ingredients for the creation of a political union many years before the event actually occurred', observes the historian Scott Bennett in one of the very few secondary works to recognise community as a precondition for nationhood.[19] They shared a language, a religion, a monarch and 'the crimson thread of kinship'. From 1895 they also shared, we may add, if not a single time zone, at least standardised clocks based on Greenwich Mean Time, following a remarkable (indeed federal) ceremony around the country where all post office clocks (except in Western Australia) were stopped or advanced simultaneously at midnight on 1 February 1895. It was a 'symbol of the gradual synchronisation of Australian society'.[20]

At least one Federalist took the opportunity to comment, if circumspectly, on the significance of this event: true Federation, wrote Maybanke Wolstenholme, demanded the growth of national spirit, not mechanism: 'Standard time may be arranged by law and altered in a night. It is but the putting on or putting back of wheels and weight, the striking of a clock or two . . . But the machinery that registers the throb of human life . . . moves by other impulse'.[21]

Despite all these cultural preconditions, Bennett continues, nationalism did not emerge until the moment when both isolation and parochialism had already been deeply eroded by widespread literacy and by new forms of communication and transport. In addition, the growth of the white population—by the mid-1890s it had passed 3.5 million and stood close to the population of the United States in 1787, as the Constitution's framers liked to remind themselves—seemed to give the country the critical mass to create its own national culture. The proportion of the Australian-born population now well exceeded those born outside the country. These Australian 'natives'—white men, born in Australia— played a role of great significance in advancing Federation. And the confident, and seemingly unanimous belief that Australia's population was set to increase exponentially in the new century, overtaking Britain's by many millions within perhaps as few as fifty years, played its part in an imaginary future for the as yet unformed nation.

Given these factors, it might seem natural that contiguous colonies should now unite. The logic of land mass, the relative ease of direct communication and intercourse between the Australian colonies, may

32   *To Constitute a Nation*

appear to be the obvious principal force. It is an invitingly simple, even elegant, image, that a nation might be defined by the ease with which its members could visit each other in trains or send each other telegrams. But the island Tasmania was included from the start in the imaginary community, and Fiji and New Zealand were invited early in the process to consider joining an Australasian Federation. These colonies were far from easy to reach, not so obvious as members of a simple geographical union. If all of these islands had been included the Australian nation would have been much larger, much harder to get around and much more geographically messy.

In other circumstances it might also have been considerably smaller. Among the many attempts to describe the nation's reach during the 1890s, the simple unification of Victoria and New South Wales was proposed at one point (by New South Wales Premier, George Dibbs). At the crucial Premiers' Conference in Hobart in 1895 it was agreed, more or less happily, that Federation might go ahead between any three colonies alone, if the people of three colonies agreed to federate. At an advanced stage in the processes, the eastern goldfields of Western Australia demanded secession from their colony, in order to join the Federation as a separate state. The nation might have stopped abruptly, its western border drawn well before Perth. This, and the willingness of five colonies, even at the very last moment when the Constitution had been completed and passed by the Imperial Parliament itself, to federate if necessary without any part of Western Australia, serve to demonstrate that territoriality as such was not the basis of community.

Edmund Barton's famous aphorism, early in the 1890s, that Federation would create 'a nation for a continent and a continent for a nation',[22] was both clever and stylish. But it was not altogether accurate. If Tasmania could be part of the nation, Federation was far from simply a matter of ruling a line around the continent, like fencing off a paddock. If Barton, then emerging as the dominant New South Wales Federalist leader, wanted to imply that the matter was simple, others emphasised the distinction between territory and population. In 1891, the former Tasmanian Premier, James Agnew, for example, argued that the name 'Australia' should be adopted for the new nation, rather than Commonwealth of Australia, since the former was a territorial title, referring to 'the material and physical country, to, as it were, the very soil itself', rather than a community title, referring 'to the mass of inhabitants'.[23] The nation's borders were not predetermined. They too had first to be imagined.

Developments in communication and transport certainly had their place, but they might just as easily have cemented instead the community of Australia and Britain, making intercourse between the colonies and 'Home' much quicker, radically improving opportunities to identify with British culture and to follow British events as if these were one's own. They might have led to an expansion of the borders of the imagined community, rather than their contraction. But the Australian colonies chose to come together, at the very time their mutual isolation was no longer extreme.

Neither communication, nor land nor people alone could serve as the basis of the national community. The community, as it was imagined, was much more than, or rather less than, 'the mass' of inhabitants. A particular type of inhabitant was included, and others excluded. Some belonged and others did not. As we shall see later, the identification of who was not in the imagined community was just as important as who was.

As the community was being imagined and the idea of Federation was taking hold, Australian nationalist literature and a distinctively Australian sporting culture were also growing. Historians have mostly failed to look for a link between these movements. They have found a thread between republican politics and the republican position exemplified in magazines like the *Bulletin* in the early years of the decade. They have also seen an association between the pastoral worker, nationalism, anti-establishment literary circles, anti-British sentiments and the emerging Labor Party.[24] And since the labour movement in the majority of states opposed Federation—at least under the Constitution Bill of 1898 (the organised republican movement had virtually faded away by then)—some have implied that the bush culture and the cultural nationalism out of which the Labor Party emerged could not have been part of the politics of Federation.

Vance Palmer's classic *The Legend of the Nineties*, for example, describes the early part of the decade as a moment of intensity, creativity and nationalism which, by the later years, flowed only along the narrowest channels.[25] The author of the other legendary 'Australian Legend', the great exponent of bushman's nationalism, Russel Ward, says little about Federation, but leaves open the question of an association with cultural nationalism. He writes, significantly, of 'the role of dreaming' in the genesis of the nation, but notes, ambiguously, that the 'dreaming of the 'nineties resulted, not in a republic embodying such noble practices as would have stupefied the actual bushman, but in much hard political horse-trading and in federation'.[26] But Chris Wallace-Crabbe, unusually, finds it 'tempting to believe, though difficult to demonstrate, that the energies which made themselves felt in the arts of the period were closely allied with the emotions which pressed the States towards Federation'.[27]

Of the three views, this is the most persuasive. How, then, might an alliance between energies and emotions be demonstrated? We may note—to begin with—that not only was the emergence of Australian culture frequently tied to political nationalism in the speeches and writings of the period, but there was also much intermingling of cultural and political circles, and the frequency with which individual politicians and activists themselves pursued literary sidelines was remarkable. Much of this output, it is true, was dubious in merit and made little contribution to a specifically Australian literature. Neither Henry Parkes's poetry nor Samuel Griffith's translations of Dante had relevance for the emergence of cultural nationalism, but the younger, native-born generation participated more in this process of simultaneous, indeed symbiotic, cultural and political nationalism.

Price Warung, author of convict stories and *Bulletin* poetry, was William Astley, organising secretary of the pro-federal Bathurst People's Federal Convention in 1896. Robert Garran, among other things, secretary to the Drafting Committee at the 1897 Federal Convention, also wrote poetry for the *Bulletin*, and John Quick, Federation Father (and co-author with Garran of the eternal *Annotated Constitution of the Australian Commonwealth*, known to all those familiar with constitutional law as 'Quick and Garran'), planned and began an original guide to Australian literature 'from its beginnings'.[28] Alfred Deakin, a man of deep and eclectic cultural learning, turned to politics because he believed himself a failure as a writer. Australian Impressionists and the *Bulletin*'s own editor were on committees for the Commonwealth Inauguration. Tom Roberts may have been paid to paint the Big Picture of the opening of the first Federal Parliament, but Frederick McCubbin painted its ceremonial arch on Melbourne's Princes Bridge (in the manner of Turner) for nothing.

The development of a 'native' population of artists was one of the secondary themes of Federation rhetoric in the 1890s. Some argued that the creation of a nation would strengthen artistic life by enlarging the cultural community, others that the growth of national consciousness would stimulate further a distinctively Australian style of art. Writing in the Federalists' journal, *Commonwealth*, about a scheme of colonial art loan exchanges, Arthur Streeton thought it seemed 'as though Federation were unconsciously begun by the artists and national galleries'.[29] Juliette Henry, when asked some years later about women's views on Federation, spoke of it as 'a step for the artistic and educational development of the country'.[30]

The *Bulletin*, that quintessential bearer of Australian cultural nationalism, itself published a good deal on Federation which, by the mid-1890s, it had come to support, describing it as representing (among many practical advantages) 'the glory and pride in assured nationhood'.[31] Federation poetry and songs with nationalist themes were produced in abundance in the period. A distinctive Australianness was self-consciously declared and celebrated again and again in cultural and political forms; these converged in the type of literary-political writing no longer encouraged or even recognised in the late twentieth century (when poetry has lost its public role), writing in which the language of romance, literary allusion and reference, description of emotion and 'poetic' outpouring mingled with serious political analysis and advocacy.

But how much home-grown culture do you need to make a nation? The historian W. G. McMinn believes that the cultural nationalism of the 1890s has been exaggerated, and that Australian enthusiasm for national products was limited, compared with the popularity in the same period of British works, including British plays, novels by Dickens, and the Queen's Jubilee.[32]

For the population in general and for a particular type of cultural product this conclusion is undoubtedly statistically accurate. But the movements for political and cultural nationalism were, inevitably, in advance of popular demand. They were led at the start by a small élite circle whose quest was to forge a distinctive Australian national character out of diffuse British references and leanings. And if the range of cultural material is extended to take in, for example, papers like the *Bulletin*, 'home-made' poetry, home-grown sportsmen (especially cricketers), *Australian music* and Australian singers (like Nellie Melba and Ada Crossley, internationally recognised as Australian), then the balance of cultural enthusiasms is probably shifted, perhaps even tilted in the direction of a popular Australian form.

A sense of community is not negated by reading or viewing foreign work. It can be captured and fostered by applying a local interpretation or eye to any cultural product. It was this distinctively Australian manner, this way of doing things, reading and responding, both culturally and politically, that was part of the process of nation-building in the 1890s. When the Australian Constitution was written, one of its distinctive features was, indeed, the borrowing of foreign models to which Australian conditions and demands were applied. This very approach—'scavenging', improvising, tinkering, taking from here and there, using material in ingenious ways, in short, the processes involved in handywork—was itself characteristically 'Australian'.

On top of the growth in national art, literature and sport, the attitude adopted by British authorities towards Australian problems fostered a general public resentment towards Britain, thus stimulating a type of negative Australian nationalism. Among the reasons for this 'current of feeling' was anger at Britain's refusal to forestall a threatened German annexation of New Guinea in 1883 and at 'the chilly indifference' of Lord Derby, the Colonial Secretary, who 'sneered at the action, [and] contradicted the rumours' when the Queensland Government attempted

36 *To Constitute a Nation*

independently to do so.[33] Along with British lack of sympathy towards the attempt to create a White Australia through restrictive immigration policy (discussed in chapter six), and the severe impact of the withdrawal of British investment in the early Depression years of the 1890s, it all began to add up to a greater desire among the Australian colonies to seek community with each other rather than primarily with Britain, and to a determination to do this by their own hand and in their own way. This feeling strengthened during the Depression of the early 1890s. Public works and private projects had been heavily dependent upon overseas, and in particular British, capital in the boom years preceding the Depression. As British investment declined dramatically, and British creditors called in their debts, Australians were prompted to question the kinship between the two countries, as well as the assumption that Britain—the mother—would automatically hold out a helping hand in time of crisis. The sense that Britain expected loyalty and obedience to its external policy rubbed salt into wounds.

But if it had all been simply a matter of cynicism or resentment, it is unlikely it would have proved productive. What needs to be added to this recipe is the 'spirit' of the age, the forward-looking, risk-taking 'vision', which subtly infused all of these factors and movements at that time. The spirit of the *fin de siècle* was the yeast that got the combined ingredients rising.

Excitement at the approach of the new century was felt across the world where the Christian calendar officially marked the years. It was, it seems, particularly potent in the white Australian population in the 1890s, because of a self-conscious sense of being 'young and free', dynamic and fresh, unlike the worn, even decaying, Old World. In part this sentiment was simply accurate. White Australia was young and democratic, free to try out much that the traditions and hierarchies of Britain and Europe would not allow. It was also in part mythical, the product of adventurous ideals attached in the European mind to Australia since well before the arrival of the British, which culminated in a period of international innovation at the moment of the ripening of other preconditions for nationalism.

Australia had existed in the imagination long before it became a nation. Well before its colonisation by the British, European fantasies had located ideal and topsy-turvy societies in its territories. Gabriel de Foigny's vision in 1676 of 'Terra Incognita Australis', in which a lone castaway finds a society of hermaphrodite Australians living in abundance without government, in a manner which 'may pass for the perfect image of the state that man first enjoyed in Paradise',[34] was part of a continuous tradition of imagining the 'undiscovered' southern lands as opposite, upside-down, and full of strange and wonderful things.

In 1756 Charles de Brosse predicted great profit and honours for the country that would penetrate the whole Australian continent. Like many others around this time, he also advocated the transportation of criminals to Australia, in his case to rid France of its vices and to turn vices into virtues in a South Pacific setting.[35] The land of opposites would transform the villain into the virtuous. It was magical, indeed Utopian.

There are effectively two types of Utopia: the one of abundance, in the tradition of *cocaigne*, the fools' paradise, where food falls ready-made from trees, where cooked pigs run around asking to be eaten, and work is never necessary. The other is the Utopia of reason, where institutions are designed to create a perfected society, where the destructive habits of human society are corrected by good design and clear thinking.[36] The combination of these two traditions appeared many times in speculations upon the use to be made of this—literally—fabulous place. There were proposals to give asylum in New South Wales to the American Loyalists, who took Britain's side in the War of Independence, so they may 'repair their broken fortunes and again enjoy their former domestic felicity', and the idea that the Loyalists could join a colony of Chinese and Indian immigrants as well as British convicts, all collectively making up for Britain's loss of America.[37] This enduring image of Australia as an ideal setting for experiment (along with the lesson from America) was to have an effect upon the processes of nation-building more than one hundred years later.

Once European explorers went further than merely imagining and then reaching Australian shores, however, once they began to take in the reality of the continent, their Utopian anticipation was mingled with real, and disappointing, experience. Although Australia's eastern shores delighted scientific curiosity with their apparently bizarre wildlife, reversed seasons, black swans, flying possums, and duck-billed animals with fur, confirming the vision of Australia as a land of unlimited possibilities, when the British arrived to stay in 1788, reports of the viability of the land and its potential for settlement, furnished earlier by Cook's voyages, were found to be exaggerated or inaccurate.

For the British the land was unyielding and far from Utopian. Convicts, transported south in the hope, among the many other reasons, that they might be transformed and build a new society, themselves attempted to escape in search of a Utopian community, 'in which they were assured of finding all the comforts of life, without the necessity of labouring for them'.[38] Explorers died searching for a fabled inland sea. Free land for the settlers, and later on gold for the taking, represented for many again the fantasy of effortless abundance, and for most the reality of harshness and scarcity.

38   *To Constitute a Nation*

Out of this continuing process grew an Australian character of resilience, with its distinctive mixture of romanticism and pragmatism. By the end of the nineteenth century, the cycles of hope and disappointment, anticipation and reality, had contributed to a culture and a national character—consistently noted by visitors—of paradoxes. It was an admixture of toughness and sentimentality, preference for cities and attachment to rural values, love of gambling and the power of endurance.

One hundred years of occupation and struggle had still not robbed the white population altogether of their attachment to Utopian ideals. But, by the last two decades of the nineteenth century, the dream of *cocaigne* had been overtaken in Utopian thought by the rationalist Utopia. It was the forerunner of public planning and social engineering, of the vision of a society perfected through education, sanitation and statutory equality.

Henrietta Dugdale's *A Few Hours in a Far off Age*, written in Sydney in 1883, and dedicated to the Victorian liberal reformer George Higinbotham, was one of the first of a new Utopian genre in which social experiment through legislation creates an ideal society. In this genre the common function of Utopias—that of offering contemporary political criticism in a fictionalised form—is made transparent. In Dugdale's work, the characters themselves describe directly to the reader the problems inherent in the writer's own society. Dugdale's time-traveller from the late nineteenth century confronts an Australia in an unspecified future, perhaps hundreds of years hence, transformed by the female franchise and women's subsequent influence on politics and education. All the miseries of war, inebriation, overpopulation and squalor have been overcome.

A similar scenario is found in the Utopian novel of Catherine Helen Spence, in which a dying woman in 1888 is granted a 'week in the future' in 1988 (to which she is transported by a dose of medication) instead of spending her remaining few years as an invalid.[40] There she has the chance to witness the cumulative effects of legislation, education and technology. She finds the working day considerably lightened and shortened to six hours, accommodation organised collectively, disease and inebriation conquered, and Australia independent, with the Empire having amicably been wound up some decades earlier. Like Dugdale, Spence foregrounds the emancipation of women through education, the franchise, 'hygiene' and birth control, as the achievement of her Utopia.

These works are just two of the many written in Australia around this time. Like the majority of Utopian writers, Dugdale and Spence also published political pamphlets and gave speeches to outline ways of achieving their goals. With Annie Lowe, Dugdale founded the Victorian Women's Suffrage Society soon after completing her Utopia. Spence was active in a range of welfare and political organisations, most prominently as an advocate of proportional representation for Australia's parliaments. She also became (as we shall see) Australia's first female political candidate, when she stood for election as a delegate to the 1897 Federal Convention.

Utopian writing was fashionable in this period, and every social reformer who fancied him or herself as a theorist seemed to want to write a Utopia. And many people, in return, wanted to read them. Indeed, the last two decades of the nineteenth century formed the great era of Utopian writing, with the combined visionary energies of the Enlightenment, socialism, liberalism and technological advances producing an extraordinary social optimism. Writing Utopias was a type of adjunct to the emerging activity of political blueprint writing and forward planning, which were to become central features of politics in the following century.

Lying right at the intersection of these approaches, Henry George's *Progress and Poverty*, published in 1879, which advocated land nationalisation and a 'single tax', went through five editions in the 1880s alone. Edward Bellamy's *Looking Backward* ranked as the second-best selling 'novel' in the United States in the nineteenth century, and has been continuously in print since it appeared in 1887.[40] Both works profoundly influenced emerging socialist and social democratic thinkers around the world, including in Australia, where Bellamy Clubs were established to discuss and promote the writer's ideas, and accounts of George's theories were published in all the new socialist and republican papers of the late 1880s. When Henry George toured Australia in 1890, he was received with great fanfare, both by the labour movement and by members of parliament, and his tour was extensively reported in the mainstream, as well as labour, press. Some followers believed his single tax theories to have much in common with the goals of the Australian Federalists.

J. A. Froude's *Oceana, or England and Her Colonies*, published in 1886, was an account of Froude's travels through Britain's colonies, in which the author 'meditated' upon a glorious future of a unified Empire, inspired by 'the dream of Sir James Harrington'. Froude had borrowed his title from Harrington's own seventeenth-century 'Oceana', a political tract addressed to Oliver Cromwell and written in the form of a Utopia, advocating the separation of powers, relative egalitarianism and small land-holding.

In the time since Harrington wrote, Froude told his readers, 'the increase of Oceana has exceeded the wildest dream of the most extravagant enthusiast'. Harrington 'would have been himself incredulous' had he known of the spread of the Empire, and the richness of its territories. But, despite what had been wrought by 'the genius of English freedom', 'the vision is but half accomplished . . . Harrington

40 *To Constitute a Nation*

contemplated that Oceana would be a single commonwealth embraced in the arms of Neptune, and the spell which can unite all these communities into one has not yet been discovered'.[41]

Froude himself clearly hoped to provide the spell, lying in an 'organic' union of self-governing Empire states, recognising that they 'will never submit again to be ruled from England', but that their union and their devotion could be fostered 'within the limits of the existing constitution'. Bestowing British honours, inviting colonial statesmen onto the Privy Council, establishing lines of political advice between colony and Crown, and above all never contemplating separation would be the means. In short, although Froude does not use the term, he sought effectively a spontaneous Imperial Federation.

Froude provided an alternative model in the Utopian panoply, the dream of an organic, peaceful and marvellous system, achieved with little more than symbolic adjustment and right thinking. Although he was warmly received on his tour in 1885, met in person at the station by the Victorian Premier Duncan Gillies, and received by New South Wales Premier Henry Parkes, and although the idea, perhaps even the name, of the 'commonwealth' was reinforced in Parkes's mind, Froude's conservative Utopia did not take hold.

Parkes himself, indirectly, explained why. 'Australian sentiment', he pointed out in 1889, was rapidly growing:

> There are disruptive organizations here in favour of pure republicanism, in favour of Henry George's schemes and in favour of organic change for change's sake . . . To those who think loosely, the lodestar is the United States. The Mother country, if she values the fidelity of these Colonies should offer something more flattering to our sense of pride and self-importance than any other form of Government can offer.[42]

This is an extraordinary statement, full of the themes of the age. One year before the first Federation Conference, called by Parkes himself, it invites the exploration of an entirely novel political system. It suggests that Australian cultural nationalism can be made compatible with adherence to the British monarchy. But it threatens, effectively, that almost anything in this visionary age might come to pass.

In the heady climate of futurism there were also dystopias, fictional predictions of an oppressive future, brought about by what would later be known as social engineering, and in some cases specifically by the good intentions of Federalists. The appeal to community and union, so frequently heard in the Federalists' rhetoric, was savagely satirised by Nugent Robertson in his dystopian forecast *Federation and Afterwards*, which he wrote in the form of a fictional lecture by a 'Dr Anias Honeybun'.

Sentiment and patriotism, and the desire to be free of the 'bondage of England', 'Honeybun' reminds the now oppressed and impoverished people of New South Wales, had led the movement for Federation. It had been recognised that 'a division of interests . . . would be an everlasting blot upon the noble picture of "one people, one destiny", an evidence of distrust . . . and of discord where there should be brotherly love'. The call, 'Honeybun' tells the reader, had been made for union, 'as it were, a marriage, where the contracting parties might have something almost amounting to a dislike of one another at first, but where it was desirable that the marriage should be consummated for the sake of the race, and the continuance of the family'. Australia was now about to 'attain to a form of government far more perfect than she had ever known', and the New South Welshmen should give up their struggle and bow to the might of Melbourne.[43] Their failure to do so, Robertson explains in a fictional afterword (following the 'death' of Honeybun), leads to the imposition of martial law. This complex, if none too subtle, scenario would find no place in the political culture of Australia one hundred years later, but in its time was a familiar form of political criticism.

In republican and labour circles, there was also a small vogue for a type of revolutionary Utopian writing, in which a class uprising leads to proletarian dictatorship. S. A. Rosa's *The Coming Terror*, Price Warung's unfinished 'The Strike of '95', David Andrade's *The Melbourne Riots*, William Lane's serial 'Yellow or White', published in *Boomerang*, appeared over the last years of the 1880s and the first years of the 1890s, in the period when the writings of British and American socialists were becoming known in Australia. In common with the more pacific Utopias, these works convey an idea of complete social transformation and a commitment to imagining an alternative, if unpleasant, Australia. Lane's own synopsis of chapter one of his dystopian serial is laughable now, but then it captured a whole fearful vision, and the conviction that the real politics of the period might bring this to pass:

> In the winter of 1908, when the colonies of Australasia had become very generally settled and populated by over 40,000,000, of whom a fourth and more were Chinese, Lord Stibbins, an Imperialistic mine owner, entertains at his splendid home of Taringa Park, near Brisbane, Sir Wong Hung Foo, the great Chinese-Australian millionaire and speculator. While the mass of the white hate the yellow race violently, the rich whites, for selfish purposes, encourage the latter and are enabled by the loss of colonial autonomy which followed the Imperialistic schemes of 1888 to over-ride the true spirit of the Australian people. Lord Stibbins, a calculating man, had devoted his life to a mysterious OBJECT, and . . . had solicited a private interview with his guest, who had fallen passionately into 'love at first sight' with the beautiful daughter of his host . . .[44]

42   *To Constitute a Nation*

Lane's scenario works within the radical republican politics of the late 1880s: employing the popular Utopian genre, it combines revolutionary socialism, the radical demand for Australian independence and anti-Chinese sentiment. It demands a revolutionary solution to forestall the radical upheaval Lane and his supporters otherwise anticipated. Soon, Lane was to attempt a microcosmic experiment along such revolutionary lines.

As elsewhere in the New World, model communities were established in Australia throughout the second half of the century, and in particular in its concluding years. Communal village settlements, including a scheme depicted by Horace Tucker in his Utopian novel of 1896, *The New Arcadia*, Moravian communities, and labour colonies—almost all short-lived—were established in astonishing numbers, amounting to nearly eighty in Victoria alone.[45] All represented the quest for a constructed, purified community, the deed following the word.

Colonial governments proved ready to absorb the Utopian ideas and experiments of this period into statutes, and into state-sponsored schemes, such as the Co-operative Communities Land Settlement Act in Queensland and the Victorian Settlement of Lands Act, both passed in 1893. For our story of the Constitution, the 1890s would see the triumph of shaping an Australian constitutional monarchy over an Australian republic, not by defeating, but by absorbing the essential goals of the republicans.

Some of the republicans perhaps aided this outcome by pursuing their Utopianism beyond Australia's borders, and therefore outside the sphere where they might have influenced the new national polity. In 1893, a year after the publication of his *Workingman's Paradise*, and two years after the first draft of the Australian Constitution was written, William Lane decided that Australia, for so many the site of dreams of new beginnings, was itself beyond reconstruction.

Although he had gained in principle support from the Queensland Government, Lane failed in his attempt to find an area of land in Australia he thought suitable for building a real Utopian community. So, with several hundred of the most dedicated Utopians, he sailed away in the *Royal Tar* and established a socialist colony, 'New Australia', in Paraguay. It had its own constitution. This laid out the rules of the colony, governing distribution and use of its land and capital, as well as the personal conduct of its members. Despite the thorough planning, the fortunes of New Australia were mixed, proving for the most part unsuccessful.[46] Its impact in Australia was largely limited to the removal from the country of many who might have contributed actively to the emerging debate about national identity.

What might these practical Utopians have made of Federation? Some years later, in the midst of the campaign for the Constitution Bill, Rose

The Imaginary Nation   43

Scott was to compare the Paraguay experiment with Federation itself. 'Do you remember the "Royal Tar"?', she asked her audience.

> I went to see them all on board and the thing that struck me most, was that all the women . . . were wretched and did not want to go and all the men were in the seventh heaven of enthusiasm and joy. I often think of that when I hear men raving over this scheme of Federation and its glorious possibilities and I consider 'Is it not better to endure and try to amend the ills we have, than to fly to others we know not of'.[47]

Scott's analogy captures more than just a metaphor. The notion that the Australian Constitution was produced out of a climate of experiment, even Utopianism, may seem altogether bizarre to those who have long seen it as entirely pragmatic, uninspiring and lacking in originality. But, although Utopianism reached its peak around the time of the Melbourne Federation Conference in 1890 and the first Federal Convention in Sydney in 1891, falling away gradually as the decade wore on, the earlier drafts of the Constitution were, if anything, more practical and restrained and the later draft, more experimental and self-confident.

Social experiment was closely identified with Australian (and New Zealand) politics in the last decades of the century.[48] Australian parliaments introduced many social novelties, including manhood suffrage, then female suffrage, alternative electoral systems, payment of members of parliament, industrial regulation, liberalised divorce laws. Where Britain relied upon tradition and precedent, Australia seemed devoted to political novelty. Not all the colonies enjoyed this as much as New South Wales, Victoria and South Australia, but by the time the Constitution was being completed, Australians were thoroughly familiar with experiment. Political 'veterans trained in the English respect for tradition', said Bernhard Wise (one of the New South Wales delegates to the 1897 Federal Convention), were, by 1880, replaced with 'younger men for whom the word "unconstitutional" possessed no terrors'.[49]

In the 1890s, the willingness to experiment in the short term combined with a preparedness to plan for the long term. What many historians have described as the utilitarian settlement of Australian Federation was much more than this; it was both pragmatic and visionary. Its achievement evoked what now may seem the strangest sentiments of rapture for those who see utilitarianism and pragmatism as devoid of emotion.

A sermon delivered at All Souls' Church, Leichhardt, in 1898, for example, foresaw federated Australia (so long as it received the Divine Blessing) as 'a great and magnificent country . . . a kind of Paradise for the world, the envy of the nations'.[50] On the day of the Inauguration of the

44   *To Constitute a Nation*

Commonwealth, John Quick told the readers of the *Brisbane Courier* that the Constitution was 'the greatest triumph of freedom and democracy, combined with cherished respect for traditional principles, that the world has ever seen'. Sublime, thrilling, and momentous, the Commonwealth,

> like a mighty ship of state, has been launched on the great ocean of destiny. May thy voyage . . . be prosperous, peaceful and glorious; ever from thy mast-head flying . . . the flag of freedom and progress . . . built to live and move with mobility far-reaching, and with lustre resplendent and immortal![51]

Such sentiments multiplied as the decade closed, and the achievement of nationhood came to be realised. Some of this was no more than the excitement of the occasion, when the Inauguration of the Commonwealth finally came about as the new century started, turning most towns for a day at least into carnivals. For others it was no doubt the expression of relief that the great and difficult task had been completed, that most, if not all, thought it successful and to begin successfully boded well for the nation's future.

And many also enjoyed the activity of planning in the imagination, forecasting by fantasy. The idea of a new nation lent itself happily to such impulses. An anonymous newspaper contribution in 1898, for example, anticipates the celebration of the centenary of Federation: 'For I dipped into the future far as human eye could see. It was June 3, 1998 and the youngest of the great nations of the earth was celebrating her centenary in regal fashion'. Scenes of great rejoicing at the peaceful achievement of the nation's 'great destiny' mingle with recollections of the crisis in 1950 when civil war over 'unequal state representation' had loomed. Over the century the large states have been subdivided many times, and the country's population now exceeds fifty-four million. Once-barren desert regions, 'only fit to support rabbits and blackfellows', now are fertile and wealthy, 'as if the wand of an enchanter had touched the country and made the transformation'. Rail links, manufacturing, and mining have multiplied greatly, and the absentee landlord has all but vanished. The education system has expanded vastly, and Australian cities are 'taken as models by many of the most enlightened communities of England and Europe'. The Governor-General, now the great and honoured 'vital symbol of the constitution which had been bequeathed' to the people, gives a speech enumerating these achievements and in 'stirring tableaux' around the country is feted and cheered by 'a great and free people'.[52]

More imaginative, Richard Werner's fictional news report of 23 August 2000 gives us the expected technological predictions of this genre. An airship has brought the writer from London in a matter of only ten days (one vessel leaves every day!), five telephone lines to Europe facilitate business, the Australian desert has been irrigated by artesian bores, and electric trams in every city carry the 'butcher, baker' and even 'John Chinaman'. The number of Australian states has multiplied, and now includes New Guinea and New Caledonia, which was handed over to Australia following the Franco-British war of 1936. With great wealth and a national population of one hundred million, greatly overtaking Britain's population, the centre of the Empire, had it lasted, would certainly have been in Australia rather than Britain. But Australia 'has long since emerged from the position of an outlying British possession'. Commercial ties alone have endured. A combination of progressive social and industrial laws and the application of rational science (including phrenology) to crime, alcoholism, and the selection of professions, has resulted in a productive, healthy people, their working day now only five hours, and industrial conflict almost non-existent.[53]

It is deeply poignant to read these predictions in the period in which they are set. They are speaking directly to the reader in the 1990s, but what they tell us is little about the conditions of our present. As with all futurism, the very attempt to predict betrays the conditions of the writer's present more than the actual future. The population, it was thought, would grow dramatically (much as the American population had done); faith in 'progress' and science, mingled with what we now recognise as racist and biologist categories of human 'types', shape the character of the Utopian optimism. Anticipated social and political conditions follow the sympathies of the time. What can be gained from these odd little pieces is a glimpse of the hopes of the age, the expectation that Federation would be the source of future greatness.

More sober contributions repeatedly made the same point. Even the Sydney *Daily Telegraph*, resolutely anti-Billite, reflected on the record of the century past, and gave its readers a *'fin de siècle'* definition of *'fin de siècle'* on the first day of the new century. The term implied 'to be clever, to be commercially useful or generally improving, in fine to be rather more than modern'. The *'fin de siècle'* implication has been, it concluded, 'richly earned by marvellous development', in commercial and industrial arts.[54] The future for Australia was to be a brilliant one.

At the noisy state banquet in Sydney that same evening, 'the greatest achievement of the century' was weighed up by one speaker: 'Mr Balfour said that it was the advancement of science. Lord Roseberry said it was the dignity of emancipation. The representatives of the United States said that it was the great advancement and the marvellous development of that continent'. But, continued Sir Samuel Way, Chief Justice of South Australia, 'there could be no doubt that the great event of that day, the federation of the colonies of Australia, had struck the keynote of the coming century'.[55] For a moment the nation imagined and the nation accomplished came together. The audience cheered.

CHAPTER THREE

Imagined Constitutions

The Constitution of the Commonwealth of Australia, signed by Her Majesty Queen Victoria on 9 July 1900, proclaimed on 17 September 1900 and activated on 1 January 1901, was not the only constitution in circulation in the 1890s. There were other drafts and alternative models, as well as detailed appeals for the Constitution to be written differently. Like the Utopian blueprints and fictional accounts of a future federated Australia, all expressed the belief that a more perfect society could be created by finding the perfect word.

The Constitution itself went through several drafts before its final shape was reached. The first Constitution Bill of 1891 was significantly different from the version completed in 1898, and that one was amended, in detail if not in essence, at the 'Secret' Premiers' Conference in 1899. The Constitution was further amended in Britain, and can only really be thought of as final in the form it had assumed by the date of its passage through the British Parliament in mid-1900. Even then (despite the long-standing orthodoxy that Australia is constitutionally rigid and unchangeable, a 'frozen continent', as Geoffrey Sawer called it[1]) the Constitution has been changed and amended by referendum, rare though this might be, and frequently by judgments of the High Court, which the Constitution itself created.

In addition many of the Constitution's sections are provisional and transitional, some covering a limited period of time only, others there 'until the Parliament otherwise provides' (which, in almost all cases, it has done by now, sometimes many times), and the states have the power to 'refer' any matter in their own jurisdiction, that is to say, to hand it over to the Commonwealth. This, as was recognised in the Federal Convention debates in 1898,[2] allows a re-allocation of constitutional powers without formal amendment.

Major changes in the constitutional relations between Britain and Australia throughout the twentieth century[3] have also altered the Constitution profoundly, leaving several sections 'dead letters'. Taken as it stood on 1 January 1901, the Constitution represented a model, as yet untried, for

Imagined Constitutions   47

a particular type of nation. The words in the document were intended, as far as possible, to fit together the mental model and the actual result. Although the Constitution's framers hoped that it would do the job, having lived through the drafting and redrafting of the document, none expected that it would remain forever unchanged.

All statutes are drafted so that their words will produce a pre-imagined outcome, and at the same time will stand up in law. Not just any words will suffice. In a constitution, the parts must not only stand as individual statutes do, but must fit together and cohere, achieving their individual purpose and, together, their common design. It is a task requiring great precision and sensitivity to words, as well as familiarity with legal language, customs, and fashions in drafting style.

It is only by thinking of the Constitution as a routine Act, or believing it to have always existed on the books, that we lose sight of the nature of the task. Regardless of how prosaic the language of the Constitution may now appear, or how commonplace the things ordained by its sections may seem, and regardless of whether or not the individual provisions of the Constitution may be to a person's liking, the skill in its drafting should not be forgotten.

Australians, convinced that they had the skill, were determined to write their own constitution. They had already had a little practice designing the Federal Council, whose Act stands as a type of pre-Federation constitution, describing not only the membership, form and frequency of meetings, but also the specific matters over which (at least in principle) the Council might exercise power: relations of Australasia with the Pacific islands; prevention of the influx of criminals; Australian fisheries outside territorial waters; the enforcement of civil and criminal court judgments in intercolonial cases; custody of offenders on Australasian ships; and the referral of any other matter from the parliaments of any two or more colonies to the Council itself. A good many of these provisions would appear in the final version of the Constitution. More important was the experience, both practical and conceptual.

By the time a real constitution was contemplated, the British authorities saw the matter as lying almost entirely in the Australians' hands. They neither wanted to repeat the dramatic experience with the American colonies in 1776, nor to insist upon following the Canadian approach where British draftsmen drew up the British North America Act of 1867. Although the Colonial Office made it clear that it would help if asked, and in the event did attempt to exercise some influence behind the scenes,[4] it would have found a most unreceptive audience had it tried to take over the process.

Around the time of the first Federal Convention, in 1891, as we have seen, an atmosphere of resentment, a suspicion of neglect, had clouded

48   *To Constitute a Nation*

Australia's image of Britain. The Victorian Premier, James Service, had told visiting British writer James Froude as much, six years before, and Froude, whose self-appointed mission was to strengthen the 'organic' links between the colonies and their mother, made a point of relating the conversation:

> If the colonies continued to be told by the press and by platform speakers that we [Britain] did not care about them, and that they might leave us when they pleased, and if official communications continued cold and indifferent, indifference might produce indifference. A separatist tendency, which had as yet no existence, would grow up. The links might be broken in a fit of irritation and impatience, and once gone could never be mended.[5]

Three years later a somewhat different interpretation was placed on this mood, by another visitor, R. W. Dale, who found that the theory of inevitable separation was an English theory, and that Australians 'universally' condemned it. Nevertheless he repeated Froude's warning that England's indifference to the colonies, and its apparent readiness to let them go, was souring imperial relations.[6]

The same theme comes up again in the year of the first Federal Convention. The 'Cockney Columbus', David Christie Murray (the only writer to have left a first-hand account of Henry Parkes's 'Tenterfield Oration'[7]), noted in his otherwise sympathetic traveller's account the 'melancholy fact' that many in the colonies were far from loyal to Britain. British neglect, the offensive attitude of superiority adopted by British visitors and the dreadful habit of sending England's 'incurable failures' out to Australia had led to resentment in even the most loyal, and active dislike among others. 'The strongest current of Australian feeling', Murray noted, 'is settling with a tide of growing power against the mother country'.[8]

What Froude and Murray sensed was a moment of real danger for Australian relations with Britain. One of the first alternative 'constitutions' for Australia was a product of this moment. In the year of Queen Victoria's Golden Jubilee, a vigorous, if short-lived republican movement emerged in New South Wales and Queensland. A Republican Union and a Republican League were formed and in various publications, including the *Australian Nationalist* and the *Republican* (edited by Louisa and Henry Lawson), the essential institutions of a republican Australia were spelled out. In a 'letter' to Queen Victoria, George Black (later a founder of the Labor Party) described these as: the abolition of the office of Governor, of the Upper House, and of British titles; payment of members of parliament; penal code reform; nationalisation of the land; 'championship of liberty'; and 'Federation of the Australian Colonies under Republican rule'.[9]

There were echoes in this movement of the much earlier 'constitution' of John Dunmore Lang, whose *Freedom and Independence for the Golden Lands of Australia* (a delightfully Utopian title) of 1852 outlined his scheme for British migration and Australian self-government. A federation of the Australian 'provinces' (with two Houses of Parliament, including a Senate with equal representation of each province) was to be achieved, along with the severing of all political ties to Britain. As in Black's model, the elements of republicanism sat comfortably within a federal framework, the radical and (what may seem) the conservative, paradoxically, co-existing.

The very crisis that stimulated republicanism helped prepare the seedbed for the vigorous growth in the years to follow of the Australian Federation movement out of which a Constitution that was both independent and dependent at the same time could be forged. The Victorian Australian Natives' Association, a Friendly Society established in 1871 for men of Australian birth (which we shall meet again), began early on to press for such a formula. At a conference in 1890 they drew up their own federal constitution in a series of resolutions which, among other things, identified the areas of federal jurisdiction: defence; a federal court of appeal; relations with the Pacific islands; naturalisation; uniform customs duties; railways; postal and telegraphic services; the public debt and federal revenue; and the division of any colony, with its consent. Although this initiative itself did not go far, and ANA interest in Federation was patchy for some years after 1890,[10] their list of federal matters resembled significantly that which was formally adopted at the first Federal Convention in 1891. In the early years of the decade, the imaginary and the real constitutions began to converge.

By the second half of the 1890s imperial relations had begun markedly to improve. In 1897, Murray found it 'astonishing' that the Australian feeling should have appeared as it had only six years earlier. Still he warned against the 'crass officialdom' of the English, who 'provided so frigid a greeting for the Australian contingent', including Australia's Premiers, who were in London with other Empire leaders in 1897 for the great celebration of Queen Victoria's Diamond Jubilee.[11]

In addition to the Jubilee, which marked the emergence of Queen Victoria from her long, drab years of mourning, a change of British government with a new Colonial Secretary in 1895 seems to have contributed to an improved climate for relations. Joseph Chamberlain, a former Liberal turned Conservative and a deeply committed imperialist, determined to keep the Empire intact, was prepared to make greater concessions to the Dominions, for example to reconsider British trading agreements with Europe in the light of colonial interests, and to hold more frequent and more relaxed imperial conferences. In 1895 the self-

50   *To Constitute a Nation*

governing colonies of the Empire also finally achieved the right to have their own members on the Privy Council, the lack of which had been the source of a long-standing grievance.[12]

By this time, however, a draft Australian Constitution had already been written, and the processes for completing a final version were well in train. Whatever their (no doubt mixed) motives may have been, the British authorities seemed to care more about their antipodean colonies and to be more respectful of the views of the colonial representatives by the time of the second Federal Convention in 1897. Australians were, by then, both skilled and more confident in constitution writing than they had been six years earlier. The evolution of Australian relations with Britain is reflected, along with many other things, in the draft constitutions that appeared over the decade.

At the beginning of the process, few Australians had the formal skill to draft a whole constitution in advance, although most delegates to the 1891 Convention were lawyers and all were members of colonial parliaments. Queensland's Samuel Griffith did, and his draft was ultimately to prevail. Both Tasmanian Attorney-General Andrew Inglis Clark and South Australia's Premier Charles Kingston also did.

With the aid of the Tasmanian Parliamentary Draftsman, Walter Wise, Clark put together a draft, the very first real draft, piece by piece, picking and choosing from among existing models: the American, the Canadian, the Australian colonial and that of the Federal Council. Before the Convention began, New South Wales Premier Henry Parkes had received an advance copy from Clark not, however, with pleasure but with 'dread', describing it as a 'literary constitution'.[13] What he meant, one imagines, was that it was abstract, a mental model, a 'paper' constitution, the very criticism some anti-Billites would later make of the real thing.

In Clark's mind was an imaginary scenario for an Australian nation that proved to be more American than the other delegates cared to accept. Clark sought the maximum degree of sovereignty for the 'Provinces' (as he chose to call what became the states), even increasing their powers in some instances over those they held at the time, by giving their parliaments the power to elect provincial governors and (following the American model) the power to confirm constitutional amendment proposed by the federal government. Added to this was a provision for appointed, rather than elected, ministers. To the assembly of constitutional parts, Clark added his own: the abolition of all appeals to Britain's Privy Council.

This idea, which would endure longer than some of Clark's other provisions, captures a much more sovereign state than the British Colonial Office was ultimately prepared to countenance. Appeals to the Privy Council and the Colonial Laws Validity Act of 1865 were the twin

Imagined Constitutions   51

portals through which an Australian law could be carried to its doom. To propose the establishment of an Australian 'Supreme Court' and the removal of appeal to a court outside Australia was to make a statement not only about the maturity of the Australian legal profession, but essentially about its right to act without interference. This section of Clark's constitution is a miniature declaration of independence, and the other delegates liked it. Behind the reception of this provision lay a long history in the colonies of opposition to the Privy Council for Australian appeals, and desire for an independent Australian Court of Appeal. The Constitution's framers hung onto something like Clark's proposal right to the very end, in 1900, when they were forced to modify it (but not as much as Britain wanted).

Kingston also offered a draft, very similar for the most part to Clark's, but more British in its inclusion of responsible government (that is to say, with ministers drawn from the parliament rather than a non-elected ministry). It confirmed the idea of elected colonial governors, only this time the electors themselves (rather than the parliaments) were to have the task, and included also the abolition of external appeals. But it added the Swiss device of the referendum (raised merely for 'consideration' by Clark) both for a popular voice on legislation and for constitutional amendment, and it gave the Federal Parliament powers over trade unions and industrial disputes. This latter provision (albeit modified to apply only to interstate rather than all disputes) was to reappear in the final Constitution and to prove central in shaping the Australian nation in the twentieth century.

Working with these drafts, and with his own supreme drafting skill, Samuel Griffith, and the others who made up the Drafting Committee of the 1891 Convention, floated on the Hawkesbury River in the Queensland Government's steamship *Lucinda* for several days, rewriting and thus reshaping the recipe for the nation. This Drafting Committee (which Clark missed joining due to having the flu) also 'cut and pasted', both from the constitutions of existing federations and from the two freshly completed drafts, Kingston's and Clark's. Their result was for the time being still more American than would ultimately transpire, but its combination of ingredients already made it an original recipe. Whether Australians as a whole were ready to cook with it remained to be seen.

The Convention's Drafting Committee, said one of the 1891 delegates not long after, went 'on a little picnic up the Hawkesbury River and returned two days later with a spic-and-span Constitution for the new nation'.[14] Shortly after the Convention concluded, Protectionist leader George Dibbs replaced Henry Parkes as Premier of New South Wales. Although he had been a member of the Convention, Dibbs had come to the conclusion that the recipe was not to his liking. Like others, he

52   *To Constitute a Nation*

attempted to write his own. It was a recipe for unification rather than Federation.

In a speech in Tamworth in 1894, launching his campaign for the next New South Wales election, Dibbs mocked the efforts of the 1891 Convention where 'everything was done in a moment with the stroke of a magician's wand to change these separate Colonies, which are competing and fighting with each other . . . into a Federation which is to resemble the United States of America'. Dibbs then painted a grim picture of Federation involving 'an additional layer of government', costing millions more pounds a year, being added to the existing six parliaments and six governors, with services including railway systems still remaining separate and the states still 'cutting one another's throats'. The people, he argued, did not want the extra cost and found the idea of additional government 'repulsive'; indeed, he concluded, having 'thought over the Federation question a very great deal', the costly duplication of the existing colonies was itself already unacceptable and this could be wiped out 'at one stroke of the pen', putting in its place a single government, like Britain's, and creating a unified nation.

The proposal for unification was greeted by the majority as fanciful. Dibbs was depicted in the *Brisbane Courier* as sailing away 'in a balloon of his own . . . towards an ideal which is beyond the farthest point ever reached in [the Federalists'] dreams', while the *Bulletin* in contrast thought his plan marred by the *absence* of 'fantasy', being instead 'a plain and dismal matter-of-fact statement of certain cash advantages'.[15] But Dibbs was far from ready to drop his plan over lack of popular approval. He went on to spell out the proposal more sombrely in a letter to the Victorian Premier, Sir James Patterson, which he then had published in the *Sydney Morning Herald*. In this letter, in which the first step of unification between Victoria and New South Wales is proposed, Dibbs's own imagined, alternative constitution is laid out.

Unlike effectively every other prominent commentator, as we shall see, Dibbs proposed a constitution resembling the Canadian model. What this meant was a central parliament, with a limited range of powers allocated to the 'provincial administrations', and 'their expenditure restricted to purely local purposes'. To achieve this, Victoria and New South Wales should come together straight away in a 'union of interests' under one Governor, one parliament, one tariff, one debt, one railway, defence, and postal administration, one land law, one principle for distributing surplus revenue, and one High Commissioner. They would be called 'The United Colonies' and afterward, when South Australia and Queensland joined, 'The Dominion of Australia' or 'United Australia'.[16]

There is nothing especially original in Dibbs's list of powers, and nothing (except the specification that there be a High Commissioner in

Imagined Constitutions 53

London) that does not appear later among the Commonwealth's jurisdiction in the final Constitution. What Dibbs had in mind was not so much a radically new conception of national powers (indeed his list was very limited compared to the final version), as a vision of a merger between the two most populous and (at least potentially) wealthy colonies. He justified this chiefly in terms of cost-efficiency, directing his appeal especially at Victoria's financial distress, the result of the Depression of the previous two years, which had hit that colony especially hard. The financial advantages were to lie both in increased trade and revenue raising as well as in economies of scale.

'There is something very alluring in the thought of making a clean sweep of all the cumbrous legislative machinery which loads the various Colonies', and 'at one swoop a clearance of all the petty aping of meaningless pomp and flourish', commented the Melbourne *Age*.[17] But still, in common with most others, the *Age* did not like the plan. There were anxieties about offending South Australia, and fears, as ever, that New South Wales would use unification to dominate Victoria.

Dibbs's constitution was a minimal, financial contract, a business merger, not even a marriage of convenience. It was an imagined constitution without an imaginary nation. It was the wrong way round, failing to capture what people hoped for from a constitution, and in its failure serving now as a reminder that Federation could not be built on financial principles alone.

The draft that was written on the *Lucinda*, modified in a couple of places by debate in the 1891 Convention, was the one that survived from these early years. It went on to serve as the point of departure for subsequent constitutions and was, essentially, reshaped at the second Federal Convention six years later. We shall examine many of its provisions in detail over the following chapters and, in doing so, reflect on why the other drafts with which it competed failed, and why it languished itself for some years. Although Federalists tore their hair in frustration over the subsequent failure of parliaments to activate the 1891 draft Bill, others may now be retrospectively glad of the delay. A quick comparison of the main differences may suggest why.

In the earlier Bill, various functions which are now the choice of the electors were to be fulfilled by indirect means: the Senate (with eight rather than six members per state) would have been chosen by the state parliaments, and Senate candidates would have to have reached the minimum age of thirty (not twenty-one). Instead of through referendum, constitutional amendment was to be the decision of elected state conventions. The 1891 Preamble did not say that 'the people' of the various states had chosen to form a Commonwealth. No guarantee of the right to vote in Commonwealth elections for those who had the right in state elections can be found. No Commonwealth powers over the custody of children, nor old-age and invalid pensions. No industrial relations powers. The Governor-General's salary might not be 'diminished' (rather than 'altered' as the 1898 version has it), leaving open the possibility of its increase during his term of office. The right of the Queen to disallow an Australian Act of Parliament extended to two years, rather than one.

About other significant differences, there may now be more ambivalence over whether their modification in 1898 represented a loss or a gain. In the 1891 version, treaties signed by the Commonwealth were to be binding on the states (the British insisted on the removal of this provision); the Commonwealth was not described as 'indissoluble'; the states rather than the Commonwealth were prohibited from making laws restricting religion; there was to be a minimum of four, not five, members of the House of Representatives per state; the Commonwealth had no power to make grants to states on terms it thought fit, and no provision for resolving deadlocks between the two Houses of Parliament was provided. Ministers were not required to be members of the parliament.

The 1891 draft, altered both by choice and (albeit in respect of external affairs only) on the eventual insistence of the Colonial Office, describes in some respects a larger degree of direct constitutional independence from Britain. It gave the Commonwealth a greater scope of power through treaties, and through the application of Commonwealth law to British ships going to and from Australian ports. It gave what it called at this stage the 'Supreme Court' the power to restrict all appeals to the Privy Council. In addition it left open the possibility of departing from 'responsible government' through the appointment of ministers outside the parliament.

But it is the 1898 draft that affirms a popular and domestic sovereignty that was not contemplated in 1891. That later draft declares that the Constitution is the work of the Australian people and that members of parliament are to be of their choice. It limits the time in which Australian Acts may be 'disallowed' in Britain. It creates a limited, but significant field of national welfare and wage regulation. In the differences between these two drafts lies the evolution of Australian political culture over the decade, and the recognition that a constitution that did not reflect this culture would not succeed.

None of the viable constitutions was manifestly republican. By the time a specifically labour position on Federation had emerged, republicanism, in the sense of opposition to monarchy, was no longer a political movement of any force. Labour movement criticism of the various Constitution Bills was rarely directed at the retention of the Queen as Head of State.

Imagined Constitutions 55

The uniformity of labour opposition to Federation under the 1898 Bill has been rather exaggerated by later historians; the labour position around the country was in fact divided roughly between the industrial working class (opposed) and the rural and mining working class (favourable), and again between those who saw Federation as a solution (via uniform national immigration policy) to the threat of cheap coloured labour undermining wages and working conditions, especially in the north and the west (favourable), compared with those whose immediate priorities lay elsewhere. Still, labour criticism, especially in New South Wales and Victoria, was articulate and detailed, and offered a meticulous critique of the Constitution Bill in which an alternative imaginary constitution is represented.

New South Wales labour policy for the 1897 Convention elections advocated: 'A one-chambered Parliament elected on the basis of one-adult-one-vote, headed by elected Ministries, and controlled by the Initiative and the Referendum', with federal powers including, in addition to those already described in the 1891 Bill, railways and the public debt, and the preservation of state control over 'Crown lands, irrigation, State banking, mining and factory legislation, education, and public health'.[18]

The Victorian *Tocsin*'s detailed commentary, published from April to June 1898, offers a more radical alternative constitution. It begins by accusing the Constitution of 'crude draughtsmanship'.[19] It dissects the existing Preamble, stipulating that the reference to an 'indissoluble Federal Commonwealth' should be replaced by a term of probation, as 'this Constitution is an experiment', and that the word 'Federal' should be excluded as it may prevent any future unification or non-federal union in which the ideal of 'one people' may be realised. Alternative sections include clarification of the reference to a 'foreign power' in section 44 (which disqualifies those owing 'allegiance to a foreign power' from standing for parliament) so that it does not disqualify Catholics 'under allegiance' to the Pope; the election of state Governors and the power of popular recall; a 'Supreme Court' subject to and not above the Constitution; clarification of the Governor-General's reserve powers; referendums for settling deadlocks between the Houses, and a means of resolving deadlocks between the Governor-General and Parliament; ministers chosen from outside parliament; assurance that the federal capital will be located in a 'virgin area'; the Swiss style popular Initiative, and a very great deal more.

What the *Tocsin*'s vision adds up to is a more sovereign parliament (with some features of the 1891 Bill) and a weaker or more flexible constitution than was settled for in 1900, with greater 'popular' access to political decision-making. We can recognise in these proposals much

56   *To Constitute a Nation*

that is still the subject of political debate one hundred years later, as well as some provisions (like direct election of the Senate) that were in fact achieved in the 1898 Bill. But we can also be confident that the small states now, just as the small colonies then, would have found this draft constitution too centralist. What it does, among other things, is reflect the tensions between federalism and centralism, between judicial and parliamentary power, between 'the people' of the states and 'the people' of the nation, all of which the Constitution's framers in the 1890s had to address and, if not resolve, at least leave in a workable equilibrium.

Other alternative 'drafts' were less realistic. As the Constitution was being written in the course of the second Convention, not only was it subjected to scrutiny, but individuals and groups also attempted to have inserted in it specific sections in which their own particular interests might be reflected. To read the petitions that were sent to the Convention sessions, particularly those written by individuals rather than organised groups, is to glimpse a world of hopes and expectations, of often naive ideas about what a constitution might contain or offer. Here in the writers' minds appeared the chance to have the things they most valued or desired entrenched in a constitution, ensured for posterity, inscribed on the nation's stone. It must have seemed a golden opportunity.

Many sober petitions were sent and presented, praying that adult suffrage should be included in the Constitution, that God should be recognised and national days of 'Thanksgiving and humiliation' be instituted, that alcohol and intoxicants should be under state control, that appeals to the Privy Council should be retained, and that Queensland be divided into several states. Much of this petitioning was successful.

In addition there were the pleas of individuals. An unusual letter from a Kyneton resident urged upon the members of the Convention 'the Imperative necessity of striving to find some means of preventing conspiracies, perjuries, vindictive and malicious persecutions, for private vendettas by the Police'. It provided detailed 'proof of their fiendishness' in a moving account of a savage beating by three policemen with blackthorn and donnybrook, fists and boots ('such Boots'), and their attempt to place stolen goods upon his (we assume) person. All of this, the petitioner went on, had led to a conviction for perjury, and six months imprisonment with solitary confinement and, to cap it all, the 'Judge's Homily on my enormous Wickedness'.[20] What pathetic hope this letter expresses, and what ignorance of the likely concerns of a federal constitution!

A more conventionally respectable petitioner, one with a greater appreciation of the Constitution if not a greater sense of the likelihood that it would radically depart from tradition, Dr Andrew Ross, Member of the New South Wales Legislative Assembly (and author of his own, unpublished dystopian 'Chronicles' of Federation[21]), asked the Federal Convention to include in the Constitution both the powers of impeachment of holders of political office and a prohibition on imperial honours, 'ribbons, stars and garters'. Unlike the outraged petitioner from Kyneton, Ross's appeal was at least presented to the Convention (if, for no other reason, in the interests of political protocol) by fellow New South Wales parliamentarian, Edmund Barton.

Perhaps the most interesting (in the political culture one hundred years later) was the petition from Mr John William Richard Clarke, living in Newtown in inner Sydney, but so enamoured of the Australian bush (especially 'the noble kangaroo') that he prayed for the protection of the native flora and fauna to be included among the Commonwealth powers in the Constitution. Having noticed, he wrote to the members of the Convention, 'that you have included the protection of our <u>Native Aboriginals</u>' in the Constitution Bill, he now asked that the protection of these other 'natives' be included. Appended to Clarke's petition are copies of letters and reports demonstrating his own long-standing interest and activism in this cause, especially in New South Wales, 'my native home'.

We shall meet our pioneer environmentalist Mr Clarke, 'the People's Stationer and Bookseller', again. What he represents here is one of the small, but significant number of individuals who attempted to hang their star on the words of a not yet written constitution. They imagined a constitution in which their most precious interests would receive national recognition. They were all to be disappointed. Most, without Dr Ross's advantage, failed even to see their petition or letter presented to the Convention.

As the Convention sessions of 1897 and 1898 progressed in their work, the Constitution took on a less fanciful and speculative character. Compromises were forged, technical details tackled, words were chosen and printed on paper. If these have the apparent drawback of lacking in inspiration, they have the virtue of lacking in obscurantism. Only two Latin expressions—*inter se* and *mandamus*—found their way into the 128 sections. Fewer than one-fifth of its sections (as the Constitution stood in 1900) were longer than two short paragraphs. Some of its sentences require concentration to follow, but none is unintelligible. Other sections, such as section 90 and section 92, which begin with the expression 'On the imposition of uniform duties of customs . . .', would have made more immediate sense in the 1890s (when the lack of uniform tariffs between the colonies was one of the burning issues of the day) and an examination of sections immediately prior to these would enlighten the reader as to the intention that 'uniform duties of customs' should quickly be imposed.

58   *To Constitute a Nation*

The Preamble, in contrast, does have an inspired feel. That 'the people' of several states 'humbly relying on the blessing of Almighty God, have agreed to unite in one indissoluble Federal Commonwealth' has a rather grand and solemn ring to it. But there is no question that the great words of truth and self-evident rights and destiny, and more perfect unions, are missing. These concepts are, it seems, now associated in the minds of many with the category of constitutions as such.

Perhaps this is because there is a widespread, if limited, familiarity with the American Constitution. More likely it is because of a common confusion, on the one hand between the Declaration of Independence and the Constitution, and on the other between the Amendments that form the American Bill of Rights and the American Constitution as a whole. The latter is, in fact, itself every bit as prosaic as the Australian. For the bulk of any constitution to be inspirational would place a severe strain upon its ability to work as a legal document.

All the same, the necessity to express the aims of Australia's (indeed any nation's) Constitution, in banal, legally viable terms, did not prevent people, including the Constitution's own drafters, from attaching high-flown and extravagant sentiments to it. It is only by understanding the temper of the age that one can appreciate the nature of this mystery. Our 'Cockney Columbus', David Christie Murray, made a little gift of a poem to the Federalists in which, as early as 1891, he tried to capture the paradox:

> Because they live among us, and we know
> The unheroic details of their days,
> Since they and we move in familiar ways,
> We scant the greatness of the deed they do . . .
> They weld an empire . . .
> . . . in calm conclave, where each citizen
> May speak his share of truth with fearless eyes.
> Blest State so founded. May their work be blessed,
> And here at last the war-sick soul of man find rest.[22]

This, it must be noted, is one of the superior poems, in literary terms, of the literally hundreds produced in the 1890s in fealty to the new nation. Songs and odes were also in abundance. Almost everybody had a poetic bent, it seems, and none was inhibited by a fear of extravagance or sentimentality. It would make excruciating reading to attempt a compilation or even a representative sample of the poems and poetic songs composed in the federal cause in this era. Established poets like George Essex Evans and James Brunton Stephens also wrote works of some slight lasting appeal. But one small example of a single stanza from the rest might suffice: 'Leagued love must dome this heritage of ours/Lest

Hate that stings, and Envy that devours/Cloud our clean air, or taint our Austral strand/"Anathema" be all but this degree:/In Union one—we claim one Destiny'.[23] What might be learned from a perusal of such literary contributions, had anyone the patience, would be the surprising fact that what seems to many now a prosaic process, resulting in a prosaic document, in its day inspired in many the impulse of poetry.

Certain constitutional provisions that in 1900 still remained unsettled, awaiting resolution in the future, individually provoked speculative fantasies and Utopian imagery. Section 125 of the Constitution, for example, tells us that 'The seat of Government of the Commonwealth shall be . . . in the State of New South Wales, and be distant not less than one hundred miles from Sydney . . . [and it] shall contain an area of not less than one hundred square miles'. It was one of the concessions granted to New South Wales at the 'Secret' Premiers' Conference of 1899 after the first referendum on the whole Constitution had been defeated in that colony. Like a map for a treasure hunt, it is both precise and mysteriously vague. What area of one hundred square miles? Did this mean a new place, or an existing town? From where in Sydney was the 'one hundred miles' distance to be measured?

Speculation, claims to the position made by individual towns, and imaginary scenarios of purified beginnings abounded. The occupants of Bathurst, Albury and Eden, as well as many others, all imagined that they might win the prize. The federal capital was the key to an imagined future: greater prosperity, national recognition, international prominence, enlarged populations, greater business opportunities, perhaps even wider circles of friends. Alongside arguments based on the virtues or shortcomings of the type of location—for example, that considerable distance from Sydney was necessary to remove the federal capital from the risk of naval attack[24]—were visions of new beginnings, of a purified start for the nation. Among temperance reformers the idea also grew of a new national city, free of alcohol and the vices that followed its consumption. Others thought of pure air and sanitation, and 'the opportunity and honour of shewing to the world the concrete results of the engineering and architectural skill of the age'.[25]

At the 1897–98 Federal Convention the debate focused on whether or not to specify the location of the new capital in the Constitution or leave it up to the new Federal Parliament to decide. Most members (except an extremely ill-tempered William Lyne, Leader of the Opposition in New South Wales) addressed the question with good humour. They afforded each other much amusement with their 'bids' for their own city or colony. Tasmanian Premier Sir Edward Braddon argued for Hobart, on the grounds that members of parliament would know 'that in going to perform their duties at the centre of government they will be making no

60   *To Constitute a Nation*

sacrifice of health or personal comfort'. Victoria's Sir George Turner countered with St Kilda in Melbourne, 'a place which is well suited, by nature . . . [with] a climate unrivalled for changes in any part of the Australian Colonies'. And Josiah Symon, pushing Mount Gambier's virtues, responded to William Zeal's question about the earthquake experienced in that town, that 'it would not be so alarming as the earthquakes my honourable friend sometimes creates in this chamber'.[26]

Their most repeated and apparently most serious concern, apart from rival claims for the capital and the insistence by some that New South Wales, the 'Mother Colony', must have it by right, was the climate. With the dark, heavy clothes they wore, the lack of air-conditioning, and the huge, hot meals they consumed, it appears, regularly, a concern such as this might well be excused. By the third session of the Convention, the delegates found themselves in Melbourne, in summer, sweltering as some of the members no doubt remembered doing at the very first Federation Conference, eight years before. Sir John Forrest, Western Australia's Premier, dreamed of

> a new city erected in some suitable place where we could all go in summer. It ought to be a cool place; indeed, the coolest place in Australia. It ought to be a place where we could build a federal city, looking forward with great ideas in our minds to the future. It ought to be a place where a city could be laid out which would be the admiration not only of the present but of future generations.[27]

Instead of a place that was cool and lovely, purified and magnificent, some others imagined a separate federal capital as threatening or unpleasant. A capital removed from the people and from public scrutiny would make 'Dictatorship not only possible, but extremely probable, as an evolution from the corruption that would segregate (*sic*) [there] . . . especially if located inland and removed from the centres of population'.[28] The national parliament, William Pember Reeves warned, must not be removed from within sight and hearing of the majority of the people, since direct access was a necessity for democratic control.[29] A letter to the labour *Worker* thought it 'against human nature to exile oneself in some lonely bush township when it can be avoided'.[30] The *Courrier Australien* was blunt in its judgement: the only really faulty aspect of the Constitution, it commented, was that the capital was to be built in 'le bush'.[31]

The Constitution Bill, written in its final form in the years 1897 to 1900, was hailed by many as visionary, ultra-democratic, 'the finest' in the world, as well as praised for its realism and pragmatism, described as the best that could be hoped for, the nearest to ideal, the product of necessary compromise. Some, like Rose Scott, thought its supporters dangerous Utopians; others believed its opponents to be 'the dreamers of Utopias, and of the reorganisation of society on a communistic basis'.[32] Others still, sometimes in virtually the same breath, spoke in Utopian terms of the great age it would usher in.

When the final draft of the Constitution was completed, it was impossible to know how it would work in practice. Should they have waited longer and gone through further drafts, some wondered, or were there greater perils in waiting? 'A choice has to be made', wrote Alfred Deakin: 'everything hoped to be achieved by waiting may be better and more easily obtained under the Commonwealth'.[33]

The nation itself had been imagined. Its boundaries had been drawn. Its powers and institutions were described or alluded to in its new Constitution. What guarantee could be given that it would work any better than William Lane's Paraguayan New Australia, into which much planning, thinking, organising and imagining had also gone? To form a nation without external pressure or crisis, without a common religious or ethnic imperative, in time of peace and ready to begin on the first day of a new century—to *write* a nation by agreement—represents if not a Utopian undertaking, at least an act of profound optimism and concentrated imagination.

To settle on a final version of the nation's Constitution, when alternatives might endlessly have been suggested, took (whatever critics may think of the product) a combination of political judgement, generosity and good fortune. For Deakin, having lived through the process in which the 'fortunes of Federalism have visibly trembled in the balance twenty times . . . its actual accomplishment must always appear to have been secured by a series of miracles'.[34]

One of the very first 'miracles' was the coming together of the representatives of seven colonies (for New Zealand was still, at this stage, part of the imagined community), upon the instigation of the New South Wales Premier Henry Parkes, at a Federation Conference in a particularly hot Melbourne summer, in 1890.

CHAPTER FOUR

Models For a Nation

Almost the first opinion expressed at the 1890 Federation Conference was on the question of foreign precedent. The first day of this august meeting began in the usual manner with the nominations of president and secretary and a word on rules of procedure. Then immediately members raised the question of whether or not the public should be admitted.

Since such a conference had never been held before in Australia, it was not at first obvious what attitude should be adopted. Although other intercolonial conferences and Federal Council meetings had taken place over the preceding years, none had set for itself the task of planning a nation. In what would prove a characteristic move in these early stages of constitution writing, attention turned straight away to what had been done in other nations. Thomas Playford, South Australia's Opposition Leader, reminded his fellow delegates that the 'Americans never admitted the Press when they made their Constitution; the Canadians at Quebec did not admit the Press', and, although he was willing on this occasion, he warned against misinterpretations that might form in the minds of press representatives during the Conference debates: 'one may think that by Federation we will be going on the lines of the United States, another that we are going on the lines of the Dominion of Canada, another the Swiss Republic, another on the lines of the States of Holland'.[1]

The desire to know how things were done elsewhere was understandable in a group of colonial politicians, setting out on the first leg of a journey that was both difficult and unfamiliar, but for which others had already drawn a map. The process involved more, however, than just following the guide posts. To begin with, there were several maps from which to choose. In looking at alternative federal models, the delegates were making a choice not only about the political model, but also about the type of political culture the new nation should embody.

They were guided by both their own constitutional knowledge of different political arrangements, and by their idea (sometimes based on direct experience, but often enough second-hand) of the cultures of other systems. The specific constitutional knowledge of federal systems was in fact relatively limited in the 1890 Conference, and although several members took pains to demonstrate at length their detailed familiarity with history (in particular that of the American War of Independence and the Civil War), most had to depend upon their image, even imagination, of these other systems, more than upon their expertise.

In short, throughout all the Conventions of the 1890s, the delegates asked themselves, not just how effective a particular constitutional system had proven in existing models, but how American Australia should be, or how Canadian, or German or Swiss. They knew that they wanted the new nation to be British, but they had then to ask themselves what were the essential ingredients of being British and how far the Constitution could go formally in the direction of America or Canada or any other model and still remain British. They needed in addition to be sensitive from the outset to the views held by the Australian public about other cultural models. Although there was no proposal at the 1890 Conference for a referendum on the Constitution, the delegates knew they would have to 'sell' their model. Many were, in addition, 'native' products of the Australian political culture themselves and shared the views of their fellows. They were keen to borrow politically, but cautious about the cultural debts they might incur.

In Melbourne, the first day's debate went on about the extent of detail they should admit in discussion at such a preliminary Conference, with some of the members adamant that they should not enter at all into details of a federal system. The point of the Conference, they insisted, was to decide on whether a future Convention to write a Constitution was or was not desired. Matters of detail would be raised then, if and when one took place.

But alternative national models would keep entering the discussion. Sir Henry Parkes warned against 'anything short of a complete Constitution', such as the American Articles of Confederation had been, and, to illustrate the virtues of a full federal authority, launched into a detailed story about a little ship laden with potatoes whose 'sturdy captain' refused to pay wharfage dues in the port of Baltimore, and whose appeal to the Supreme Court was upheld in the name of 'entire freedom' of trade throughout the United States.[2]

Sir Samuel Griffith, from Queensland, made a characteristically erudite early contribution, by listing all the federal powers found in the Canadian Constitution and suggesting a couple of additions. Mr Playford gave a lecture on the particular historical reasons for Federation in several nations, including the difficulties of 'intercourse with the mother country' during Canada's winter months when its rivers, lakes and canals were

64   *To Constitute a Nation*

frozen. He then firmly rejected the Canadian model, suggesting that 'if we are to build up a Federation on the Canadian lines, the colony of South Australia will never agree to it'.[3] South Australian Premier, Dr John Cockburn, then took up this theme, later adding his own rather peculiar entry to the list that was developing in the course of the debate:

> We want to see a union of strong colonies, each with its own local traditions, each with its own local affections, each with its own peculiarities . . . a brotherhood of infinite diversity would be much better than a homogeneous union of colonies without a proper amount of differentiation . . . [Australia] could not follow Canada in this respect.[4]

As with the issue of admitting the public, the debate over whether or not to embrace the Canadian model went on and on, each successive speaker addressing the question as if there were fierce argument, their level of determination not to follow Canada growing as they did, but no one in fact wanting to put the opposing case for a full-scale copy of that country's Constitution.

Henry Parkes, who had in fact quite recently supported such a scheme, was accused of as much for a while, until in a burst of outrage, he took this and other slights on board: 'I have never alluded to the Canadian Constitution in any way that would justify the inference that I have any intention . . . of copying it'.[5]

So, what was wrong with being Canadian? Everyone agreed that the Canadian Constitution was too centralist, that it was not really a Federation properly speaking. In brief, its crime was to define specifically the powers of its provinces, thereby limiting them, and to include the statement that anything else was left to the power of the central parliament, thereby giving it a larger scope for power. The Canadian Parliament, as the Australian framers saw it, had virtually unlimited power. All were convinced that it rendered the provinces weak and oppressed, little more than municipalities over which a dominant central government held constitutional sway.

It might be imagined that the Canadian example would have been attractive. The Australians' dedication to retaining close ties with Britain while federating, and the recognition that British draftsmen had shaped the British North America Act of 1867 (Canada's Constitution) in such a way as to leave a strong role in it for the Imperial Parliament, would seem to have provided an obvious model to follow. But two things worked against this. The Australians' desire for states' rights, for one, was greater than their commitment to being British. And, secondly, the need to imagine Australia as a distinctive, independent nation, not just a copy of its 'sister', was at work in the members' cultural armoury.

Although details of the Canadian Constitution were referred to fruitfully on occasion throughout the Convention debates of the 1890s, its overall example was consistently treated with a tone approaching scorn. In debating the division of power over finance at the Federal Convention held the following year in Sydney, Richard Baker from South Australia told fellow members that 'the greatest frictions and the greatest jealousies and contentions' characterised the relations of the Canadian provinces. These are

> held together by what is euphemistically defined as 'better terms'—that is, each province of the Dominion of Canada is constantly trying to get the better of its neighbours, trying to obtain more from the federal government . . . [T]he authors of the Canadian federation . . . have laid the seeds of the dissolution of that union.[6]

In Adelaide seven years later, William McMillan implied that something even more sinister lay in an apparently successful feature of Canada's system. Addressing the issue of whether the Australian Constitution should allow ministers to sit in the Upper House as well as the Lower, he mentioned almost in passing, that

> Sir John Macdonald—who had the fathering and, if not the fathering, the nursing, of the Canadian system of government—was sufficiently shrewd to make a sort of mosaic of the Ministry . . . by selecting men representing different States and interests, and so successful was he—and I think it is a very dangerous thing to be so successful—that for fourteen years that eminent statesman carried on without any interruption. Therefore the position of Canada in some matters at the present time . . . is no exact analogy for us.[7]

Press commentary adopted a similar attitude. On the need for Federation to ensure Australia's defence, the *West Australian* commented that large funds were needed, and although 'it may be urged that Canada gets along with a smaller sum . . . the less said about Canada as an example of the benefits of Federation from the point of view of military defence, the better'.[8] In New South Wales, the labour *Worker*, although scathing about Australia's draft Constitution, commented that no one would 'pretend that Federation has favoured democracy in Canada, for during twenty eight out of the thirty years since the provinces were united the Conservatives have been in office and jobbery has been rampant'.[9] During the first referendum campaigns in 1898, a further fault was outlined by Sir Joseph Abbott, one of the Convention delegates, in a letter to the press: the Canadian Constitution was much less 'liberal' than the Australian Constitution Bill, since Canadian Senators were nominated for life by the Governor-General and, among other things, the people could not amend it.[10]

66   *To Constitute a Nation*

Canada had, it seems, the simultaneous vices of nondescript provinces overawed by the central power and disputatious provinces threatening that power, of over-stable ministries and an unstable union, of a domineering centre and a weak defence capability. It was unimaginable to be Canadian in the 1890s. Except, perhaps, on occasions when the constitutional structures were not the issue and the example of a relatively recently federated nation could prove useful. Thus, for example, the Victorian Premier, Sir James Patterson, speaking at Corowa in 1893, held up the Canadian example. What practical advantages were to be gained from Federation?, he asked, rhetorically, replying that Canada's remarkable growth since its Federation, in employment, in railways, in property values provided 'the best answer'.[11]

Only a year after the Corowa meeting, however, invited by New South Wales Premier George Dibbs to join his colony in a scheme of unification based on the Canadian Constitution, Patterson did not find the example so convincing and he declined to investigate Dibbs's proposal further. At the Bathurst People's Federal Convention of 1896, President Thomas Machattie, who naively referred to Canada as a model for Australian Federation and an argument in its favour, quickly learned from others, like Edmund Barton, that Canada's had a crucial 'weak spot': 'the system of Government in Canada will more and more, day by day, decade by decade, approximate to a unification, wiping out States altogether'.[12]

George Dibbs was one of the few in Australia to hold favourable views of Canada's Constitution in the 1890s. Indeed, Dibbs criticised the 1891 Bill (although he had been a delegate at the 1891 Convention) on the grounds of its dissimilarity to the Canadian model, the very thing, of course, the other Australians had attempted to achieve. The unification, promoted in Dibbs's model, was precisely what they feared. Throughout the constitutional Conventions of the decade, almost everyone else wanted to have his chance to show that he too did not care for the Canadian model.

Only the New Zealanders at the 1890 Conference, themselves faced with the question of imagining their country as a state of Australia, failed to see the point of going over the Canadian model. Captain William Russell, Member of the New Zealand House of Representatives, advised fellow Conference members to avoid a choice between the American and the Canadian: 'There is no reason why Australia should not adopt that which is best from every kind of Constitution', to fit its particular needs. 'Are you not one people with identical interests', he asked, people with 'no natural difficulties—no boundaries . . . [except] the imaginary boundaries which separate the great colonies of the Australian continent'?[13]

But, Russell added, New Zealand was not part of this picture, its boundaries were not 'imaginary'. Indeed, so different were the conditions of life and the circumstances of their history, that New Zealand was, he said, likely to develop a 'different national type' from Australia's. Despite clear and persistent indications from the New Zealand representatives that they did not see themselves joining the Federation, the Australians continued to act as if this were always an immediate possibility. Only late in the decade was there, in fact, any serious public interest in New Zealand itself, but this, the historian Keith Sinclair has pointed out, amounted to 'a three months' flurry' in 1899. A Royal Commission was appointed, its report recommending that the Australian Constitution Bill be amended to allow New Zealand to enter the Federation later but still as an Original State. In the meanwhile New Zealand should have the right to appeal to the Australian High Court, and to form a united defence force with Australia. But it was, Sinclair argues, no more than a nervous reaction to an imaginary future Australian tariff against their colony, and the New Zealanders did not actually convince themselves that they should join: 'It had always been said that the New Zealanders would be a distinct and superior people and many of them believed it'.[14]

If Canada was unacceptable, might Australia be something else altogether: Swiss or German, for example? These were federal systems and only federal systems could be tried out in the imagination, for other Federations formed a type of extended family within which one might metaphorically marry without going altogether outside the community.

Germans, as people, were very familiar to Australians of British origin in the nineteenth century. In South Australia, and in parts of Queensland, German names and churches and community organisations were common. Up to the disastrous reversal of the First World War, Germans were spoken of with trust: the *West Australian*, for example, described the contribution of the New South Wales German community to the Inauguration of the Commonwealth in 1901 as 'truly typical of the sturdy enterprising German, whom Australians feel it an honour to regard as fellow countrymen of the commonwealth'.[15] In Queensland, at the time of the second Constitution Bill referendum, in 1899, 'the desirability of some influential German citizen taking the stump among his teutonic countrymen' was treated as 'admirable' since the 'German vote will be a large factor in the approaching referendum'.[16]

The Germans were also related—indeed very closely related—to Britain's Royal Family. Nobody minded in those days. The German Constitution was raised as an example from time to time in Convention debates. One of its provisions—national powers over old-age pensions—got into Australia's Constitution as section 51 (xxiii). And it is perhaps no coincidence that the German system of state-run old-age pensions was introduced into the 1897 Convention by a South Australian delegate.

68   *To Constitute a Nation*

Switzerland's contribution to Australia's Constitution is much better known. It is the referendum, as the means of constitutional amendment. The Swiss example almost always got good press, whether in mainstream commentary, labour movement publications, public debate, or Federal Conventions. There were occasional snide references, during an anxious moment for states' rights proponents, for example, in the debate on constitutional amendment at Melbourne in 1898, when South Australia's James Howe complained that in 'this vaunted land of liberty— Switzerland . . . the people allow their women to become scavengers in the streets of the principal cities'.[17] But to express such a view was unusual.

During the second referendum campaign on the Constitution, the labour *Clipper* in Hobart reproduced a lengthy English article on the virtues of the Swiss Constitution, including the claim (particularly appealing to labour critics) that it 'has made the law so plain that lawyers are already nearly useless'.[18] Mr Forbes, a New South Wales Member of Parliament, told a meeting in Hay during the same campaign, that the Swiss Constitution 'provided for equal state representation, and there it worked satisfactorily' despite large differences in populations in each 'state': 'in Switzerland there had been no complaints, no difficulties, no fights, and nobody wanted to alter the existing state of affairs'.[19]

Although the 1891 draft Constitution did not include the referendum as the means of constitutional amendment, not only was the referendum embraced in the final draft, but the Constitution Bill itself was put to a referendum for approval before it became an Act of Parliament. But Australia was not to be Swiss. That particular Federation was too culturally and linguistically alien to provide a full imaginative model for the Australian Constitution writers. Commenting on the powers of the Houses of Parliament in Adelaide in 1897, South Australia's Sir John Downer noted that Switzerland recognised

> that the States Council must be quite as important as the National Assembly . . . The Americans followed the English precedent as it existed at the time, the Swiss followed the American precedent . . . and they did what every Federation except Canada has done . . . The Swiss approached the matter with great thought and scientifically framed a Constitution . . . We, however, do not want to go there.[20]

The problem was, said Downer, that Switzerland did not have responsible government. But if responsible government (that is to say, where the ministry is chosen from among the elected members of parliament) was the stumbling block, America's Constitution surely had the same fault, and Canada's (which had responsible government) should have been, for all its shortcomings, more appealing, if only as a point of departure.

Alone among the various federal models on offer, the Canadian Constitution appeared entirely unattractive. This is all the more striking because sections of the British North America Act (like the German and the Swiss examples) were in fact borrowed for Australia's Constitution, and the Commonwealth's power over marriage and divorce was inspired by Canada's example.

The decision to grant the divorce power to the Commonwealth Parliament rather than leaving it exclusively to the states was indeed one of the cases where, despite their general admiration for the American Constitution, Australians rejected the prospect of being American, by seeking to avoid what they saw as a culture of scandal and domestic distress resulting from differing state divorce laws.

Amid the public disparagement of the Canadian federal system and admiration of the American, many doubts were openly expressed about American history and culture. In the 1890s, popular images of America were, as they have remained, very mixed. America may have been 'the standard of modernity' throughout the nineteenth century,[21] but it was also characterised in Australian eyes as brash and materialistic, afflicted by economic inequalities and by racial problems mercifully (it was thought) absent in Australia. Four decades before Federation, the Americans on the Australian goldfields were already considered loud and obnoxious (as well as republican).[22] American politics were tainted with associations of self-interest and corruption. The expression 'Tammany Hall' was in common circulation, used to convey this association, as well as to warn Australians away from such a culture.[23] Social policy and working conditions were deplored: 'America is the workingman's Paradise Lost', quipped the *Worker*.[24] That the War of Independence was the prompt for America's own nation-building was also frequently mentioned by Australians, who were proud of having undertaken Federation without bloodshed. At the 1897 Convention, South Australia's Patrick Glynn even doubted that the War of Independence had been 'the outcome of a wild and ennobling impulse of patriotism': unlike in Australia, it was in fact 'the method of commonplace and calculating men, of commercial instincts and narrow ambitions'.[25] In all of this, the overriding negative example, one which the Canadians had also sought to avoid in their Constitution, was the threat of Civil War.

It has to be remembered that the Civil War, so historically distant to us now, was a matter of living memory for even the youngest of the delegates in 1890. Even as late as 1898, detailed debate was going on in the Australian press about the causes of the Civil War and its lesson for Australia. Before the referendum of that year, A. B. Piddington, the New

70   *To Constitute a Nation*

South Wales free-trade liberal and advocate of 'popular government', mounted an attack upon the Constitution Bill with an analysis of the American Civil War. The War had been caused, he said, by equal state representation in the United States Senate. Subject to the will of the states rather than the will of the people, the Senate had encouraged the growth of slavery. Through the principle of equal representation, Piddington argued, individual allegiance to a state had overriden allegiance to the nation.[26] Thus it would be in the new Australian Commonwealth.

Letters to the editor in reply attacked Piddington's claim as 'notoriously unfounded', and 'absurd'. One argued that what the American Civil War demonstrated was the need for the smaller states to be protected against the larger ones. It was the imposition of oppressive tariffs on the small states, not slavery, that had caused the War in the first place, its writer claimed.[27] Another asserted that the abolition of slavery was not a serious issue before the Civil War and the United States Senate was much more powerful than the proposed Australian Senate, as the latter could be 'sent to [its] constituents' in the case of conflict with the government.[28] In return, Piddington replied that 'the American type of federation which is copied in the [Australian] Convention Bill would justify the smaller colonies in breaking up the union'.[29] In this exchange what was being debated, more than any specific historical interpretation, was the manner and the degree to which Australia could follow the American political model and avoid being American at the same time.

The Australian Constitution would ultimately include its own protection against settlement by 'the sword', as the long shadow of the Civil War hung over debates throughout the 1890s. But since Australians did not want to be Canadian, the only other real federal alternative, in their eyes, was that symbol of modernity, wealth and the type of civilisation about which most felt ambivalent: America.

Only one delegate in 1890, Andrew Inglis Clark from Tasmania, was openly enamoured of both American politics and American culture. Clearly worried that the dramatic example of the Civil War might put people off the American model, he suggested, unsuccessfully as it turned out, that fellow members of the 1890 Conference should simply forget about the Civil War. The War had, he assured members, nothing to do with the respective powers of state and central governments, but was a struggle of passions, between good and evil, the result of the 'serpent in the way', that is to say, slavery. 'Well, Mr President', Clark declaimed, 'we shall be cursed with no such question in Australia'.[30]

Clark had got down to the business of national comparisons straight away, expressing the wish that the delegates would 'state more or less precisely what kind of confederation we would individually advocate, and also what kind of confederation each colony . . . would respectively be satisfied with'. 'For my part', he added (what they must have already known), 'I would prefer the lines of the American Union to those of the Dominion of Canada'. Clark expanded on this theme at some length, describing the great variety of American life, the wealth and industry, the variations in climate, population and social life, the strength of community and local public life. If America's system had been 'constructed' on the same lines as Canada's, it would have instead produced 'danger, dissension, irritation, and disunion'.[31]

Clark had not yet been to America. He had, however, already formed a strong impression of its culture and an expertise in its constitutional history. His first visit later that same year confirmed his enthusiasm.[32] The following year, at the 1891 Convention in Sydney, Clark renewed his efforts to see the American example adopted, including offering, as we have seen, his own draft Constitution along its lines.

Later commentators have suggested that Clark's influence was the reason for a close resemblance between Australia's and America's Constitutions. The degree of resemblance must remain an open question. Let us note here at any rate, that the Australian Constitution is not nearly as American as Clark hoped it would be. Several small differences between Clark's draft and the draft Constitution were there from the start; similarities (such as the appointment of senators from state parliaments and an independent 'Supreme Court') made their way into the 1891 version of the Constitution but did not survive its later reworking. But Clark had also hoped to persuade fellow delegates of the virtues of America's alternative to 'responsible government'. While he had some support for exploring this system from Sir Samuel Griffith, and the wording of the 1891 draft Constitution captures a slight ambiguity on this matter (where the final draft does not), Clark's preference did not get very far. It was not just that he literally missed the boat, being deprived of the chance to join the Drafting Committee on the steamship *Lucinda*. It was, at the end of the day, the overall belief of the Convention that a departure from 'responsible government' would make Australia too American.

They wanted to be American to a degree, indeed they had to be American in following a particular federal model that suited their strong colonial jealousies, and they admired the way America's Constitution had done this. Those who shaped Australia's Constitution also deeply admired the work of the American 'Founding Fathers' and, although they were too diffident to apply the term to themselves, they sought to emulate them from time to time. Some of the speeches, especially in 1890, mentioned the American Founders in great and portentous tones, as if trying to convey the comparable weight of the Australian occasion. There were a couple of attempts to produce something along the lines of the mighty *Federalist* of 1787–88,[33] but, culturally, the Australian

72   *To Constitute a Nation*

Federalists chose to remain British. The wish to embrace the American federal system politically made the need to distance the new nation from the American cultural model all the greater.

In the course of shaping a nation, in imagining the identity of the national community, the process of sorting out resemblances and dissimilarities was crucial. Creating a nation politically entailed an interconnected and simultaneous reflection on the new nation's character, or the 'national type', and this was often expressed in terms of what Australians were not as well as what they were. There were frequent comments on the Australian type, as if British settlement in Australia were an experiment now coming to fruition, as if the results of one hundred years of incubation or of the admixture of different components could now be recorded. Not infrequently, overseas visitors noted that Australians, while friendly, were highly sensitive about criticism. Given the attitude of condescension often reflected in these visitors' accounts, this is hardly surprising, but it is even less surprising given that Australians were also in the process of reflecting on, while shaping, their own type.

It is perhaps premature to speak of a 'national character', began an essay in 1899 but, unlike the 'nation of shopkeepers', 'we are a nation of athletes', a 'gambling people' and a 'reading-people' (although whether a literary people remained to be seen); a 'music-loving people' and—what comes as a surprise one hundred years later—a 'flower-loving' people. Australians disliked convention and displayed a 'want of veneration', the account goes on; they were 'sensation-loving', craving newness: 'Old customs and traditions rapidly make way before the sturdy march of progress', older people's opinions were mocked, and the constraints of politeness and etiquette, especially towards women, were (along with dancing) avoided. The new type emerging would be progressive, full of 'self-reliance and resourcefulness', and 'able to hold its own . . . whether it be in the Legislative Chambers, in the Court of Law, in commercial life, or on the field of sport'.[34]

At the same time, Australians were also assuring themselves, both in writing their Constitution and in reflecting on their character, that they were British. It was partly a test of loyalty, stated because it was expected to be stated, just as certain statements are expected now, not insincerely, but ritualistically. Henry Parkes, who was prone to outrage, was particularly overcome at the 1890 Conference, by what he took to be an imputation of disloyalty on his part because he had forgotten to include the words 'Under the Crown' in one of his draft resolutions in favour of Australian Federation. To appear 'disloyal' was not only bad form, it was politically unacceptable, no matter how critical one might also be about aspects of Britain's system. Sometimes, one suspects, to declare oneself British was to allow the space for criticism, virtually in the same breath.

What then did they mean by being 'British'? The term captured a set of political values and traditions more than cultural or social practices. It meant, in rhetoric at least, a commitment to parliament, and rule of law, to a benign, even lovable monarch, and minimal interference in people's liberty, combined with an imperialistic notion of progress and destiny meaning, roughly, the expansion of trade, education, Christianity, and rationalism at the expense of tradition, superstition and emotion.

Commenting on the completed Australian Constitution, the Chief Justice of New Zealand tried to capture some of this in a comparison (as usual) with America: although it might appear that the Queen's constitutional right to disallow Bills gave the Monarch great power, he argued, the 'Kingly Power' in Australia was in reality less than the President's power, because the British tradition was one of non-interference in the parliament. So, Australia had 'practically all the powers of self-government possessed by the United States', but was 'more democratic', because its people were more 'in touch' with parliament. With high levels of education and 'no great race question', 'the hopes of democrats as to the future of the Commonwealth are high. If it fails, then democracy must be said to be unsuited to a people who are mainly of British descent'.[35]

Britishness was also minimally cultural. To be British meant to be civilised, that is, materially more advanced and therefore culturally superior to the native populations whose territories the British forces felt destined to occupy. It meant being clothed rather than naked despite the heat, and having wives who were quiet and orderly, and also clothed. It meant also going about things without too much fuss or self-advertisement. But beyond these minimal notions, the (white) Australians' way of being British culturally was already significantly different so that tensions, as we have seen, were beginning to occur. By the end of the century, it was no longer necessary for Australians, if it ever had been for more than a handful of people, to pretend to the manners of the British upper classes in order to make themselves culturally British.

It might also be thought that to be 'British' was to be white. This was true to a point, but it was much more literally true for Australians than it was for Britons. There were shades of 'whiteness' for the British, with the English themselves being as 'white' as was possible. There was also a sort of honorary category of 'coloured white'—the 'white man', who was decent and educated and civilised in the English manner. Within this category was a further hierarchy, partly determined by degree of 'pigment' and partly by cultural indicators. But most white Australians did not accept a hierarchy of 'colour', and, as we shall see, they were criticised by a minority in Australia for failing to be 'British' in their attitude to race, and lectured over their lack of subtlety by the Colonial

74   *To Constitute a Nation*

Secretary as they attempted to write a literally 'white' nation into their Constitution.

The Australian Constitution was written to be both American and British at the same time. The British part of the Constitution was responsible government, a hereditary Head of State, the Australian Parliament's acquisition of the privileges of the House of Commons, the prohibition on money bills originating in or being amended by the Senate, the absence of a bill of rights, and much unstated convention, like the existence of a Prime Minister in the Lower House, and a Cabinet. Many more *unwritten* details (such as the Governor-General's practice of taking advice from his ministers) were assumed.

The American part is the distribution of powers so the Commonwealth gets the specified, and therefore limited powers, and the states get what is at least in theory an unlimited rest. It is the existence of a High Court with a capacity for constitutional review, and a Senate with similar powers to the Lower House, representing each state in equal numbers.

As everyone knew at the time, this combination was unheard of, and might even be full of perils. The issue was not so much the clash between a supposedly sovereign Lower House, and an Upper House with the power to override it (a conflict that emerged almost as soon as the Commonwealth Government came off the blueprint and began to operate), for after all this was still, at that time, more or less the relationship between the House of Lords and the House of Commons, nor was there a widespread appreciation of the likelihood of the Senate's turning into a Party House, which largely contributed to the ongoing conflict between the Houses, and was also to happen almost overnight. It was the problem of unequal representation, the triumph, it seemed, of the representation of states rather than the representation of persons, that most worried critics of the final Constitution.

The idea that British democracy was essentially about the representation of individuals (even though, by the 1890s, the category of people able to exercise the vote was limited in Britain compared with Australia) was a persistent image. This issue will come up again later when we look at the type of 'compact' Australians thought themselves to be entering at the time of the referendums on the Constitution Bill. We should note here that the problem of welding or weaving together the American and the British models was perceived, in the main, as a problem of representation.

Metaphors are important in politics. Whether it was welding or weaving that had to be done was a significant indication of an overall perception of the differences between these systems. The British Constitution was seen by many as 'organic', as having grown rather than

Models For a Nation   75

having been constructed, mechanically, as it were, as the American Constitution had necessarily been. It helped no doubt to have at hand the cultural imagery of America as mechanised, urbanised, fast and artificial, and of Britain as green and pastoral, its Constitution growing like a venerable oak. This imagery was employed at the Federal Conference in Melbourne in 1890, where Dr Cockburn, in his 'brotherhood of infinite variety' speech, raised doubts about following the American model, as well as the Canadian, since the former was 'so far different from anything which has ever obtained under British rule', and the 'whole principle' of the latter was 'a gradual growth and not a manufacture'. The American model would be 'so utterly different from any of those traditions which have enwrapped themselves around the growth of the British Constitution'. The result, then, interjected Henry Parkes, 'would be another growth of that prized variety'.[36]

How could members of a conference destined to set the course of constitution writing in train convince themselves that they were doing no more than tending a slow-growing plant? Mr Deakin appeared to resolve the dilemma, at least for himself, and at least for the moment, in a characteristically philosophical contribution towards the Conference's conclusion. The American Constitution, he pointed out, in fact had grown, as 'a closely-allied offshoot from the British Constitution':

> The task which lies before the Convention is not that of creating a new Constitution. Any assemblage meeting with the design of shaping out of the inner consciousness of its members some novel form of government, which might appear to be theoretically perfect, would fail . . . I trust that the members of the Convention will shape the Constitution they propose . . . to our national characteristics and capacities so that it may unfold with their unfoldment, expand with our expansion, develop with our destiny.[47]

It was not clear how this would help practically, since either the members had to measure and define Australia's 'national characteristics', 'mechanically' matching future constitutional provisions to these, or they would need to rely on their intuition—their 'inner consciousness'—to give them a feel for the appropriate constitutional form. In the event, they did a bit of both.

A lot depended on anxieties about how far the American model would lead them. Aside from its attractive federal arrangements, it was, of course, a republic, not a monarchy, and the essence of being 'loyal' lay in expressing affection for the monarch. Not everyone minded a little bit of republicanism, and many found ways of being republican—that is to say, supporting (as a present or a future goal) full Australian sovereignty against British interference—at the same time as remaining loyal. But few

76 To Constitute a Nation

in the population and none in the Conventions wanted to be radically republican, and they reminded themselves that the Americans had gone down that route because they had been pushed to war with the Mother Country. Henry Parkes, always happily anecdotal, told the 1890 Conference that the great historian of American and English history, William Lecky, had personally assured him that Americans most probably would not have 'quarrelled' with the English, if they had had at the time a federal system like the Australian system proposed now by Parkes himself.[38]

The following year, Parkes supported the adoption of what proved to be, in republican versus monarchist imagery, the most ambiguous name possible for a united Australia: Commonwealth. J. A. La Nauze has traced in detail the likely provenance of the term, first proposed by Parkes and urged by Deakin early in the Convention of 1891. It was, he concludes, most probably suggested by James Bryce's great work *The American Commonwealth*, recently published and soon to serve as the 'bible' of the Australian framers.[39] But the exact source, if indeed there was a single one, is now beyond discovery and matters little. It is what the name subsequently conveyed that is interesting. The big question was: did Commonwealth smack of republicanism?

Letters to the newspapers throughout the 1890s declared that it did, and many of the Convention members continued to think so too. The term at that time readily evoked, it seems, that brief period of English history in which Oliver Cromwell, as Protector, occupied the place of the King. The name, wrote someone calling himself 'Australian', has 'a smack of socialistic tendencies . . . Further, it reminds us first of the reign of Oliver Cromwell, who, although a good general, was somewhat of a cruel tyrant'.[40] 'We do not want a word of political signification of any sort', wrote a Mr Selwyn, 'neither Commonwealth, nor Dominion, any more than Republic or Democracy; we want Australia for all Australians'.[41] A Mr Ronald added a piece of information for Melbourne readers, that the word 'commonwealth' was translated into French as 'république' and vice-versa, and he asked 'What serious complications might not this lead to in international affairs?'. Unaware, it is clear, of the lengthy attempts at the name's interpretation undertaken in the Convention debates, Mr Ronald added that its choice was 'evidence of that slipshod hurry-scurry way' in which the Constitution had been handled.[42] From time to time, a defence of the name Commonwealth also appeared in the press, one accusing its opponents of being 'imperfectly informed Tories', who had not taken the trouble to discover that 'commonwealth' was 'in ordinary use in England in the ultra royalist days of the Tudors, when nobody dreamed of a Republic'.[43]

These epistolary exchanges were echoes of the Convention debates. Almost immediately after it was adopted in 1891, James Munro from

Victoria tried to have the name altered. It was not 'a happy title', he said; it 'raises rather serious questions—questions that suggest a good deal of controversy in the minds of many people'. Deakin took up the defence. It was 'a distinctly English word', to begin with, he said, 'with a pacific signification' which suggests that the state was formed for 'the common good of its people, for their common-weal'. Then Sir John Downer made the perfectly reasonable point that it might be 'a very nice word indeed, but . . . we have to consider, not only the technical meaning of the law, but also the popular understanding of the law'; 'the popular understanding of the word "commonwealth" ', he insisted, 'is certainly connected with republican times'. (Mr Deakin: 'No!'.)[44]

And so the debate went on, Deakin declaring the Protectorate to be, in any case, 'the most glorious period of England's history', and Western Australia's John Wright demurring, with Thomas Playford counter-attacking by accusing him of believing 'in the glorious memory of Charles I!'. Edmund Barton raised once more the honourable association of the term with Shakespeare (something his brother would describe at greater length that year in a published annotated edition of the draft Constitution of 1891).[45] All sorts of alternatives were proposed: 'Dominion of Australia' had been freely used in 1890, but how could they have settled on this, after all they had said about the Canadian Dominion? 'Federal Australia', 'United Australia', 'the Federated States of Australia' were also offered, while William Marmion (also from Western Australia) continued to insist that plain old 'Australia' was good enough. His fellow delegate, Sir John Forrest, made the interesting observation that the term 'commonwealth' might be appropriate to 'founding an independent nation', but not a Federation of independent, sovereign states, the object of their Convention. Then Barton and Playford, as well as New Zealand's delegate, Sir George Grey, all in turn testified that while they had at first been, if not 'prejudiced against the word', at least unhappy with the choice, they had quickly converted, and now liked it very much indeed.[46]

In following the tug-of-war between states' rights and 'nation-building' that continued throughout the decade, it still comes as a pleasant surprise that the term Commonwealth survived. Only late in the day was it discovered that Queen Victoria herself did not care for it,[47] but it seems unlikely that the Constitution's framers learned directly of this and, in any case, it was by then well beyond the moment for any reversal, even if a satisfactory alternative had been found.

Many hopes are attached to names bestowed by parents on their children. The name chosen for Australia and defended so warmly, even by those who put the interests of the sovereignty of the states ahead of the idea of nation in other debates, clearly captured an imaginary future, the happy ideal of a peaceful, generous nation. It was 'the only really first-class thing' about the Bill, said the labour *Hummer*. 'Commonwealth means common weal, or the general good, the well-being of the community . . . Let us keep the good homely pure English word "Commonwealth", and make Australia the first nation in the world to work and legislate for the *good of all*'.[48] For conservatives as well it had the virtue of being an English name, one they were eventually persuaded had classical more than modern affinities.

It was a name that, ultimately, seemed to suit almost everyone. Having assembled their Constitution from a collection of parts, having borrowed and improvised and at times forced pieces together, it was reassuring to be able to call this collection something that was both familiar and uncommon. Something quite different from the name of all the models the framers had 'tried on' for their new nation.

CHAPTER FIVE

Things Properly Federal

While the Australian community was being imagined, another process went on: the specific identification of those political matters the nation had in common. Throughout the processes of constitution writing, members of the Federal Conventions sought the key to what belonged 'properly' to the national, or federal, sphere, those things that made the colonies a nation as well as, or more than, separate states. Adherence to the American, rather than the Canadian, model required the listing of national powers and, because they were not placed on the national list, the definition (by implication) of what remained as domestic or state powers. Some things, it seems, fell 'naturally' or spontaneously into the category of national, others into the category of state. A range of matters was contentious, neither clearly one nor the other and considerable effort went into the debate over where to place these, over which level would get the power.

Some of the federal powers were immediately obvious, given the pressing practical concerns of the Federation movement. The most urgent national matters were made exclusive to the Commonwealth Parliament, that is to say, laws in respect of these matters could only be made at the Commonwealth level. Defence was the obvious first candidate to become an exclusive power.

One of the major prompts for the Federation Conference in 1890 had been, as we saw, Major-General Edwards's report the year before, which concluded that Australia's independent defence capability was as good as non-existent. With the fact that Australia offered 'such a rich and tempting prize', reported Edwards, 'without a proper supply of arms and ammunition—with forces which cannot at present be considered efficient ... and without any cohesion or power of combination for mutual defence among the different Colonies—its position [if threatened] would be one of great danger'.[1] It would make no sense to create a nation unless defence were considered naturally to fall under the nation's jurisdiction.

80   *To Constitute a Nation*

The rows of customs houses along the colonial borders were also a constant reminder that intercolonial tariffs would need to come under matters of national concern; border tariffs, imposed over several decades by all the colonies except New South Wales on goods imported from all the others, would be swept away and replaced, perhaps, by a national tariff. Before Federation, and in the days before income tax, tariffs generated the bulk of a government's revenue. A constant political reality and a common intercolonial problem, they were, as former Victorian Premier James Service so memorably put it in his home-town speech at the 1890 Conference banquet, the 'lion in the path' that must either kill Federation or be killed by it (to be precise, he said the 'lion in the way', a colloquial expression of the time, but 'path' it has become).

'On the imposition of uniform duties of customs', as the Constitution says (meaning immediately following their imposition), the customs houses would be placed exclusively in the ports. The collection of customs and excise duties was made, therefore, an exclusive power of the Commonwealth, complemented by section 92, which declared that 'trade, commerce, and intercourse among the States . . . shall be absolutely free'. This section, now almost legendary for the judgments to which it has given rise this century, seems at the time to have meant, essentially, that the states should once and for all cease imposing tariffs against each other. It would appear, after all, a rather weak idea of a nation, whose own members had to go through customs controls when they travelled around their own country.

The new nation, the protectionists argued in addition (successfully, as it turned out), must protect its nascent manufacturing industries and its level of wages at the same time, by imposing a uniform tariff on internationally imported goods. It was to be (although the metaphor would not have been appreciated) like building a modern-day Great Wall of China, encircling the continent (as well as Tasmania) with a barrier through which foreign interests could not pass unscathed.

Immigration controls too would reinforce the walls, while behind them (even the Free Traders, who did not want tariffs on imports, agreed), the movement of goods and money and persons, all now part of a new nation, would be 'absolutely free'. Although immigration was not made an exclusive Commonwealth power, it effectively became so as soon as the Commonwealth had passed its first Immigration Act, which it got straight down to doing, in 1901.

The settlement reached in the first decade of Federation, where protection of industry from cheap imports and labour from cheap workers was mutually agreed, endured almost unscathed in its essential form until the last two decades of the twentieth century, and did more to shape Australia's political and economic destiny than almost any party policy. But this was not just the idea of new national governments, bent on social experiment. It was deeply embedded in the culture of the 1890s and in the characteristic commitment to strike a bargain, and out of this, to forge a compact. This settlement is inscribed in the Constitution as among those things 'essentially federal': free trade within, and the option of tariffs without, along with powers over industrial arbitration in matters 'extending beyond the limits of any one State'.

Tariffs, defence and immigration. These are the issues commonly considered by historians to be the causes of Federation. Sometimes, along with postal and telegraphic services, these are the problems of the time identified retrospectively as needing a national solution, as pressing the otherwise unwilling colonies into an awkward union. No one can doubt, looking at the campaigns and the rhetoric of the last two decades of the nineteenth century, that these issues featured prominently. They were the things most obviously 'properly federal', the first on the agenda when it came to describing the powers of the new Commonwealth.

What these issues have in common is not just (or even not essentially, as some might think) that they are the material and financial interests of capitalism, but, at a more general level, that they represent concerns shared by all modernising and emerging nations in this era. Under the combined influences of capitalist expansion, rapid development of communications and transport technologies, movements of populations and democratisation, nations on an entirely new scale were exploring political relations with each other and finding themselves forced into formalising these relations. It was the era of nation-building, when the pre-First World War borders were being drawn in dark ink on the maps. One by one, new nations were formed in the second half of the century: Germany, Italy, Canada. Immigration, quarantine, naturalisation, exports, diplomacy, military relations all assumed an unprecedented importance.

Australia's founders were far from unique, nor were they especially materialistic, in seeking a constitutional expression for these matters, indeed in making this their point of departure. These were the issues of the age. It is astounding to realise now that passports, for example, were not required for travel to and from most European countries, and Australians freely left their ports for Britain and its colonies without 'papers', until the time of the Great War, the event that altered almost everything in international relations as well as individual lives.

Passports may now be the expression of an established nation-state, but they do not in themselves make a nation. Nor do tariffs or military infrastructure. The colonies were not compelled to federate in order to solve their material problems. The twentieth century has given us many examples of how this might otherwise have been done: a customs union between the colonies, a defence treaty, common policy on immigration, all leaving the original political nation or colony intact.

82   *To Constitute a Nation*

Such arrangements were already beginning to develop as modern nation-states formed in the nineteenth century. In Australia, an agreement had been concluded as early as 1855 between the three relevant colonies, New South Wales, South Australia and Victoria, over duties on goods transported along the Murray River, and discussions, albeit inconclusive, about achieving a full customs union had continued over the following decades. Regular meetings of, among others, intercolonial Postmasters-General had attempted to reach common policy and standards for decades.[2] On immigration, all the colonies in 1888 agreed in principle to a common approach, and, although Queensland subsequently departed from the agreement, the structure for its renegotiation was there and was reactivated in 1896. 'The whole year round', said Alfred Deakin, one of the delegates at the 1895 Federal Council meeting in Hobart, 'there are different federal conferences, now a federal gathering of commandants, then of health officers, next as to maritime affairs, with, at this very moment, a postal conference and a caucus of Premiers. So it goes on, from year's end to year's end'.[3]

A colonial defence treaty was imagined at times in the last decades of the century. Captain Russell, at the 1890 Federation Conference, contemplated a naval defence union among all the colonies including New Zealand, and assured the Australians 'with absolute certainty', that his colony would be happy to belong (although, unsurprisingly, he also doubted the value of a federal army to his country).[4] For some time advocates of a federal union for defence purposes had promoted the establishment of a federal defence force as a priority before political Federation, rather than as a consequence of it. Major-General Edward Hutton, Commandant of the New South Wales Military Forces, pressed for a 'military federation' throughout the early part of the 1890s,[5] and his successor, Major-General George French, wrote at the end of the Federation process that he had been 'somewhat disgusted' at the decision 'that political federation must first be accomplished'.[6]

In 1889, with the dismaying realities expressed in the Edwards Report brought home to them, the colonies might well have sought an immediate defence treaty. Instead, they sought Federation. It was a process that would take over ten more years and that would grow to cover a field of matters way beyond the limited practical issue of defence.

The views of Majors-General Hutton and French reflected the consistent British commitment to a military union prior to Federation, and their repeated attempt to have this plan adopted by the colonial Premiers. Hutton was successful only in convincing George Reid in New South Wales, but Reid himself failed on several occasions, including at the crucial Premiers' Conference in Hobart in 1895, to win over the other Premiers. At issue was the British plan, semi-clandestine, but understood, to bring the colonial forces under a central Imperial command, a scheme which went hand in hand with Imperial Federation, and for which the majority of Australians had no sympathy at all.

The Colonial Office had gone as far as to attempt to persuade the Constitution's framers to change what is now section 68, so that 'the Queen' rather than the Governor-General would be Commander-in-Chief of the naval and military forces. This, as historian John Mordike has pointed out, would effectively have placed control in the hands of the British Government (upon the advice of which Her Majesty was constitutionally bound to act).[7] The strategy was obvious to the Australians, for whom federal control of defence was an incontestable part of Federation, a matter irreducibly federal, and therefore scarcely debated at all in the Conventions.

But, 'strong as is the temptation' to believe that Federation would enable Australia to defend itself, commented the *West Australian* on the eve of Federation, 'not even the question of national defence can be considered wholly from its sentimental and picturesque side. Federation possesses no alchemist's power of mystery by which through the mere act of union insufficiently defended States can be made impregnable'.[8] There was no respect in which, at least in the short term, full independent defence was to be achieved by the process of federating any more than it might have been achieved prior to Federation. Australia would remain dependent upon British naval forces, and its military policy subject to British powers of disallowal. In federating, what the country did gain was greater political and strategic legitimacy to assert and ultimately win the right to such control. For this reason, as the Colonial Office found to its frustration, the political will to accomplish an intercolonial union such as a defence treaty, in the absence of full Federation, could not be generated.

There was no shortage of suggestions for other forms of union in the decades prior to Federation. At the 1890 Conference, alternative schemes were closely under scrutiny. There, as well as a defence treaty, the possibility of an immediate customs union without full Federation was raised. It was thought by at least South Australia to be premature. The colonies, said Dr Cockburn, must at present be free 'to follow their own inclinations, and to work out their own destinies'.[9] In his turn Sir Samuel Griffith argued forcefully for the advantages of Federation, even without a customs union: 'If possible let us get a complete Federal Parliament and Federal Executive, one dominion with no rivalries—no customs rivalries at any rate, amongst ourselves. If we cannot get all that let us get as much of it as we can'.[10]

What were the things which the separate colonial parliaments simply could not do by themselves?, Griffith asked. Defence, external relations,

84   To Constitute a Nation

foreign trade and commerce, copyright and patents, he responded. They could get by without a customs union:

> And there would be this advantage, that under the new arrangement the absurdity of fighting one another by customs tariffs would become so apparent that before very long they would be given up . . . The collection of such duties is a most disagreeable thing, but it is not inconsistent with Federation— not a perfect form of Federation, but an arrangement very much better than anything we have at the present time. That is the 'lion in the path', and it seems to me to be a very harmless creature after all.

Then Griffith added:

> Matters such as those of fiscal policy are, after all, only means, not ends, in themselves. Whatever conclusion may be arrived at in regard to such matters, it is our business not to lose sight of the one great end in view—the establishment of a nation. The moral effect upon the people of Australia of the accomplishment of such an object would be very great indeed.[11]

Griffith's argument offers an alternative perspective to those historians for whom Federation begins and ends with the tariff, or indeed with commercial relations outside the continent. Although Griffith listed external trade and commerce among the concerns he found self-evidently national, he elevated the creation of a nation above these. Its creation, he argued, would give scope to the 'legitimate and noble ambition of those who desire to take part in the affairs of a great nation', men whose energies are 'cramped' when limited to internal matters. Being a player on the world stage, a nation among nations, 'practically commanding the Southern Seas', realising a destiny, thinking big. These goals, as much as, and often more than, financial or material interests, prompted Federalists and gave them to imagine a nation, not just a treaty of mutual convenience between the colonies.

The material advantages and the moral achievement were to be played out both against and alongside each other throughout the whole decade, and the perennial question of whether the colonies could federate without a customs union or whether a customs union could be achieved independently of Federation was symptomatic of this debate. But the range of responses underlines the larger dimension in the imagined nation. However much material interests motivated the promoters of Federation, the nation was to be more than a treaty.

Attempts to create an intercolonial union that fell short of full Federation had in fact already been made. The best known is the Federal Council. It was formed, recognising 'that the time has not yet arrived at which a complete federal union of the Australasian Colonies can be attained, but considering that there are many matters of general interest, with respect to which united action would be advantageous'.[12] It seemed, briefly, full of promise, but its birth was attended by two bad fairies— intercolonial jealousy and political rivalry—and, despite a patchy but consistent existence, which only terminated with the Inauguration of the Commonwealth, it is remembered (if at all) as a failure.

The idea of the Federal Council was to give the colonies a direct means of reaching common policy on matters beyond the scope of individual colonial parliaments, in particular defence. It allowed at first two members per self-governing colony and one for each Crown colony (these were Fiji and, until 1890, Western Australia), with members nominated by the colonial parliaments. It was to convene at least once every two years, with the power to 'legislate' on a range of matters as referred to it by two or more colonies, and it met more or less regularly along these lines, until 1899 always in Hobart. Victoria, Tasmania, Queensland and Western Australia joined at the start and remained members. Fiji also belonged but never attended meetings. South Australia, hostile at first, belonged for a time, then withdrew after 1891 and did not rejoin. New Zealand and New South Wales never joined.

The Federal Council was intended as 'the forerunner of a more natural system of Federal Government', said Henry Parkes in promoting the original idea.[13] What a 'more natural' system might mean he did not say. Proposed by New South Wales, the Council was then abandoned by that colony and never had the opportunity to prove itself, either natural or otherwise. It is commonly argued now that the Federal Council failed because it had no executive powers, and because New South Wales, the Mother Colony, refused ever to join it. But this is to mistake the symptoms for the cause.

The overriding concern with the (external) matter of European incursions into the South Pacific, which prompted the Federal Council's establishment at the beginning, the absence of customs and tariffs from among the Council's areas of legislative competence, and the perception that the Council was strongly associated with Victorian interests, contributed, as W. G. McMinn has shown, to problems with its legitimacy as a body concerned with national and internal matters.[14] The vanity of Henry Parkes, who did not want to involve New South Wales in something he had not directly orchestrated, no doubt played its part and South Australia's discontinuous membership also contributed to the Council's inability to act properly as a national body.

But the Federal Council's impotence and its failure to be a magnet for all the colonies must itself be explained in the first place. It was a matter of too little and too early, on the one hand, and too little, too late, on the other. The Council was formed just before that burst of nationalism

86   *To Constitute a Nation*

which accompanied the beginning of the ultimately successful Federation movement. It missed these beginnings.

In the early 1880s, at the time of its birth, sentimental and constitutional attachment to Britain was still strong enough to hamper any movement seeking constitutional independence for the nation. Support for Imperial rather than national Federation was at its peak and suspicion that the actual goal of the Federal Council was Imperial rather than national Federation was, not without reason, attached to it. While many of the powers of the Council in fact appeared later in the Australian Constitution, their enumeration was not in itself adequate to make a nation, or even to inspire the rhetoric of union and nation-building found continuously from 1889. At this stage the idea of what was properly federal focused, not upon internal matters, but on, in Alfred Deakin's words, 'the protection of Australian interests in the surrounding seas'.[15]

The role and identity of the Federal Council was therefore an important subtext and frequently also a direct subject in the Conference of 1890 where the baton would change hands, passed from the Council to the series of Conventions that marked the 1890s, and also, for a while, from the Victorian Premier's hands to those still steering New South Wales, Henry Parkes's. In a major speech at that Conference South Australia's Thomas Playford, having gone over all the available federal examples, came to the difficulties confronting Australia: greater difficulties, he argued paradoxically, than 'in any country in the world in which Federation has taken place'. Australia had 'no enemy at our doors', and could therefore 'only appeal to injuries that might be occasioned by our hostile tariffs, and to the advantages of union'.

This situation would, he went on, require the slow and careful development of public opinion and the demonstration of the worth of Federation, in the face of the fact that the current colonial system seemed to work successfully. The Federal Council had been part of this evolution, and Parkes himself had all but written its Bill. Why then, asked Playford, had New South Wales refused to join?[16]

Despite his attempt to reply immediately, Henry Parkes had to sit, fuming, through several days of further debate, much of it focusing on the value of the current Federal Council, before being allowed his right of reply. In the meanwhile, in a lengthy speech on the American system, Andrew Inglis Clark saw the Council's value as lying in the lesson it might 'even actually' provide since it had in it 'a provision not possessed by any other Federal Constitution in the World', the power for two or more colonies to refer any subject to the Council for legislation. Even his beloved American Constitution, he said, might have been improved with such a clause. The lesson, it seems, was learned since, in a modified form, this power of referral (first proposed in a Privy Council report in 1849) turned up again in the final Constitution.[17]

Things Properly Federal   87

If the Federal Council was not adequate in itself at present, why could it not be used as the basis for constructing a Federation? Some considered this a possibility; others, for example, Griffith and Tasmania's Treasurer, Bolton Bird, considered the obstacle to such a scheme to be the absence of an institutional structure in the Council. There was no executive, and no possibility of legitimacy unless the executive was democratically chosen. Bird thought the Council might work if it had two Houses, rather than just the one that was undemocratic and had 'too much power over the purse'.[18]

When Henry Parkes finally got his chance in Melbourne to reply to Playford's question, he could scarcely contain himself. He had been, he believed, accused of disloyalty to the Queen and he fulminated on this before turning to the question of why New South Wales had failed to join the Federal Council. He had repeatedly explained, Parkes told the Conference, that ('Upon reflection, and after further examination of the great and complex question') he had simply changed his mind. The likelihood of a body such as the Federal Council succeeding in the objects for which he had first suggested it was small. The Council was, he now believed, too limited 'in number and authority, and consequently so powerless to acquire prestige' that it could never work harmoniously with any 'hostile' colony.[19]

It must have seemed the weakest of arguments, since the colony most hostile to the Council was that of the very Premier who had advocated the Council's establishment in the first place. What Parkes appears to have meant, essentially, was that he wanted and would settle for nothing less than a full Federation, a nation rather than simply a union. This change of heart must have been stimulated by his voyage to America at the very moment of the Federal Council's conception, and his perception, while there, that something greater had been done under similar circumstances to those prevailing now in Australia. No doubt Parkes also meditated on the idea that a larger place for men 'of legitimate and noble ambition' could be carved out in the doing. He must also have sensed a shift in the winds of Federation's fortunes. Public sentiment was now turning away from Imperial Federation and from the pursuit of limited, non-sovereign bodies like the Council. Parkes decided to abandon the Council and go for all or nothing.

Only a year later, the colonies met in Sydney in order, this time, to establish the framework for something greater. As they discussed what the something would be, the Federal Council's fortunes were once again contemplated, but no one would claim much more for it now than Dr Cockburn did: 'affection' and a vague hope for its future. Joseph Abbott, in passing, provided here the most original (and perhaps most convincing) explanation for the absence of New South Wales from the Council: that it was 'Victoria's fault'. When the vote came up in

88 *To Constitute a Nation*

parliament, he said, it was 'just about that time the Melbourne Cup was run . . . and members ran away to it, with the result that when the division took place the Government were in a minority, and so the Federal Council had to do, from that day to this, without the colony of New South Wales'.[20]

But, despite its low stocks, the Federal Council surprisingly did not die an early death, as other attempts at pre-Federation union had done. It met regularly, indeed more frequently in the 1890s than in the decade of its birth, being actually enlarged in its membership in the mid-1890s, and it was only terminated by the passage of the completed Constitution. It outlived old Henry Parkes himself. Although it legislated on very little (its major success was the regulation of pearling and bêche-de-mer fisheries in Queensland and West Australian coastal waters) and on nothing that now appears to be of overwhelming national importance, it did provide a forum for discussion and resolution on all sorts of matters of common interest.

Even late in the 1890s the idea of reinvigorating the Federal Council, even using it as the basis for full Federation, circulated from time to time. At the Bathurst People's Federal Convention in 1896 William Lyne regretted 'that an attempt had not been made to build a federation from the Federal Council'.[21] As late as the day of the Commonwealth's Inauguration, James Drake (ardent Queensland Federalist and soon, although he did not know this even then, to be first federal Postmaster-General following the death of James Dickson) spoke with a tone of trepidation about the seemingly narrow passage for true Federation between supporters of unification on the one hand and 'not a few adherents' (indeed quite influential ones) on the other, who were 'in favour of continuing the Australian Federal Council and of infusing into it some slight tincture of the representative principle'.[22] That such a scheme could not have succeeded must, however, have been apparent to all but the most optimistic by the end of the sixth session of the Federal Council meeting in Hobart, in early 1895.

'Hobart has been the centre of various Intercolonial Meetings', wrote the journalist and lawyer James Backhouse Walker in his diary on 15 February 1895: 'first in importance', he noted, was the Premiers' Conference, then came the Federal Council. There was a Postal Conference, a Mining Conference, even a 'Temperance Convention',[23] and to his list Walker might also have added an Australian Natives' Association special meeting to form a Hobart branch of the Federation League. The Tasmanian capital was a point of colonial convergence in the days of sea travel, a 'convenient centre', said Alfred Deakin, and also happily 'isolated from influences which might at other centres be brought to bear'.[24] It was also 'The Season' when the heat of the mainland drove many who had the means south. When the Federal Council got together that summer, its members joined with those of the other intercolonial meetings for a reception and a ball at Government House, and a picnic in Fenton Forest. Such informal gatherings should not be underestimated as opportunities for establishing intercolonial political trust, official and unofficial networks, indeed for fostering what was, by the second half of the decade, generally known as the 'federal spirit'. Even though it could not be expected to resolve much, the Council meeting was to prove of great use.

In late 1894, anticipating this forthcoming Council session, George Reid, recently elected Premier of New South Wales, called a special Premiers' Conference in Hobart to discuss Federation. The Council meeting would bring together, among others, the Premiers of the four member colonies. Although New South Wales did not belong, Reid's own presence could naturally be guaranteed and the remaining non-member Premier, South Australia's Charles Kingston, had been urging Reid to move on the plan.

The Premiers' Conference was scheduled to begin on 29 January 1895, the day before the Federal Council, and to run for a couple of days after its completion. The Conference (meeting virtually next door in the Tasmanian Chief Secretary's Office) immediately overshadowed the Council. The Federal Council had on this occasion 'no business' to complete, that is to say, several resolutions, but no proposals from member colonies for legislation, so it spent much of its three days arguing about its own identity.

From the start the very existence of the Premiers' meeting evoked outrage among some of the Council members. On the first day of the Federal Council, following the customary opening formalities, Tasmanian member Henry Dobson proposed that they establish communication between the two meetings, with the prospect of a further joint conference to plan 'united action' on Federation. He was met with vehement protest. Western Australia's James Lee Steere immediately objected that it was 'hardly wise' for the Federal Council to be involved with 'informal discussions . . . This is a legally constituted body'. Then came the other Tasmanians. Adye Douglas: 'Let them go on their own track'; then Andrew Inglis Clark: 'Yes, let them go their own way'; then Mr Douglas again: 'We are a legally constituted body'. And Edward Braddon, Tasmanian Premier and Council President: 'I certainly do not see at the first blush how I can interfere with the matter in the way proposed or . . . bring our proceedings into collision, or any sort of contact, with the proceedings that are being separately concluded by the Premiers elsewhere'.[25]

But if Braddon failed to see at 'first blush' how this could be done, he must have seen at the end that it could not be avoided. To begin with, four of the Premiers who were meeting 'elsewhere' were there in the

90   *To Constitute a Nation*

very Council meeting, and even though two of the Premiers, Sir John Forrest and Sir Hugh Nelson, were opposed to the plan adopted by the other Premiers for an elected constitutional Convention and referendum on the completed Constitution, they did not prevent the Conference from meeting. In addition there were a significant number who were sympathetic towards both the Premiers' meeting and Plan among the remaining Council members.

Queensland's Attorney-General, Thomas Byrnes, led the attack on the Premiers' Conference from the Council meeting. Opposing the idea that the Federal Council should even talk about Federation, Byrnes declared, amidst other vituperation, that he and others 'had come a long distance to do business, and not to be thwarted or overshadowed by a meeting of individuals elsewhere'.[26] Speculation about the Federal Council's purpose was raised in the press; would the Councillors discuss the Premiers' Plan or would they attempt to ignore it? But, how could they have ignored it? And what 'other business' did they have?

There was one hurried attempt, by Queensland Federal Councillor, Edward Archer, to circumvent the Premiers' Plan, by moving that the dormant 1891 draft Constitution should be put immediately before the colonial parliaments, but this only turned inevitably into a debate on the Plan. The Victorian delegates, convinced that Archer's motion was intentionally antagonistic and an affront to the Victorians who had already debated the Bill in their Parliament, walked out. In their absence, the motion was passed.

But the 1891 Constitution Bill was not put to any other parliament, and the motion now has only passing historical interest. In the course of the meeting, however, discussion of the Federal Council's worth yielded several instructive conclusions. Mr Douglas thought they should be honest, and admit the Council had been a 'ghastly failure'. Even while the Convention of 1891 had been, he thought, an 'unnatural' attempt to create a 'paper constitution' without any wider community action or understanding of the principles of Federation, the Federal Council had not provided an alternative. It had failed, Douglas said, through lack of unity, and lack of strength, and its only prospect now was to combine its labours with those of the 'more powerful' Premiers.[27]

Others agreed that the Council had problems, but declared that these were not its fault; rather they were caused by the parliaments in the member colonies having failed to provide the Council with things to do, and/or the fault of New South Wales keeping 'aloof'. An increase in its numbers, perhaps even an elective basis for membership, might, they felt, reinvigorate it.

A third group, some strenuously, depicted the Council as still energetic, even as, in the words of Queensland's Attorney-General, the 'true germ of the greatest Federation that Australasia can have'.[28] Alfred Deakin (who later supported the Premiers' Plan vigorously and called the Federal Council a 'mere creature of the colonies'[29]) rejected the epithet 'ghastly failure' as well as the proposal to confer with the Premiers, and asserted that the Federal Council had great potential—even that it had done great things, such as influencing the French Government's decision to cease transportation to New Caledonia. But, if the opposition to the Premiers' Plan was carried by the Federal Council on that day, this would be its last victory. We know now that the Premiers triumphed, and that the idea of popular approval of Federation (discussed in chapter eight) was a necessary precondition for the success of the movement.

At the ANA special meeting in Hobart in that same week of 1895, Deakin told his audience that the 1891 draft Constitution had been 'a splendid attempt', but like Robinson Crusoe's canoe, 'the largest that he built—when he built it the difficulty was he could not get it into the water'.[30] Perhaps the Federal Council, with its statutory identity and its relative maturity, might once have served as the body to get the canoe in the water, but by this stage in the decade the nation had begun to be conceived as an internal community and not merely one with interests 'in the surrounding seas'. In the event, the Federal Council played its part, providing a useful model of how *not* to go about federating and, in quite a simple sense, bringing together regularly the senior politicians of the majority of colonies, including those most reluctant to embrace a Federation. It also helped shape the idea of what was and what was not properly federal, both in terms of the law and of the polity. Its legislative powers were among those drawn, in some cases literally, into the 1891 Constitution Bill, along with powers from other federal constitutions, and much on this list turned up again in the final Constitution.

Those powers finally settled on as national can mostly be viewed in section 51 of the Constitution. Although almost all are formally 'concurrent' (that is, able to be exercised by the states as well as the Commonwealth), they become effectively exclusive once the Commonwealth has passed legislation under such a power. This is the case because, by force of section 109, any state law inconsistent with a Commonwealth law is invalid.

The powers found in section 51 represent what was thought of in the 1890s as proper for national, rather than local, legislation. As one progresses down the list, most, along with defence and immigration (tariffs are found later in the Constitution), will appear 'naturally' national: trade and commerce across borders, postal, telegraphic, telephonic and 'other like services', lighthouses, quarantine, census and statistics, currency, external affairs. But some things are there that do not quite fit and,

92   *To Constitute a Nation*

having been noticed as unusual, they invite us to reflect also on what is not there.

Marriage and divorce, for example, find their way into the list just as they do in the Canadian Constitution, but not in the American. Given the strong preference among the Australians for the latter model on states' rights grounds, this needs to be explained. In the 1890s the situation around the colonies was far from uniform on this matter. Existing divorce laws in Victoria and New South Wales were considerably more liberal than they were in the other colonies and in the United Kingdom (for this reason, the Queen's assent had been withheld, although never finally refused, on Australian divorce Bills a number of times in the preceding two decades). In Victoria and New South Wales, divorce was becoming 'feminised' in this period with women able to seek legal release from marriage on the grounds, for example, of their husband's adultery alone, or of habitual drunkenness, or a period of desertion of four or more years.[31] In the other colonies women were not entitled to sue for divorce on single grounds.

The idea of the new Commonwealth Parliament having the power in this matter raised alarm both in the liberal colonies, where it was feared that the conservatives would reverse existing progressive legislation, and in the small colonies, which were concerned that they would be infected by the moral pollution of the larger colonies. The *West Australian Church News*, for example, argued that under the Constitution, West Australian divorce and marriage laws which 'are not nearly so lax as in the other colonies . . . will become assimilated' to those of the eastern states, where divorce was more common, and where there was often 'a deliberate connivance at adultery and other sins', with the weakening of 'family life, sobriety, and the State', and the sin of illegitimacy 'steadily on the increase'.[32] The claim was repeated in the 1897 Federal Convention by West Australian delegates, concerned that the marriage and divorce power would 'drag down' the marital tie 'to the level of New South Wales', undermining the 'morality and respectability' of the new nation.[33]

Here, however, strong argument was mounted against the federally variable divorce laws, which had caused such 'pain and grief' in the United States. In the view of those great constitutional commentators, Quick and Garran, the 'one defect in the [United States] Constitution more conspicuous than [any] other' was 'its inability to provide a number of contiguous and autonomous communities with uniformity of legislation on subjects of such vital and national importance as marriage and divorce'.[34]

So, what some claimed as a state matter, and what might easily have been considered domestic (since it belonged to that realm of the family, morality and personal relations, which were otherwise almost all

Things Properly Federal   93

untouched by Commonwealth powers) appeared in the eyes of others as a matter 'of national importance'. Sir John Downer summed up the latter view with his claim that no subject was 'more fitted for general legislation' than marriage, because it concerns 'not merely the individuals who are parties to the contract . . . but also those who are to come afterwards'.[35]

But, while children—'those who are to come'—made divorce a national matter, the general custody and guardianship of children was defined as non-national, and left to state control. The Commonwealth gained powers over children 'in relation to' divorce and matrimonial causes, but not over the custody of children born outside legal marriage, nor over orphans or 'wayward' or homeless children. Joseph Carruthers, from New South Wales, argued that granting the Commonwealth powers over custody generally might lead to its taking over 'the whole of the benevolent institutions of the various colonies which have to deal with children' and turning these into federal institutions, whereas there was 'a decided objection' to any 'federal interference with what the people conceive to be matters most sacred in the family'.[36]

Until 1946, when one of those rare events—a successful referendum—occurred, social welfare powers in general were not considered properly national. Maternity, widows', unemployment and family allowances, among others (the very areas of greatest concern for women), were left to the states until almost half a century later. It was not until after the Great Depression and the Second World War that a broad shift in thinking began, which allowed such matters to be seen as part of the nation's political responsibility.

Up until the last decade of the nineteenth century welfare was almost exclusively a matter of charity and philanthropy. It was the special sphere of women who served on the committees and boards of benevolent societies, or 'visited' welfare institutions as 'Biblewomen' or informal inspectors.[37] 'Domestic' and 'private' converged in their multiple connotations. Social welfare, much of it distributed in the family itself, was the 'private' sphere in which women made their particular contribution, while men acted on the public stage of parliaments and, increasingly, unions. In the evolution of a specifically feminist critique of politics, which was emerging at this time around the campaign for the suffrage, women recognised and began to articulate the cultural implications of the political distinction between public and private.

Arguing against the common view that the suffrage would take women away from the home, Mrs Ruffy-Hill from the West Australian Women's Suffrage League wrote that it was 'for the sake of the home that we wish a voice in the formation of laws which rule the community'; it was because of 'man's forgetfulness, or neglect in the past to legislate

94   *To Constitute a Nation*

fairly and justly for the homes' that women must agitate in that sphere.[38] Against the assertion of many women that the right to vote itself was a national issue, the suffrage was frequently defended by others as essentially a state matter. One prominent New South Wales judge, for example, responding to an appeal by Rose Scott for the entrenchment of universal suffrage in the Constitution, wrote that 'the framing of the constitution must not be made the occasion of settling questions not essentially connected with federation'.[39] This debate, as we shall see in chapter ten, was continued with important consequences in the 1897–98 Federal Convention.

As the perception of welfare as essentially private began slowly to change, male inspectors started to replace women, and colonial and then state governments began to legislate in the field of welfare; very gradually the provision of welfare would become identified with the nation. In the 1890s the slow transition was beginning. In New South Wales state funding for hospitals and asylums for 'the sick and necessitous poor' at this time 'generously' complemented charitable subscriptions, and schemes for children's industrial schools and reformatories, as well as boarding-out in private homes, were under the supervision of a State Board.[40]

The emergence of a shifting taxonomy of domestic versus national matters appears often between the lines in the debates over what was and what was not properly federal. The ambiguity was sometimes delightful. In the Sydney session of the 1897 Convention, an amendment was moved to include 'lunacy' among the Commonwealth powers listed in section 51, along with 'Bankruptcy and insolvency'. Mr Carruthers argued that this power was necessary, because 'the lunacy question . . . has to be dealt with outside the limits of a particular colony . . . [T]he exclusion of lunatics is as much a matter of federal concern as is the exclusion of criminals'. South Australia's John Gordon objected. His colony, he said, had an agreement with New South Wales concerning lunatics: 'We took care of their lunatics, cured them, and sent them back, and, for all I know, some of them may have become members of parliament'. 'That shows it is a federal matter!', cried Mr Carruthers. Then Richard O'Connor repeated the sober warning found throughout the whole attempt to untangle the 'federal' from the 'domestic': they should guard against loading 'the commonwealth with any more duties than are absolutely necessary', and the motion was lost.[41]

For the most part, the things thought self-evidently federal belonged to the sphere of male politics, while women struggled first to conceptualise their domestic concerns as political and then to have these recognised. What, then, are invalid and old-age pensions doing in section 51, listed among the essentially national matters? They came from neither the

Canadian nor the American Constitutions; they are not to be found on the Federal Council's list. The old-age pension was German. But the inclusion of this section was not accidental; it must be understood alongside that other apparent anomaly, national powers over 'Conciliation and arbitration for the prevention and settlement of industrial disputes extending beyond the limits of any one State'.

Some labour critics, like the Brisbane *Worker*, argued that pensions and arbitration powers were 'really matters of domestic concern' but had been redefined as federal to curb the tendencies of progressive states.[42] But in the Convention the majority of those who argued for such powers to be seen as federal did so in order to support national progressive policy. Those wanting to include old-age and invalid pensions sought to make the case that these were not in fact charitable matters (because if they were, they could not be 'national'), while opponents sought to demonstrate that they were. Edmund Barton, for example, claimed that supporters had failed to establish that pensions were 'a federal and not a provincial concern'. That, he added, 'is the whole question we have to decide . . . to distribute the powers and functions with which we are dealing, so that things which are properly federal will go to the commonwealth, and those which are provincial will go to the provinces'. If the Commonwealth took over invalid pensions, he said, it might as well take over 'the treatment of the sick poor generally'. But the latter was not only a provincial matter, it was 'an intensely local matter', a charitable matter where relief is distributed 'in the districts concerned'. Old-age pensions, Barton concluded, fell into the same category; 'until I came to this Convention I never heard it argued . . . that it was a federal matter'.[43]

Responding to Barton, the mover of the motion, South Australia's James Howe, pointed out that men who had worked and served all their lives were being reduced to destitution in their old age. Because the Australian labour force was particularly migratory they could not be protected by state pensions. In Germany, he told the Convention, it is compulsory for employers and employees to contribute to a government pension fund. 'Then when a man comes on the fund he does not come upon it as with us . . . upon the charitable institutions of the country. He can hold up his head among his fellow-men.' The old-age pension prevented a man 'who has fulfilled all the obligations of citizen, husband, and father, from becoming a pauper in his declining days'.[44] 'Is not this purely a state matter?', asked Henry Dobson from Tasmania. 'If I thought so, I would not bother the Convention about it', replied Howe.

In the course of this debate, Western Australia's Premier Sir John Forrest said he hoped that the term 'migratory' would not apply after Federation, 'that we may always consider ourselves at home in our own country', and that everyone 'surely must see that the Federal Parliament,

96   *To Constitute a Nation*

having control of the whole of the people of the colonies, will be in a far better position to deal with this difficult question [of pensions] than the states'.[45] Forrest's position is striking, not only because it comes from a representative of the conservative small colonies, indeed of the colony most reluctant to join the Federation at all, but particularly because it captures the idea that the new Commonwealth was a union of all of the people, rather than simply a contract between the states. The rights of citizens of the nation are evoked. A claim to regulate the lives and relations of the people, not just the administration of trade and communication inside and defensive strategies outside the nation, is made.

Charles Kingston's inclusion of a national arbitration power in his original 1891 draft Constitution covers similar ground. It took three attempts in the 1897–98 Convention finally to have this power included, with opponents arguing that it would interfere with private property and with the right of contract. There was no such provision in either America's or Canada's Constitution but, it turned out, South Australia's arbitration board was a useful existing example and there was a valuable lesson in New Zealand's experience. The Australian Constitution, said Victoria's Henry Higgins, who took up Kingston's efforts at the later Convention, absolutely must have 'recognition in it of the momentous change in regard to industrial matters which is now taking place all through the world'.

What was new was not just the growth of industrial disputes and their frequent impact beyond the borders of colonies, but essentially, the rise of agents other than individuals in politics and law. Although the framers were persuaded to agree to this power because of the potential for interstate disputes and the need therefore for a federal body to resolve them, there is a glimpse in this debate of the class politics which, almost from the moment Federation occurred, would characterise Australian political life for many decades.

'Legally speaking', said Higgins, 'a dispute between employer and employee is a dispute between man and man', but disputes may in fact concern 'hundreds and thousands and tens of thousands of people . . . [and] hosts of people and families dependent upon them are affected'. Opponents again argued that industrial relations was not a national concern, that 'the industrial life of the state is . . . a thing of purely domestic concern'.[46] 'What I say', added Sir John Downer, 'is that this is not a federal question at all . . . Even the argument that New Zealand has done something is not sufficient to satisfy me'.[47] In the event, the motion survived to live on as one of the key components of Australia's political culture in the twentieth century. Its impact could scarcely have been over-estimated.

A range of other matters did not make it onto the national stage. Commonwealth powers over the Aboriginal people, as we shall see, were not only not granted, they were specifically ruled out. A statement of citizenship, even a head of power on the subject, was dropped because it was both too difficult to define and too complex to tie together with the British subject status of Australians. But nothing else was included that could have the effect, eventually, of ruling out Commonwealth powers over legal citizenship, and the Commonwealth Government was able to pass the first Nationality and Citizenship Act, in 1948, with only political, not constitutional, objections from the Opposition. Franchise laws were not written into the Constitution, although there had to be a national franchise Act as well as individual state Acts, in part because entrenching a particular type of franchise, defining a particular category of voter, was not thought by the majority of Convention delegates to be essential to shaping the nation's polity.

A declaration of human rights and powers over international affairs missed out, in the first place because of fidelity to the tradition of English Common Law, in which rights are protected through the assumptions and practices of the courts, and with this the desire not to be too American, and in the second place because Britain retained the right to regulate Australia's external affairs under the Colonial Laws Validity Act, at least until 1931.

But did human rights miss out altogether? The 'external affairs' power did not imply, as it might appear, a divestment of British powers over Australian external affairs. But, while its original purpose remains 'singularly vague', as Quick and Garran themselves describe it (prophetically suggesting that it might 'prove to be a great constitutional battleground'[48]), it has now turned into a general power, among other things, to conclude international treaties (including those covering human rights). A single Bill of Rights may not be there in one piece on paper, but it may be emerging from behind the scenes in the course of High Court interpretation.[49] All of this is another story. What it illustrates, however, is the principle Alfred Deakin expounded, that the Constitution would evolve and 'unfold with the unfoldment' of the nation's characteristics.

Not everyone, however, agreed over what the 'nation's characteristics' were, nor on the exact division between national and domestic. They argued over whether the nation's share of powers would be small or great, with Henry Higgins (who, only ten years later, would preside over the famous Harvester 'living wage' decision in the federal Industrial Court) opposing a £400 annual salary for members of parliament on the grounds that 'the Federal Parliament will have much less to do than the ordinary local Parliaments', and the labour representative, William Trenwith, objecting that the Federal Parliament, 'instead of having less to do as time goes on, will have a great deal more to do'.[50] On issues such

98   *To Constitute a Nation*

as rivers and rails, lines were both confused and divided. Should the Commonwealth control river navigation, or general use of water, all river systems or only those crossing state boundaries? The South Australians, sharing the Murray River with two other colonies and fearful of New South Wales, wanted a Commonwealth tribunal to ensure riparian rights, while the New South Wales delegates resisted a generalised characterisation of rivers as a federal matter. In the end all the final Convention could agree upon was that the Commonwealth should not be allowed to 'abridge the right of a State . . . to the reasonable use of the waters of rivers',[51] and Australia's rivers remain to this day a constitutional muddle.

Although Henry Parkes had spoken of the new rail link with which the four eastern colonies were joined in 1889 as 'without any exaggeration of language . . . superior to anything that has ever occurred in the history of these great colonies' and a symbol of future Federation,[52] the colonies were in fact joined politically long before any national rail system would be contemplated. Rail transport, it was agreed at the Convention, was to be controlled by the Commonwealth when it came to military purposes, and railway construction undertaken by the Commonwealth only upon the request of a state. The West Australians in particular would depend upon (and soon be disappointed by) the latter provision, in their hope that the construction of an intercontinental railway would be an immediate priority following Federation. In the attempt to allocate such powers either to the national or the domestic realm, some delegates thought the gauge was the issue, others the control of transportation, or the construction of future lines. On the intra-state railway systems, 'Federation and nationhood had no impact'.[53] In the final Convention session, arguing for Commonwealth control of future construction, Patrick Glynn expressed the hope that Australia 'is not going to be stagnant—that the possibilities of the future do not end with the passing of this Bill'.[54]

But it was much easier to draw upon existing examples of how things were done in other colonies or other countries, than to imagine in realistic terms 'the possibilities of the future'. Many things we now think, or may come to think of as properly national were not part of the picture in the 1890s. Mr Clarke from Newtown thought that protection of the environment (although he would not have used the term) was a national matter. He thought alone. Phenomena like radio and television, matters not even conceptualised technologically, let alone as political subjects one hundred years ago, have in some cases found a place in existing constitutional provisions such as 'Postal, telegraphic, telephonic, and *other like services*'.[55] Civil aviation (only imagined in the fictional Utopias of the time) came eventually under Commonwealth control, but only by a combination of recourse to international treaties (through the external affairs power) and referral from the states. Other things sit in a constitutional no man's land: are matters such as space exploration or bioethics properly federal, or should they, because they were not imagined among the subjects debated in the Conventions, remain under the control of the states?

The framers were shaping the Constitution with the conceptual tools they had at hand. They agreed in the main that the things that women did were not national, and that private enterprise should be left to state regulation if it were regulated at all. Personal freedom, as they saw it, and freedom of 'trade, commerce, and intercourse' were not just things for the centre to leave untouched. Such freedoms were part of the character of the nation itself.

CHAPTER SIX

White Australians

Among the many models that were tried on for the new nation, one was rejected outright. Australia, it was almost universally agreed, must not be Chinese. It is hard now to appreciate fully what was meant by this in the 1890s, and how absolutely necessary most people then believed it to be for the new nation to be 'white'. Cartoons, caricatures and purple prose images of Asians were drawn so crudely and repulsively, that they represent now a barrier to understanding the imagination of the nineteenth century on this issue. The issue of 'colour' was unequivocally a racist issue, but it was much more than this. As much as anything, it was a type of cultural strategy in the processes of nation-building.

While the historian R. Norris has argued that White Australia was 'at best no more than a peripheral issue in . . . the federation movement of the 1890s',[1] the lack of urgency attached to the matter in campaign literature and Convention debates (to which Norris points) is only persuasive as evidence if the wider political culture of the period is overlooked. While every other question raised during the Federation campaigns and debated in the Conventions produced several lines of major disagreement, no significant group of opinion favourable to Chinese immigration existed in Australia by the 1890s. The most liberal and the most conservative colonial politicians, members of labour organisations, female suffragists, pro- and anti-Billites, republicans and monarchists expressed the conviction that the creation of the nation meant controlling the level of the 'coloured' population in Australia.

A great deal of this rhetoric went on, however, in the background, sometimes indirectly, because, among other things, there was a certain, paradoxical reluctance to appear openly racist. It is 'of no use', said Sir John Forrest in the middle of a Convention debate which had drawn forth some entirely unashamedly racist views, 'to shut our eyes to the fact that there is a great feeling all over Australia against the introduction of coloured persons. It goes without saying that we do not like to talk about it, but it is so'.[2] If one compares, for example, the careful and statesmanlike approach of Charles Kingston on the issue of coloured immigration during debate in the Convention, with his unsubtle, even populist, denunciations in the South Australian Parliament,[3] the unreliability of official Federation sources on their own is seen more forcefully. There were, it appears, two main reasons for the relative (although far from complete) official silence. One was that the White Australia issue was so much a part of the background, so widely embraced and uncontroversial, that it did not need to occupy much specific attention. The other was the uncomfortable feeling that it was not quite 'British' to display and act upon prejudice based on colour.

In the eastern colonies in the second half of the 1880s, there occurred an outburst of popular emotion against the Chinese which was so intense that it bordered at times on riot. Governments of the hour were placed in an awkward position. As individuals, many shared the virtually hysterical fear of coloured 'invasion', but they could not officially be seen to give encouragement to unlawful behaviour or gestures threatening the sovereignty of the parliaments. They had to comport themselves in a 'British' manner, applying the law (even, as far as possible, the rule of law) dispassionately, and not offending the British authorities themselves any more than could be avoided.

Often quite sincerely, legislators attempted to fashion an approach to the Chinese in Australia that discriminated against them as immigrants, but was not discriminatory in other respects. But they were also listening to the demands of their electors. And in the simultaneous creation of a nation out of an existing group of separate units, the identification of a common enemy was culturally and politically invaluable. The official commitment to act grew steadily as the 1890s progressed. Australia was increasingly imagined as a white community.

At the height of the anti-Chinese feeling, what might have been a regular intercolonial Conference of Premiers in 1888 was turned into a Conference specifically on 'the Chinese Question', with resolutions passed in favour of a uniform policy that would severely restrict Chinese immigration and make the unauthorised passage of Chinese persons from one colony to another a misdemeanour. In a cablegram to the British Secretary of State, Lord Knutsford, from the Conference President, Henry Parkes, these resolutions were conveyed along with the request for 'diplomatic action' on the part of the Imperial Government to complement Colonial legislation.

The British, it was well known, did not favour immigration policy based specifically on colour; the Conference had already received a telegram from Knutsford warning the Australians that measures 'placing Chinese emigrants on different footing to subjects of any other power' would offend the Chinese politically and might endanger commercial relations with China. Knutsford asked that the Conference consider

102   *To Constitute a Nation*

instead legislation 'equally restricting immigration in Colonies of all foreign labourers, with powers of relaxing regulations in special cases', and assured them of his confidence that they would 'endeavour to conciliate susceptibilities of the Chinese Government as far as possible'.[4]

It was a view, at that stage, shared also by the Tasmanian Premier, Philip Fysh, whose expression of dissent at the Conference is valuable in conveying, among other things, how much other Australians were prepared to depart from British traditions in their hostility to the Chinese. Fysh's memorandum captures both a desire to conciliate the British and also to be 'fair', an attitude thought by many to be essentially British. He was not alone in experiencing such compunction. Where the popular response was almost altogether lacking in subtlety, the political response to the 'Chinese problem' was far from simple, and fairness was sought by at least some of the politicians as they attempted to write a white nation into the Constitution.

It 'behoves these Colonies to remember', Fysh told fellow delegates, 'that their preservation is maintained by British forces and that Colonial Acts must be justified by the Home Government'. His concern, however, was not only about the British response: the draft bill they had drawn up made no allowance for Chinese residents to improve 'their social condition by the introduction of their wives' and it ignored the rights of naturalised British subjects of Chinese origin, as well as disregarding 'the climatic characteristics of [Australia's] northern territories . . . which are a barrier to successful occupation, except in pursuit of avocations peculiarly tropical and unsuitable to European labour'.[5]

Fysh had effectively described the full range of issues confronting Australians on the Chinese question: opposition of the British authorities; the problems, both legal and moral, of differentiating between British subjects (who were all, in theory, supposed to have equal standing across the Empire); concerns about degrading conditions imposed upon Chinese persons within Australia; the issue of the suitability of 'white men' for work in the tropics. But he had not gone as far as to agitate for an open-door policy and, indeed, only the year before, the Tasmanian Government had itself passed legislation restricting Chinese immigration along similar lines to those of other colonies (one Chinese only to every hundred tons of a ship's tonnage) and imposing a poll tax of £10 on each Chinese person arriving. The details of this legislation had already been communicated to the Colonial Office, with the explanation that Tasmania, while not having itself experienced an 'influx' of Chinese on any alarming scale, desired to co-operate with the other colonies, especially to avoid Tasmania's 'being used as a temporary residence by Chinese immigrants for the purpose of obtaining letters of naturalization so that they might thereafter obtain admission into other Colonies'.

White Australians 103

The memorandum of explanation, written by the Attorney-General, Andrew Inglis Clark, further defended Australia's right in international law to impose immigration restrictions, and it painted a picture of large numbers of Chinese immigrants wanting inevitably at some stage in the future 'to establish separate institutions of a character that would trench on the supremacy of the present legislative and administrative authorities', or alternatively accepting 'an inferior social and political position', and creating racial divisions in Australian society, leading to a 'degraded estimate of manual labour'. With racial divisions came the risk of civil war.[6]

To Australians the Chinese appearance, language, script, way of working, dressing, worshipping, relaxing and eating were all utterly unlike anything they understood. The modern study of anthropology had only begun to expand in this period, and intensive field-work accounts, based upon immersion for long periods in the daily life and rituals of other cultures, were virtually unknown. But travellers' tales, popular prejudice and popular Social Darwinist theory of the evolution of racial types built up imaginary ethnographies. People believed they knew what Chinese life was like. Almost without exception, they believed it to represent a threat to their cultural universe.

Not all were comfortable, however, with the clash of principles involved in being British or Christian while reviling the Chinese. Mr Allen, a Member of the New South Wales Parliament, attempted to meet such concerns by explaining to a meeting of the Anti-Chinese League in Sydney in November 1887, that the claim that the Chinese 'were not a race capable of running hand in hand with Australians . . . was [in fact] no breach of broad Christian principles'.[7] At the Sydney Chinese Mission annual tea that same year, the Anglican Bishop reassured his audience that Christians 'were at liberty to depart from what had been the glory of all English-speaking races, [which] was, that provided law be obeyed and order observed, they admitted to their shores, freely, men of every colour and of every race'. But, he said, they were still obliged to remember that Europeans had exploited China, and Chinese policy should proceed 'from pure statesmanship, and not from base individual or class jealousies'.[8] Chinese individuals who were victimised or tormented were from time to time defended in letters to the press on 'Christian' and 'English' principles, and press commentary frequently deplored the public hostility towards them.

At the 1890 Federation Conference Henry Parkes was also adamant that his view that Federation offered a defence against Asian invasion was not based upon 'any feeling of loathing' towards the Chinese. 'I am not', he told the Conference, 'one of those who wish to look down upon them as a people who are in their habits particularly inferior to us. On

104   To Constitute a Nation

the contrary, I believe them on the whole to be a law-abiding, industrious, frugal and peaceable people'. His reasons, he went on, were the preservation of 'these Australian lands which were acquired according to the rights of nations, for a people modelled on the type of the British nation'.[9] The strategy of explaining away moral scruples by reference to 'self-defence' would prove an effective one.

By the mid-1880s, when concerted colonial action was first sought, the Chinese population had in fact begun to fall from its peak of previous decades. The 'defence' was no longer against literal numbers within, but against what was thought of as their disproportionate impact. Certain occupations and certain regions had relatively high concentrations of Chinese and this galvanised labour movement opinion in particular. The raw numbers were still high enough for the Chinese to be more visible than any other non-white group, but even so, many Australians would never have seen an actual Chinese person. The *idea* of the 'Chinaman' shaped their views, however, as if they had.

Since the Chinese population in Australia was almost exclusively male, they were rarely softened by being seen in family groups, living 'normal' lives, displaying human attachments. As single males, it was often assumed that they threatened the purity of white women by desiring them sexually. This imagery was typical of the caricature of the 'Oriental': a mixture of fascination and repulsion. Paradoxically, decorative orientalism—chinoiserie, japanning and the mixing of oriental and Australian bush motifs—was becoming fashionable in this period in art and in craft work, as well as costume. When the American Woman's Christian Temperance Union campaigner, Jessie Ackerman, toured Australia, she is reported to have lectured on the pagan habits of the Chinese and the evils of drink at the same time, while dressed in a Chinese costume.[10] The Oriental, in the context of an international movement in design, was exotic, seductive; domestically, as a familiar part of Australian culture, he was degraded.

British colonial authorities did not appear to understand how important the Chinese issue was in Australia at the time, and, more than this, how much their lack of empathy might endanger Australian relations with Britain itself. The impasse was not only political. Among literary accounts written by British visitors a regular theme was Australia's need to introduce and tolerate large numbers of Asian labourers, or else to accept the reduction of their own wages. 'Coloured' men, accustomed to tropical conditions, should be used to develop the north, to build up industries and agricultural exports, to make the country flourish to its full potential.

The refusal of white Australians to follow this course was, it was implied, neglectful and selfish. 'The vision of the Australian Continent peopled entirely with a white race is magnificent', wrote one commentator, but how, he asked, could Australians answer the charge that they had failed to develop the land's resources? Australians must 'justify their possession of the north', for it 'was not [their] land in the first instance' and they must not be 'dogs in the manger'. If Australians would not accept Asians, commented this particular writer, an alternative would be immigrants from Italy who would work more cheaply than Australians. Failing this, Indian natives, who were British subjects, 'like the rest of us', should be introduced, and 'over all would be the managers of the British race'.[11] Another British commentator, who thought the Chinese had done 'great service on the gold-fields' in growing vegetables, and who believed that only the 'Kanakas' could cut cane, thought the legitimate interests of the north were being overridden by the majority in the south where coloured labour was not needed. He speculated that there would be 'useful interests sacrificed . . . to the god Demos'.[12]

One unusual local proposal for employing 'a million' Chinese labourers, as well as Japanese, Javanese, 'Hindoos' and others, claimed that, while whites could not work in the tropics, 'the acclimatised sun-coloured man' could. It defended the Chinese, however, as 'human beings, like ourselves': 'A good Chinaman [may be] brown in colour it is true, but in intellect, heart, and soul, [is] in no way different from a good white man'.[13] By way of illustration, the author, E. W. Cole, related the story of having travelled around twilight in the same carriage as a young man with whom he conducted a lengthy conversation and who, he discovered only when the man got out and under the light, was Chinese. Like the exemplary New South Wales business man and philanthropist, Quong Tart, this young man had been raised and educated in Australia, in contrast to the majority of Chinese, who presented 'the worst side' of the Chinese character and gave, Cole argued, a misleading example.

Men like Quong Tart, Chinese Australian 'citizens', were themselves conscious of the example of large numbers of uneducated labourers, mostly from peasant backgrounds, who had come to Australia during the gold rushes and who worked in the market gardens or the furniture industry, many seeking escape in opium-induced dreams outside their long working hours. A petition to the Government of New South Wales in 1883 from Chinese 'Citizens' and 'Residents' prayed for a ban on the importation of opium into the colony, and expressed the desire 'to point out that the use of Opium in China is confined to the very lowest orders of Chinese Society, and that those using it are unfavourably regarded by their fellow-countrymen'.[14] Addresses of loyalty and praise to the Governor of New South Wales were regularly sent from 'the Chinese Residents', 'the Chinese Community of New South Wales', and 'the Natives of the Empire of China residing in Sydney and its suburbs', with

106   *To Constitute a Nation*

the latter assuring the incumbent of their belief 'that you will distribute justice with an even hand irrespective of creed and nationality'.[15]

They were fighting a losing battle. Their desire to represent themselves as respectable in comparison to their more numerous unassimilated 'fellow-countrymen' may have worked in a limited number of cases, but the desire itself was indicative of the problem. The degree of respect Quong Tart commanded in commercial and political circles—when he died in 1903, two years after the introduction of the White Australia policy, 1500 mourners walked behind his coffin—was both a mark of his own personal qualities, and of the surprise his example elicited. Arriving with his uncle at the New South Wales goldfields in 1859 at the age of nine, Quong Tart had been thereafter educated in English-speaking circles, quickly becoming almost an Englishman in a Chinese body. He became a businessman, with tea-rooms in Sydney, where he welcomed almost every prominent visitor throughout the 1890s (including Henry George, Jessie Ackerman, and the members of the 1891 Federal Convention). A convert to Christianity, Tart was naturalised, married to a Scottish woman and was a member of the Foresters, the Oddfellows and the Masons.

But, although he might have attempted to do so, Quong Tart did not erase his Chinese identity. He was regarded as 'practically . . . the acting, if not official, Chinese Consul', by fellow Chinese residents,[16] as well as recognised by the white establishment for the award of Mandarin of the Crystal Button, two levels of which were conferred upon him by the Emperor in 1887 and 1890, at the very height of public anti-Chinese sentiment in Australia. Tart was prominent in both the Lin Yik Tong Chinese Benevolent Society in New South Wales and the Masonic Lodge, and he had acted as mediator between the New South Wales Government and Chinese officials during the visit of Chinese Commissioners in 1887 (who came to investigate the conditions suffered by the Chinese in Australia), and on his visit to China in 1889 where his diplomacy had, said the press, 'the effect of softening considerably the bitterness entertained towards the [Australian] people'.[17]

Dressed in his Mandarin costume, Quong Tart was buried in an Anglican crypt, with the Masonic Apron laid on his coffin. Masses of floral wreaths and messages of condolence were sent by prominent men, including the State Governor and the Prime Minister, Edmund Barton. Tart was, 'in the best sense of the word a good citizen', said the *Sydney Morning Herald*; 'a citizen who had always acted up to citizenship in the highest sense of the word', said the *Town and Country Journal*; 'A man of sterling worth/Though not of our nationality—proud of Chinese birth', sang an otherwise deservedly obscure poet.[18]

But could a 'Chinaman' be an Australian citizen? This is a much more complex question than it first appears. Quong Tart was a naturalised

British subject, but this fact did not feature in the paeans of praise to his exemplary 'citizenship'. He had earned his citizenship, it seems, through his ability to assimilate and to embody the qualities of commercial success, philanthropy and Christian family life held up as a middle-class cultural ideal. And so long as he manifested his Chinese origins, he reminded white Australians of the remarkable transformation this entailed. Citizenship was an honour; not even every white person could achieve it.

While they contemplated laws to standardise the membership of their imagined national community, the colonies were beginning to introduce Acts prohibiting the naturalisation of Chinese residents.[19] The legal door was rapidly closing. But, naturalisation, even where it was possible, did not in itself mean acquiring Australian citizenship. By the 1890s, it was almost universally agreed that the Chinese could not be citizens. The justification was put in both practical and moral terms:

> Both the virtues and the vices of the Chinese are bred in them by a civilization stretching back in unparalleled fixedness of character and detail to an age more remote than any to which the beginnings of any European nation can be traced, and . . . no length of residence amidst a population of European descent will cause the Chinese immigrants who remain unnaturalized to change their mode of life.[20]

Alongside crude public depictions of degradation, disease and moral pollution, such views as these of Andrew Inglis Clark were repeated frequently by other politicians, many of whom we recognise as having been, like Clark, progressive liberals in all other areas. Their argument was, essentially, that the Chinese were so different in history, political culture, religion and character that they could not be assimilated into the type of community developing in Australia. Clark's statement strikes in particular a contrast between the antiquity of Chinese culture and the newness, and, therefore, the greater vulnerability, of the emerging Australian nation.

By the second half of the 1890s, this argument began to take in all coloured' peoples. Men from the South Pacific had been employed for decades under conditions of virtual slavery in Queensland's sugar industry. Now they too became included alongside the Chinese in the rhetoric employed in the southern colonies to construct an imaginary scenario of cultural upheaval. But the uniformity of opposition to the Chinese is made all the more remarkable by the division of opinion on other coloured peoples, in particular on the 'Kanakas' in the north. Queensland's apparent reluctance consistently to fall in line with the rest of Australia on this matter was the source of considerable nervousness throughout the 1890s. In the late 1880s Queensland had introduced

108 *To Constitute a Nation*

legislation allowing indeed an increase in Kanaka intake, and, at the Premiers' Conference of 1888, Queensland excluded Pacific Islanders from the range of coloured races the other Premiers agreed should be prevented from immigrating. It must remain in the realm of speculation whether, had Queensland participated in the Federal Convention of 1897–98, the presence of that colony's delegates would have substantially affected the outcome of debates on the Commonwealth's power over race and on the nature of citizenship.

But, increasingly, the other colonies expanded their category of unacceptable coloured immigrant. The risk of creating a 'class of servile labourers as an institution' was outlined at length in a paper prepared for the Bathurst People's Federal Convention in 1896. Earlier that year a further Intercolonial Conference debated, among other things, the extension of the various Restricted Immigration Acts passed in almost all their colonies nine years before. Here, with little controversy, a commitment was made to preventing virtually all future coloured immigration, including from the South Pacific islands.

The particular focus in 1896 was, however, on Japan, a nation with which Britain had concluded a commercial treaty the previous year. Rather than reassuring the Australians, this treaty served merely to highlight what the Premiers (with only the subsequent exception of Queensland) interpreted as a further threat. Adherence to the treaty would entail an agreement to allow free movement of each member nation's people within each other's country. The 1896 agreement may be seen now as a forerunner to the Coloured Immigration Restriction Act of 1901, one of the very first policy initiatives of the new Commonwealth Parliament taken in the year of the Commonwealth's Inauguration.

In the process of identifying itself as a nation a community does not simply look to the practical advantages of enhanced defence or enlarged industry or financial protection. Many historians have assumed that defence remained one of the central issues of Federation, and the Edwards Report on the colonies' defence capacity one of the principal catalysts for Federation initiatives in the early 1890s. But, although European incursions into the South Pacific and in particular Germany's annexation of north-eastern New Guinea in the 1880s caused some considerable alarm about Australia's vulnerability to attack, military defence soon fell away as a central Federation issue, and a different type of 'defence' emerged.

The enormous populations of Asian countries presented an awe-inspiring spectacle when compared with the tiny population of Australia. The idea of a wave of invaders had first been stimulated by the novelty of large-scale Chinese immigration during the gold rushes. But, by the 1880s, any potential threat of real military invasion came from European countries, not from Asia. Fear of Chinese invasion was more metaphorical than based in reality.

The metaphor was one of 'pollution'. Pollution was a common object of fear of the period, embracing a range of what people considered to be related matters: unhygienic practices, contagious (especially sexually transmitted) diseases, sexual impurity, 'miscegenation', inebriation, vermin. A frequent theme of public campaigns, especially in the field of social welfare, was the 'cleansing' of society, the purifying of its morals, the control of impure practices. Social Purity Societies, as well as Hygiene Departments within temperance organisations like the Woman's Christian Temperance Union, were formed.

A profound cultural battle raged at the end of the century between the bearers of a sober, domestic, hygienic ideal of life and the raw, freewheeling, itinerant life of the *Bulletin* bushman.[21] This battle was most likely the product of increasing levels of education and organisation among women, who by this stage were demanding more control over the domestic context of their lives, and of the rationalism and Evangelicalism of the age translated into an Australian setting. Perhaps pre-eminently, the processes involved the modernisation of a former frontier country, which was now becoming urbanised and 'civilised', both materially and culturally.

There is no simple key to understanding this process. But the place in it of the idea of the Chinese, more than any other coloured people, was central. It brought together the rural yalues typified in the *Bulletin* and the urban values of the respectable middle class. Earlier stereotypes of the Chinese as thieves—of gold and possessions and jobs—were by the end of the century overshadowed by fears of pollution. Chinese immigration represented, it was believed, a contagion. The Chinese themselves were seen as 'impure', and the spectacle (both imaginary and real) of opium dens and squalid living quarters reinforced this view. One strategy employed to restrict Chinese immigration without running the risk of British opposition to restrictive immigration Acts was the imposition of quarantine controls against entry from China.[22] When Chinese cases of leprosy were reported in Australia, the fear of contagion seemed confirmed.

But it was a rationalist age, and just as often the excesses of prejudice and hysteria had to be tempered by science: a report of the repatriation of Chinese lepers from the Little Bay Lazaret in 1896 made the point, for example, that 'Scientific opinion no longer holds leprosy as contagious in the ordinary sense of the word, but the average man likes to have lepers kept at the greatest distance possible'.[23] The advantages were financial, since the cost of keeping the lepers was a not inconsiderable burden on the New South Wales Government, as well as humanitarian;

110   *To Constitute a Nation*

it is not 'hypocritical to say that these people will be, many of them, far happier in China [where] no law of segregation exists'.[24] Other commentators agreed with the latter conclusion (as did Quong Tart, who undertook the negotiations with the lepers), but cast doubt upon the conclusion that leprosy was not contagious, and raised the question of why, in European countries where there were very poor and unsanitary conditions—but no Chinese people—leprosy was dying out.[25]

At this stage, in forming Chinese policy and attitudes, scientific opinion was secondary. A 'leper' is much more than an individual suffering from a disease, whether or not it is contagious. Cases such as these and the publicity they attracted because of the New South Wales Government's policy of repatriation confirmed the association between China and leprosy. Dismaying though it is to acknowledge one hundred years later, to the majority of white Australians then, the Chinese were 'lepers'. There can be no more powerful social metaphor.

If Australia was engaged in an experiment, building a realist Utopia, moulding a golden future, as so many believed, the serpent must be kept out of the garden. It was the serpent of slavery in America's federal Eden that had led, Andrew Inglis Clark had argued at the 1890 Federation Conference in Melbourne, to the disastrous Civil War. A similar problem must not be allowed to mar Australia's debut as a nation.

As we have seen, before his departure to Paraguay, radical labour leader William Lane wrote a dystopian forecast of the early years of Federation in which a Chinese dictatorship, assisted by wealthy European backers, had turned white Australians into slaves. Kenneth Mackay's *Yellow Wave*, published five years later, tells a similar tale of 'invasion'. These racist allegories reverse the slave–master scenario, and demonstrate that the fear of slavery was probably as much a fear of mastery. Growing concerns about the power of the Japanese, which found their expression in the 1896 intercolonial immigration agreement, capture in particular the fear of domination by a superior race, rather than social degradation. The contrast is typical of the ambivalent culture of Orientalism[26] in which the East is depicted by European writers in the form of mysterious and sinister individuals who are both stupid and cunning, both degenerate and masterful.

The place occupied by the Chinese in Australian culture in the last decades of the nineteenth century was multi-dimensional. Like other coloureds they were understood as a counterpoint to the visible progress of the white and especially the Anglo-Saxon race. Progress was an article of faith, like purity and hygiene, to which it was directly related in the culture of the period. Measured against the domination (often meaning destruction) of the natural environment, progress was evidenced in military power, in the building of cities, the conquering of wilderness, the enjoyment of material goods. Those who conquered had, therefore (it was believed), self-evidently better systems of law, political organisation and morality.

This line of thinking, however, put white Australians in an uneasy position in the evolution of their own nationalism. Progress was happily claimed as part of a share in British Imperialism. As long as Australians imagined themselves a direct part of the Imperial community, they could rejoice in its conquests of armies and wilderness. But within Australia itself, defence and development were a weak point. Beautiful cities had been built, it is true, of which white Australians were justly proud. But the country's ability to defend itself without British assistance had been publicly shown to be virtually non-existent, and it was implied from time to time that Australians had failed even to attempt to 'conquer' the interior, disappointing their own early expectations as well as their fellow members of the Empire. Some thought it Australia's duty to employ coloured labour in this task, since white Australians, it was argued, had shown themselves, if not necessarily by their own fault, at least partly through selfishness and the decline of the 'pioneering spirit', to be incapable of doing so. How could Australian nationalism make a claim to be distinctive and at the same time claim its part in progress?

In response, some denied that the failure to occupy central Australia represented a failure of progress at all. Indeed, it was even asserted that the Australian pattern of land development was itself a sign of progress, compared to the 'Arabian nomadic or squalid kind of way'. Although it was admitted that the development of the land was still comparatively slow, Australia's industry and civilisation were 'such as is furnished by the denizens of no real Sahara', and belied 'any notion that there are not very material foundations for future nationhood—much more solid than the sands of the desert to which our land is compared by the opponent of union'.[27] Chinese agricultural methods employed in Australia in market gardening were, despite their manifest success (perhaps because of it), rejected as primitive and unsuitable. To have adopted the nomadic or oriental techniques of using the land would have confirmed the failure of white progress and reduced the Australians in their own eyes to the level of the coloured subjects of the Empire.

A central, if unconscious, cultural strategy in demonstrating a share in progress involved the comparison between white Australians and 'backward' people. This group could not be white, or English-speaking, since the exercise might lead to conclusions unfavourable to the Australians. Why not, then, the Australian Aborigines? The Aboriginal example was indeed employed quite often to illustrate a range of positions, including the moral and material superiority of white Australians. But at

112   *To Constitute a Nation*

times, the Aborigines were also employed to illustrate the virtues of the 'noble savage' in contrast to the materialistic life of the whites; at others to show what followed from Aboriginal dispossession. The Chinese should be kept out of the cities, said one writer, but might be allowed to live 'in our glorious land which we stole from the native black people who lived here before us'.[28]

But in constructing a white community through writing a constitution, the Aboriginal people upon whose land the nation was to be built featured scarcely at all. Although the merits of Commonwealth versus state citizenship for white Australians were debated at length, and a rough conclusion was reached that 'dual citizenship' would operate (that is to say, people would be 'citizens' of both state and Commonwealth) in the new nation, Aboriginal Australians remained until 1967 citizens only of their state, to the extent that they were regarded as citizens at all. Until the referendum of that year, the Commonwealth was prohibited, by section 51 (xxvi), from making special laws for the Aboriginal people. Although there is no reason to believe that Commonwealth governments over this century would have passed more progressive laws in respect of the Aboriginal people than did the states (since they controlled the Northern Territory and still failed to do so until the 1970s), what this constitutional position implied at the time of Federation was that the status of the Aborigines was to be defined according to their membership of a state, not of the nation as a whole.

Neither this section, nor section 127, which originally ruled out counting the Aboriginal people in the Commonwealth census, attracted much original debate at all in respect of their implications for Aborigines. A reader may search the records of Convention debates, and find barely a mention of the Aboriginal people, except in 1890, where in a remarkable speech one of the New Zealand delegates summed up the attitude that was to prevail throughout the Federation processes.

Enumerating the varied reasons for which he felt it unlikely that New Zealand should join Australia in federating, Captain William Russell discussed at some length the difference in approach to 'native administration' in the two countries. The Maori race, he said, has been 'treated in a manner so considerate that the condition of no other native and savage race on the face of the globe can be compared to it'. Their land rights had been recognised from the start and fear of war had forced peace-making between the white and the Maori populations: 'The whole of New Zealand politics for years hinged almost entirely upon the native question'.[29] It was quite the opposite in Australia, Russell declared; the proposed Federal Parliament would be a body 'that cares nothing and knows nothing about native administration . . . the members of which would have dealt with native races in a much more summary manner' than New Zealand. Whether or not Russell's characterisation of a sympathetic history of relations between the Maori and white New Zealanders was accurate, these views raised no protest at all from the Australian delegates. 'Native administration' was, although an issue in some of the colonies more than others, a matter of scant concern in building the Australian nation.

Section 127, dealing with the census, was inserted in the course of debate in 1891 and attracted little discussion. Its explicit intention was to make the calculation of the population of a state 'fair', so that, for example, South Australia, which included then the Northern Territory, and which had the largest Australian population of Aborigines (estimated—although certainly underestimated—at 23 789 in 1891),[30] would not be required to contribute its future share of total customs revenue to the Federal Government above the sum calculated on the numbers of its white population.[31]

Some, including delegates at the 1897 Convention, believed that section 127 related also to the calculation of the number of House of Representatives seats to which a state would be entitled. John Cockburn objected to what he considered to be the potential disenfranchisement of Aboriginal voters by this section. He pointed out that in South Australia there were significant numbers of 'natives' on the electoral rolls, and believed they 'ought not to be debarred from voting', and as a matter of principle therefore they 'ought to be preserved as component parts in reckoning up the people'.[32] In the course of this debate, however, Cockburn was reassured that the numbers of Aboriginal people were too small to affect the state's entitlement to representatives in the Commonwealth Parliament, and he was reminded of the problem of inflating South Australia's future per capita costs.

For such reasons, among others, South Australia was anxious to give up the Northern Territory as soon after Federation as possible, and some white Territorians were equally anxious to be rid of the south, to 'obtain those many adjuncts to advancement which South Australia has denied' the Territory.[33] In this way, although Aboriginal affairs was not recognised as a national issue in the Conventions, it was to become a Commonwealth matter soon after Federation, when administration of the Northern Territory was taken over in 1911. The implications of this shift of responsibility were, however, not fully confronted for decades.

Like the Chinese and other coloured persons, the place of the Aborigines in the constitution of the nation was a negative one, addressed only as antithesis of the white Australian. Thus, in the first Commonwealth Franchise Act, passed in 1902, the right to vote in Commonwealth elections was denied to 'aboriginal native[s] of Australia Asia Africa or the Islands of the Pacific except New Zealand', and

114 *To Constitute a Nation*

subsequent citizenship law continued to define Australian citizens as those who were not members of 'coloured races'.[34]

But the Aborigines, widely assumed at the time of Federation to be declining in numbers, were not imagined as a threat in the manner of the Chinese. 'Compared to the Aborigines', historian Andrew Markus argues, 'the Chinese were seen as a civilised people . . . Unlike the Aborigines, who could be ignored once they had been subdued, the Chinese could not be ignored, for it was believed they would triumph if allowed to compete in a free market environment'.[35] Even more than this material threat, the Chinese were used, culturally, to identify the type of citizenship the future Australian nation would not embrace. In the example of the 'Chinaman', Australians believed they had found the starkest example of what 'Australians' were not.

The fact that this imagined Australian community, 'modelled on a type' of people, also embraced other whites, including the Germans, Scandinavians, and French (who were all in Australia in sufficient numbers to publish their own weekly newspapers at the time), highlights the function played by the Chinese of identifying a community by what it was not. The white populations of Australia metaphorically became British together. Community was emphasised. 'We are invited to believe', a press rebuttal of anti-Federalist arguments put it, 'that some radical and racial distinction exists' between New South Wales and the other colonies. If this were true, and the others were 'so evil', then the people of New South Wales should 'surround our superior virtues with such special safeguards as would render them impossible of contamination from outside'. But, the colonies were all 'English communities . . . Our political institutions and our public men are formed on the same familiar models, we cherish the same ideals of national life'.[36] To imply that there was a racial distinction between British people was dangerous ground in this period, and it was a charge the anti-Federalists had to deny if they were to maintain credibility. The view that the 'crimson thread of kinship' ran through all white Australians would inevitably triumph.

These cultural imperatives found their way into the Constitution. The 'contamination' of coloured races, rather than of fellow Australians, was addressed as the problem. There were two main constitutional issues. The first concerned the power of the nation to define the 'alien' and to restrict the influx of aliens on any terms it saw fit. The ongoing conflict between Australia and Britain over immigration policy throughout the 1880s and 1890s involved, to a significant degree, conflict over both the current sovereignty of the colonies and the future sovereignty of the Australian Commonwealth.

A nation, to be sovereign, must be able to regulate its own community, in part through its immigration laws. Against Australian claims that immigration was their concern alone, the British Government maintained that immigration policy fell under foreign affairs. The field of colonial foreign affairs was to remain under the control of the Imperial Government, although acting 'only to protect the interest of the United Kingdom or as Trustees for the Empire at large'.[37]

However, by the last two decades of the century, uniformity of law around the Empire had begun to erode. Uniform tariff policy and common trading agreements were beginning to fall apart and the British had conceded that variations would have to be tolerated. An Anglo-Chinese treaty, urged in 1888 by Henry Parkes, which would induce China itself to restrict emigration, and which might have broken the impasse between Australia and Britain, was not pursued by the British. Australian politicians took the opportunity to assert their right to an independent immigration policy.

Although Britain had not gone as far as to disallow previous colonial Bills imposing entrance taxes on incoming Chinese persons or restricting their numbers, some of the considerable disaffection that characterised relations with Britain at this time involved an Australian feeling that concern about coloured immigration was not appreciated by the British authorities. A decade after the 1888 Chinese Conference, the British response to the hardening White Australia policy was much the same. In its desire to keep the Empire together, the British Government attempted to be more conciliatory in general, giving undertakings that it would improve imperial trading relations (for example, terminating commercial treaties with Germany and Belgium), and allow Colonial representatives (at last) onto the Privy Council. The Colonial Secretary, Joseph Chamberlain, assured the Australian Premiers in London in 1897 that he sympathised with their determination 'that there shall not be an influx of people alien in civilisation, alien in religion, alien in customs, [which] would most seriously interfere with the legitimate rights of the existing labour population'. Nevertheless, Chamberlain reminded them, this determination could and should be met 'without placing a stigma upon any of Her Majesty's subjects on the sole ground of race or colour'.[38] But the Australians were only moved to the extent that they were prepared (by imposing a European languages test in the first Immigration Act, rather than a colour bar as such) to disguise their intention of 'placing a stigma' on individuals, whether British subjects or not, precisely on the grounds of their 'colour'.

The second constitutional issue involved the question of how to treat aliens once they had arrived in Australia. By the late 1890s, as all potential coloured immigrants were targeted, the issue of creating a distinctive national community began to focus on the specific conditions of that community, and the protection of a high level of employment and

116   *To Constitute a Nation*

wages came to be seen as a crucial part of the imagined new nation. As labour representatives gained seats in colonial parliaments, and as labour demands became increasingly articulated, coloured labour, especially that of the Chinese and Pacific Islanders, came to be increasingly perceived as a threat to white labour, both in terms of numbers and of conditions.

Commonwealth powers over immigration, section 51 (xxvii), and over 'naturalization and aliens', section 51 (xix), would provide adequate means to achieve a white nation. In addition power over 'the people of any race . . . for whom it is deemed necessary to make special laws' was to be included in the Commonwealth's list, in section 51 (xxvi). Special discriminatory laws (or, in the unlikely event, laws to create special, favourable conditions[39]) could be passed by the Commonwealth in order to deal with the coloured immigrants already in Australia (although not with the 'Aboriginal race'). There was to be a national community, the members of which would come equally under the law, and the others, people of special 'problem' races, and Aborigines. The 'race power' was written into the Constitution with almost no opposition.

But was this power to be exclusive to the Commonwealth, or concurrent (able to be exercised by both state and Commonwealth parliaments), the delegates asked. In the Melbourne sitting of the second Convention, in 1898, with the support of Tasmania and Western Australia, the Victorian delegates in particular put the case that the race power should be concurrent. Alfred Deakin, Henry Higgins, Isaac Isaacs, John Quick and William Trenwith all asserted the need for states to regulate coloured labour according to their own individual conditions. If the Commonwealth had exclusive powers over race, the states' existing legislation would be invalid, perhaps for some years, until the Commonwealth brought down uniform legislation, and the latter, they argued, might overlook the special needs of individual states.

Opponents of concurrent powers put the opposite case, that coloured labour was a national issue, a matter, said Edmund Barton, that related to 'the whole body of the people, to the purity of race, to the preservation of the racial character of the white population'; these, he told the Convention, are 'Commonwealth questions' and 'should be so exclusively'.[40] But Barton was (somewhat typically) arguing at cross purposes with the others. No one disagreed with his characterisation of preserving the 'purity' of the race; they simply wanted to put it into effect according to the particular demands of their own state and, if anything, they were concerned that the Commonwealth would be too liberal in its protection of a common white citizenship. In addition they were concerned that the Commonwealth might find itself subject to British treaties, and have its hands tied by non-discriminatory conditions attached to these.

Individual states must at least be free, it was argued, to apply discriminatory laws in industrial relations. In particular, delegates wanted to retain states' rights to prevent coloured employment in certain industries and to regulate the holding of miners' licences. Concern over states' rights in such matters was, as usual, where the bulk of the debate lay. So much was the commitment to a white nation taken for granted that the Convention debates reflect concern with its being inadequately provided for in individual states, rather than an exchange of ideas about its desirability.

Virtually alone, South Australia's Charles Kingston engaged in a complex analysis of the issue, recognising that the question was concerned with much more than industrial conditions or immigration policy, but in fact was a matter of shaping Australia's citizenship. Then, as now, a lack of clarity surrounded the issue: was it legal citizenship, that is to say, the power to grant naturalisation, or access to political rights that was at issue, was it a question of civil rights within a state, or the wider problem of the character of the community and its membership? Kingston in conclusion insisted that White Australia should be almost exclusively a function of immigration policy, not of restrictive laws applying to coloured residents who had already entered the colonies. Immigration restrictions should be employed, he argued, to circumvent a future coloured population, but the coloured residents already here should be treated as fellow citizens—not quite to the point of allowing them to vote, he implied, but decently at any rate.

Others thought that both the weapons of immigration policy and the race power should be wielded in the quest for a White Australia. Pointing to the 'cruel and inhuman' treatment often received by Chinese in Australia, New South Wales Premier George Reid argued that when 'a man is allowed to come into the country he should be treated on perfectly level terms'. But, he added, the latter cannot be achieved, since 'we know, as a matter of experience and fact, that there is no desire on the part either of the whites or of the coloured races to merge in a common citizenship'.[41]

For all their increasingly marginal status throughout the 1880s and 1890s, there remained in Australia a small population of Chinese residents, some of them 'subjects of the Queen' who, like Quong Tart, managed to live and work without persecution. They ran businesses and societies, and they published Chinese-language newspapers. Not only did they petition the Governor and the Parliament to demonstrate their difference from the mass of undesirable Chinese, they also petitioned at least one member of the 1897 Federal Convention, James Walker from New South Wales, seeking an assurance that their freedom of movement within a Federated Australia would not be restricted. They were, it was reported, given that assurance.

118   *To Constitute a Nation*

At the time of the second referendum, one of the proprietors of the *Chinese Australian Herald*, James Philp, declared that nine-tenths of the 'Chinamen' in Australia were in favour of the Constitution Bill. They wanted the abolition of intercolonial tariffs, he said, and anticipated that the removal of customs officers at the borders would 'free them from the harassing inquiries and restrictions they are now subjected to'. They did not believe Federation would increase restrictions against aliens, but if it did, and the numbers of Chinese declined, it would enhance the value of remaining Chinese labour, pushing up the price of vegetables in particular. The labour movement, they concluded, would soon demand an amelioration of current restrictions, as working people saw the price of Chinese-produced commodities increase. Far from dreading Federation, Philp concluded, the Chinese 'hail it with pleasure'.[42]

It was, one assumes, the representatives of this point of view who contributed a magnificent silk-draped arch and a giant dragon to the Melbourne celebrations for the reception of the Duke and Duchess of York and the opening of the first Federal Parliament the following year. The motto on their arch read 'Welcome from the Chinese Citizens'. They would not have used the term so confidently, had they heard the Convention debates.

What exactly might be meant by Reid's 'common citizenship', other than that it should be 'white', was never fully resolved. What *was* resolved was that, one way or another, the new nation was to have a 'purified' beginning, freed from the threat of pollution and disorder that, in both the popular and political imagination, came from coloured people in numbers. If, as anthropologist Mary Douglas has shown, people in the nineteenth century saw 'primitive' religions as characterised by fear and 'confused with defilement and hygiene', their own rituals, designed to confirm community and create unity, were no less 'confused'. 'In chasing dirt, in papering, decorating, tidying we are not', Douglas argues, 'governed by anxiety to escape disease, but are positively re-ordering our environment, making it conform to an idea'.[43] To her list we might add: performing the political rituals to constitute a nation.

CHAPTER SEVEN

Australian Natives

A good form of government . . . should
fit the people easily, as the bark of a tree fits
its trunk and branches in every stage of growth.[1]

'A new land is for new ideas', said Victorian Suffragist Vida Goldstein, and in 'a vast continent, whose strange native inhabitants, fauna and flora, seemed literally to transport [people] to a new world of thought', big, broad ideas developed quickly.[2]

The idea of a special, formative relationship between the Australian environment and individuals of the British race, one that gave rise to a new form of person, a new type of society that would be the seedbed of social experiment, was persistent in nineteenth-century Australia. The strange native environment stamped its character on the settlers. Their children became a new kind of 'native'.

This observation was made by visitors almost as soon as the first generation of native-born children began to appear among the white inhabitants. By the end of the nineteenth century (perhaps partly through a process of transmitting their ideas and expectations to each other down the years) visitors to Australia invariably looked for, found and identified a distinctive 'native' type.

Again and again, travellers (most of them British) embarked upon a great voyage to the Southern Colonies, or to the New World, or even around the whole vast British Empire and then, back in London, immediately published an account of their experiences. This genre—a combination of travel tales and popular anthropology—seems to have been particularly popular in the 1880s and 1890s, when the moral and social conclusions so readily drawn by the visitors could also be related in their observations to the experiment in progress as Australia's colonies undertook their transformation into a nation.

A visitor is, of course, subject to a range of false impressions. The 'natives' may be on their best behaviour; an experience that is rare may be mistaken for one that is commonplace; superficial impressions may remain uncorrected because the visit is brief. But an outsider can sometimes also see things with clarity that are less visible to those close at hand, and when outsiders repeatedly agree with each other, their observations accumulate in force as well as number. What they describe,

120   *To Constitute a Nation*

whether accurate or not, is as interesting and meaningful as the reality. Through the eyes of those who wrote about their visits in the Federation decades, we know now that white Australians were already a distinctive type, that they did not just make a hopeful claim to distinctiveness themselves, but that others also saw them this way. They could not be mistaken for their British cousins, even where they might have wished it. Australians, said one visitor in 1889, are 'rooted in quite a different soil'.[3]

Although, in order to argue for his 'Commonwealth' of Oceana, the British writer James Froude wanted to emphasise the similarities between Britain and Australia, he also saw in 1886 the differences. Above all he noted the extent of pleasure-seeking and love of material comfort among Australians. While he admired the relaxed hedonism of the colonists, he found the intellectual life deficient and he warned against the effect of too much enjoyment: 'men and nations require in reserve a certain sternness, and if anything truly great is ever to come out of them this lesson will in time be hammered into them'.[4]

Similar observations, with less implied censure, were made by visitor Max O'Rell:

> You will not find in the Australian that dogged, obstinate perseverance, that bull-dog tenacity which has helped the English to do so many great things . . . The Australian has quite a passion for amusement. There is no country in the world whose people flock in such numbers to . . . places of recreation; there are no people who take so many holidays, or enter with so much keenness into all national sports; there is no society that dines and dances quite so much as Australasian society.[5]

The American writer, Samuel Clemens (Mark Twain), who 'followed the equator', was struck most forcefully by the democratic temperament and politics of Australians, by the power of the working man (especially in 'his paradise', South Australia), and by the strength of independent sentiment. Although, Clemens commented, Australians like to call England 'home' ('in an unconsciously caressing way', like a young daughter, 'stroking mother England's old grey head'), the country 'is so jealous of its independence that it grows restive if ever the Imperial Government at home proposes to help'. He was also much struck by the cleverness and the ingenuity of the Australian 'aboriginals' and poured scorn on 'the white man's notion that he is less savage than the other savages'.[6]

Like other visitors, Clemens was deeply impressed by the degree of hospitality and friendliness accorded to him. This, said John Clifford, another British visitor, was in fact what he had found in his own search for 'a distinctively Australian "type" of man'. He had studied the physique and had not found it there, although, he added, there were more 'cornstalks' than in Britain, and 'an interviewer persuaded me to confess that Australian women possess a rare opulence of beauty'. He had failed to find it in Australian speech. But, there it was 'in the boundless generosity and overflowing hospitality to the stranger from the Homeland!'.[7] Clifford was also taken by the relative lack of 'caste' and the degree of independence and individual 'self-reliance' among Australians. There was 'freer initiative': 'Greater inventiveness in methods of work is possible'. In particular, Australia (and New Zealand) had adopted the 'greatest happiness' principle and, because of this, universal education had been made a state priority and social problems like inebriation were approached scientifically, with the view that the state (unlike in Britain) should be 'the protector of the feeble, a shield for the tempted, and a builder of disciplined and serviceable manhood'.[8]

There were also visitors who found the glowing picture promoted in official literature to be too 'rose-coloured' and lavish, the reality less attractive. While the relative egalitarianism struck some as an advantage, others like John Foster Fraser were unimpressed by Australia's industrial relations and by the association between high wages and tariffs on imports: 'British investors are chary: rightly or wrongly, they dread Labour legislation in Australia'. The young Australians, Fraser found, tended to avoid hard work, preferring town or station life to agricultural labour. Australians were 'the most pleasure-loving people I have come across', he commented, and the 'warm climate, the pleasant conditions of life, are already removing that doggedness which was the hall-mark of the brave men who first adventured in Australia'.[9]

No other visitors of the 1880s and 1890s, however, surpassed the prominent British Fabians, Beatrice and Sidney Webb, in their distaste for both the Australian 'character' and the Australian life-style. Their comments, it is true, were written in personal diaries and were presumably not intended for publication, but nevertheless, for all their frankness, the Webbs' observations of Australia confirm much that is found in other visitors' published reports.

During their tour of eastern Australia, Beatrice Webb's entries in particular complain unremittingly of vulgarity, provincialism and materialism in the population, as if she had found herself in a drawing room full of upstarts trying to pass themselves off as aristocrats. She observed a consistent lack of policy, compounded by an absence of public spirit and lack of statesmanship among the politicians. Australian women in particular were appalling: uneducated, bad-mannered, 'dressy' and idle almost without exception and they were, 'to my mind', the principal reason for 'the low tone of all classes'.

While Sidney Webb's entries are more focused on the statistical dimensions of Australian work and products, and less concerned with

122   *To Constitute a Nation*

human attributes and social relations, both the Webbs pour constant scorn on the lack of idealism, low level of education and the unmitigated materialism they encountered. At the same time, both finally find something to praise. The quality of Australian journalism was, they concluded, easily equal, even in cases superior, to British journalism.[10]

What is one to learn from such an account, apart from irritation at the attitude of breathtaking and undisguised snobbery towards those whose hospitality the Webbs also recorded, and who (despite their supposed lack of education) had heard of the couple and their work? At one point, Beatrice comments critically on a farmer with whom they travel, as having 'that curious sort of tolerance for political opponents which seems characteristic of these colonies'.[11] This perhaps is the common thread through all the Webbs' complaints: a level of tolerance they find unacceptable and experience as apathy or indifference. The line between indifference and tolerance is a thin one, as is the line between incrementalism and conservatism. One may well be mistaken for the other, and both may merge into each other.

The Australian society the Webbs observed in the late 1890s was lacking in the extremes of class division and ideological warfare with which they were familiar in Britain. They interpreted this to mean a lack of intellectual energy and political ideas. They were not the only contemporary observers to draw this conclusion. The touring theosophical leader, Annie Besant, who thought Australians lacked mental alertness;[12] Albert Métin, who found socialism 'without doctrine';[13] and, a little later, James Bryce, whose own work, *The American Commonwealth*, had served as the 'bible' of the 1891 Federal Convention, also considered Australians thin on ideas and 'doctrine', motivated by material goals more than ideals.[14]

Why the goal of material amelioration cannot itself represent an ideal is another issue, but for the Webbs the lack of energy went much further. Even the countryside itself seemed inadequate; both the people and the land displayed 'a desolate combination of restlessness and ennui', and the scenery was 'crude and monotonous'.[15] In this climate, one is tempted to ask, how could Australians produce the high quality journalism the Webbs also observed?

The answer may well lie in the comparatively early introduction, from the 1870s, of universal, compulsory education in the Australian colonies (a feature of the country's life unnoticed by these visitors), as well as in the general willingness to experiment and to challenge authority, noticed by others. The Webbs find only that Australian children were left to 'tumble up' and, as adults, they were happy to 'muddle along'. The Australian 'native' politician was, it seems, a rather relaxed, inefficient creature, honest, but ineffectual. He was, they emphasised, utterly unlike the American model, yet was also a poor shadow of the British standard.

This habit of easy-going tolerance the Webbs picked up no doubt allowed many moments where outrage should have been expressed to pass without protest, but it had also allowed, by this stage of Australia's development, a series of incremental reforms. It was not simply a matter of apathy; where Australians in the 1890s held rigid, intolerant views themselves—such as on the necessity for Australia to be white—they were impassioned and active, to a degree Beatrice Webb did not observe. Instead, she saw only what she detected as political indifference and found appalling. Among the other attributes many of the visitors regularly noted was a tendency of Australians to be over-sensitive to criticism. It can at least be said that Australian readers responding negatively to the Webbs' views could not be accused of being thin-skinned.

In a published account of the visit, Sidney Webb displayed both greater politeness and an appreciation of the advantages of Australian reformism. There was, he told an interviewer, much to be learned from Australia. It was not 'an infant community just out of the gold-diggings stage, but . . . an adult Anglo-Saxon Democracy, full of interest and instruction to the political world'. In particular was the lesson—one that was 'unsettling to the Conservative mind'—that the extension of democratic rights, such as the suffrage, did not necessarily produce corruption, as it appeared to have done in America. Great interest lay in the way the 'separate democracies at the Antipodes, British by race, have taken our English Constitution and adapted it to their own circumstances'.[16] Australians may not have been great political thinkers, but they were great improvisers, and on the right track.

Among all the observations of the Australian type and the speculations on its evolution in the future, one constant theme emerges: the love of the outdoors, the mingling of people and nature. In the 1890s an entire book was written in which the anticipated impact of the semi-tropical climate and outdoor life was 'matched' to the type of food, personal hygiene and exercise needed for Australia to develop. As early as 1893, Philip Muskett was arguing that Australians ate badly, consuming too much meat, not enough fish or salad or Australian-grown wine—it 'should be the national beverage of every day life'—and that 'the real development of Australia will never actually begin till this wilful violation of her people's food-life ceases'.[17] With a lengthy defence of the theories of Montaigne on the relationship between national character and climate, Muskett concluded that the 'Coming Australian' could be safely predicted as:

> more nearly akin to the inhabitants of Southern Europe than to his progenitors in the old country . . . The ample opportunities for outdoor life will

124   *To Constitute a Nation*

do much towards ensuring physical development. And, finally, the imaginative faculties will be very active, and it is quite permissible to hope that in time there will be a long roll of artists, musicians, and poets.[18]

Depending on the tastes of the commentator, the closeness to nature was either a good or a bad thing. It was thought by some to be the reason Australians as a type were easy-going and democratic, and by others the reason they were intellectually lazy, rebellious, and rough. It was perhaps, for some, a bit of both. White Australian children seemed to the visitor's eye a little feral, but they grew up to be sturdy adults, open and friendly. Being 'native' meant growing up with this legacy. The white population happily used the term, free it seems of any sense of paradox.

In the late 1880s Henry Parkes wrote to an English journal to complain of being asked by an Englishman if Australian natives were black. Everyone knew, Parkes said, that 'natives' meant the whites: the blacks were called Aborigines. It was an example, the story's narrator tells his readers, of the English tendency to look down on Australians and to fail to understand their values.[19] To be *native* was a matter of pride, above all in the years leading to Australian Federation. To be native was to be young and free, with new ideas and lots of energy. It was, so thought the great bearer of this view at this time, the Australian Natives' Association, to be democratic. All of this meant white. The Natives were White.

Australian Natives were native-born men. These were the first two qualifications for ANA membership. Later, 'virtual' Natives, residents of Australia for more than twenty-five years, were admitted to the Association, but their membership was not allowed to compromise the native profile, nor the rhetoric that went with it. Natives had also to be of good character, and this was assured by a process of membership by nomination. Nomination ruled out, among other things, the coloured native-born. White women, who might otherwise be thought native, were also excluded from the main organisation, although at times in the 1890s their membership was advocated by individuals within the ANA. If the full picture of 'nativeness' captured not only place of birth and colour, but also a certain prominence in the community, women were not yet native enough. Simultaneously in this decade, however, women themselves began to seek recognition for their contribution to the community and, at the very moment of Federation, among other things, a sister association was established.[20]

The requirement of native birth meant that the majority of members were relatively young in the 1880s and 1890s, the sons of the gold rush generation of the 1850s. Natives were young, home-grown and respectable. Theirs was a mutual help, mutual improvement society, which in

Australian Natives 125

the 1890s became a powerful political pressure group. Between the early years of the decade, marked by the first two constitutional meetings of 1890 and 1891, and the completion of the Federation project with the Inauguration of the Commonwealth, the ANA emerged as the exemplar of what the nation wanted in federating. It also became one of the central actors in the transformation of the federal movement from a parliamentary process, dominated by a generation of older men, into a process which can be called in contrast—for the moment—popular.

The direct involvement of the ANA in Federation organisations was chiefly confined to Victoria, although the large Victorian branch forged important links with New South Wales and South Australia in bringing about significant intercolonial meetings.[21] The Association held its own major Federation conference in 1890, and co-sponsored both the Corowa Conference of 1893 and the Bathurst People's Federal Convention in 1896. Overall the influence of the ANA model was immense. Or, rather, the model itself came to represent the imagined parameters of the emerging national community.

Even more than the Association's involvement in specific events or the actual level of its membership, it was the prominence of individual members that contributed to the ANA's association with Federation. A significant number were members of colonial parliaments and also delegates at the Federal Conventions, especially the later ones. Despite British predictions that 'the larrikin' would soon be 'master' when 'the governing men had to be taken from colonial classes',[22] the Native men had proven themselves well and truly capable of leadership by the mid-1890s. The very consciousness of such British attitudes increased their resolve to explore a native identity separate from, if parallel to, their Imperial identity. The new native identity had to be distinct from both the Aboriginal native and that other distinctly 'Australian' type, the convict.

The ANA adopted the strategy of shifting White Australia's lineage away from the convicts, identifying Australian birth with patriotism rather than dishonour, creating in effect a new category of nativeness. Although one ANA speaker was probably going too far for broad cultural acceptance, when he contrasted the ANA activities with 'the deification of sport (Cheers)—of bone and muscle at the expense of intellect',[23] the Association's strategy included the cultivation of intellectual and cultural pursuits through lectures and discussions, elevating Natives above the rough masses, stressing self-improvement both of individual and, metaphorically, of nation.

In Victoria, at least, the Association saw itself as almost single-handedly responsible for pushing patriotism in the direction of nation-building and in particular for opening the movement to the people. It was the ANA, the Bendigo League told its members, that had prophetically recognised after the 1891 Convention that the Constitution should be removed from parliamentary business and written by popularly elected delegates. Election gave the process a democratic status, allowing both the myth and the real experience of direct popular involvement to grow. Since native had come to mean young, progressive, and democratic, in contrast to the older, more conservative British-born men who dominated the parliaments in the early years of the 1890s, it gave Federation a much greater claim to be a 'native' product.

Much was made in such rhetoric of the numerical prominence of the native-born in the Federation movement. One letter to the press accused the New South Wales Protectionist leader, William Lyne, of holding an incoherent position as an anti-Billite; Lyne's protectionist motto, it said, 'is "An Australian policy for an Australian people"', but 'Where will we get the Australian people except through federation? Let us hope that in the coming fight the native born will assert their nationality by voting for Australian union'.[24] An editorial in the same paper referred to the 'Australian born population of the country, of whom [opponents] speak with contempt but who . . . are admitted to be strongly on the side of union, and to be animated by the patriotic aspiration to raise the status of their country . . . to a great nation'.[25]

Among proposed amendments to the 1891 draft Constitution debated at the Bathurst People's Federal Convention in 1896, it was resolved that for a naturalised Australian to be eligible to stand for the Senate, 'citizenship' should have been held for a minimum of ten years, rather than five (as the 1891 draft Constitution specified), and five years, instead of three, for the House of Representatives. The idea was to keep 'the new Commonwealth . . . in the hands of those who had given practical proof of their devotion to Australian interests'.[26] Devotion and commitment to Australia were the attributes by which a person's political capacity would be judged and, it was assumed, these were best demonstrated by being as far as possible a native.

When the ANA was formed in 1871 in Victoria, it was 'maligned in the press', a Tasmanian Branch meeting was later told, treated as 'an attempt' by its founders 'to take the reins of political power' from their fathers, 'the old pioneers', and 'to sever the silken bonds that . . . tied them to the old country'.[27] In the 1890s, the reins of power were taken from the older generation, but the 'silken bonds', if a little worn, remained intact. It was part of the ANA genius to represent a nativeness that remained at the same time British.

In appropriating the word native, the ANA also claimed a right to the land once owned by the original 'natives', as well as affection for and pride in the symbols of this land. The Association advocated both the celebration of 26 January as Foundation Day in New South Wales and

Australian Natives 127

the adoption of the wattle as the national flower. The idea of protecting the native symbols became a significant theme in the second half of the century, with the protection of native flora and birds advocated by a growing number. In addition the 'protection' of the Aborigines began to be institutionalised.

The 1897 Queensland Aboriginals Protection and Restriction of the Sale of Opium Act, the model upon which other states later based similar Acts, was the product of a report by the Protector Archibald Meston,[28] who would later arrange the Aboriginal display in the Commonwealth Inauguration celebrations. This Act provided for the establishment of Aboriginal reserves, into which the remaining 'full-blood' Queensland Aborigines would be gathered. It targeted in particular 'the great and widespread injury' being caused to Aborigines by the consumption of opium (which was associated with the Chinese, more than alcohol, associated with the 'white' man), and it restricted, among other things, the movement of whites onto reserves, as well as the amount of money Aborigines might have and the employment and residence of their 'half-caste' children.[29] As historian Henry Reynolds points out, Aboriginal 'protection' often amounted in fact to authoritarian control of the Aborigines' lives, with reserves used also for the incarceration of convicted or insubordinate individuals.[30] But institutionalisation 'not only catered for a whole range of dominant racial concerns, it was also the usual mechanism for the state provision of welfare'.[31] The decision to leave Aboriginal affairs to the states, rather than placing it in the hands of the Commonwealth, was significant in allocating such welfare to the discretion and judgement of individual officials, and making the Aboriginal people 'vulnerable to the political agendas of officers' with their own personal notion of 'protection'.[32]

The view that those in receipt of welfare, those needing 'protection' were not full, participating citizens, capable of exercising the full range of political rights, was also emerging at the time. If the white Australian Natives were at the forefront of creating the nation, being an original 'native' was soon to rule out the right to political participation in that nation. In 1902, with the first Commonwealth Franchise Act, Aboriginal natives (except those already on the electoral roll in their state) lost the right to vote, and, thereby, the right to stand for parliament, along with bankrupts and public servants, persons owing allegiance to a 'foreign power', and those attainted of treason or convicted of offences attracting a year or more of imprisonment.[33]

While Aborigines were not disenfranchised by the Constitution as such (as many people continue to believe) they might as well have been. Among the many arguments advanced by suffragists in support of their cause during the Federation years, the women pointed to the fact that

128   *To Constitute a Nation*

'the franchise was enjoyed even by aboriginals, but was denied to women, criminals, and lunatics'.[34] In 1902 the situation was reversed; white women gained the Commonwealth vote, Aborigines and coloured residents (with the exception of Maoris) lost it. For many years afterwards, as in 1901, the Aborigines were not thought sufficiently 'native' to have a stake in the new nation.

While white Australians were beginning to identify with the native environment, they did not make the imaginary link between themselves and the Aboriginal natives. Indeed, they repudiated the idea of a common or symbolic identity between the Australian Native and the Aborigine. This paradox was the product of a combined ruling notion of progress and the emergence of Australian nationalism. To identify with the Aborigines as 'natives' in common would have represented a symbolic threat to the assumption of white superiority, and perhaps also an unconscious threat, in competition for ownership of the land. Flora and fauna were less culturally problematic, more yielding and easier to protect.

Mr John Clarke, whom we met in chapter three, captured the paradox of this view in his petition to the 1897 Convention: 'I am glad to notice', he wrote, 'that you have included the protection of our Native Aboriginals' in the Constitution Bill, and 'humbly prayeth that the Honourable the Federal Convention will draft in the Constitution, a clause protecting the Native Animals', as well as the flora and trees. He was, of course, mistaken about the Convention's intention towards the Aborigines and was to be further disappointed in his own prayer. Clarke's petition failed even to find a sponsor and was thus not presented to the 'Honourable Convention'. He was sent a note of thanks from the President, and his petition marked 'declined to present'.

We do not know what originally inspired Mr Clarke. But we do know that he wrote tirelessly to the papers on the subject of the protection of native species, and his work was acknowledged in American naturalist circles. His father, Jacob Clarke, was a fine arts publisher and importer, who specialised in views of natural scenery, 'for beauty and variety unequalled', (as well as 'Portraits of celebrated Personages' and Modern Statuary).[35] John Clarke was already in late middle age by the time of the Federal Convention, and had practised as 'The People's Bookseller and Stationer' in the George Street Market Buildings in Sydney for many years. His degree of success, like his home address, seems to have been unstable. Although he attached a list of his letters to his petition, he appears to have had less, rather than more, success with seeing them published than he hoped to indicate. His was not a lone voice, and his appeals reflected the degree of attention to the issue of environmental protection that was slowly emerging in this period, with the establish-

Australian Natives 129

ment of naturalist and ornithology clubs, and Native Bird Protection Acts in the 1880s and 1890s, following on from the declaration of limited shooting seasons and national parks in earlier decades.[36] But, for the most part, Clarke's specific concerns did not echo far.

In 1895, Clarke had warned against the destruction of both native trees and native fauna. Responding to 'A Shady Customer', whose plea had been to stop the ringbarking of roadside trees in the country because this practice was robbing the poor tramp and 'weary wayfarer of some respite from the heat, some relief from the monotony of the road',[37] Clarke hoped for government attention to the matter: 'Rather than pursue the policy of cutting down and destroying trees, one would think their growth would be encouraged'. He supposed that city trees were being cut down 'to show off our buildings, which are nothing compared to the beauty of nature'.[38]

Later that year Clarke argued for legislation 'to prevent the wholesale annihilation of our native fauna', whose skins were transported in 'great waggonloads' for shipment to London, and which would otherwise soon be extinct. The 'noble kangaroo, which is unique to the continent', was, Clarke believed, already extinct in Tasmania and a government attempt to introduce one hundred young kangaroos for breeding had failed.[39]

One possible source for Clarke's idea of government action may be detected in this letter: the supplier of the young kangaroos was Mr Joseph Stringer, 'bird-fancier' and, it happens, sometime fellow tenant of the George Street Markets. We may imagine their daily conversations, joined perhaps by Mr O. Le Bon, the other bird fancier in the Markets in 1893. Perhaps Clarke also argued with the Messrs Gelding, florists and nurserymen (in the building, at no. 1), on the value of native flora. But more significant is the letter's reference to 'a very laudable' attempt being made in the New South Wales Parliament at that time to introduce a Native Flora Protection Bill.

The ultimate failure of this Bill was imminent by the time Mr Clarke turned, with renewed hope, towards the Federal Convention two years later. It had been introduced as a Private Member's Bill by the Member for Ryde, Frank Farnell, three times between 1894 and late 1897, modified at the end in both its scope and its projected penalties. Like Mr Clarke, Mr Farnell had warned of the extinction of many species, and hoped 'to earn the gratitude of the people hereafter for having done a little to preserve to them something of the natural luxuriance of our native flora which they can appreciate'.[40] Farnell wanted there to be both sanctions against uprooting of certain species on Crown land, and botanical reserves set aside, as well as, if possible, a clause preventing the holding of the wild-flower shows, which appear to have been responsible for much destruction, root and plant, of native flowers.

130   *To Constitute a Nation*

Mr Cotton (representing Clarke's own inner city electorate) protested that the Bill would create 'artificial crimes': 'I like to see men going home', he said, 'with wild flowers for their wives and children, and it is ridiculous to make this harmless pleasure a crime'. Mr O'Sullivan suggested an amendment to the Bill, to apply the sanctions only to dedicated public reserves, a measure he believed could prevent 'the wholesale destruction of our native flora', and he added: 'We have already destroyed many beautiful objects in Australasia for want of care'. Most thought the Bill too sweeping; some argued that the flowers and ferns were actually in abundance; others believed that current national reserves were adequate to protect all the relevant species.

But opposition in the debate was directed at the Bill's expected effect, rather than its intention. Chris Watson (the future first Labor Prime Minister) argued, for example, that the Bill would deprive those who did not have 'big gardens and plenty of money at their disposal' of their only opportunity 'to enjoy nature's beauties', and would place 'restriction [*sic*] upon the ideas of persons who could not afford a series of gardeners to cultivate the art of the beautiful'. Some objected that it would deprive flower sellers of an income, or curtail the cultivation of backyard gardens, some thought that sheep and fires and insects did more damage than 'human infusoria'. No one put the case that the flowers were worthless, or that non-native cultivated species were superior, or that the matter was trivial. Indeed, it was in defence of the ordinary person's love of native flowers that the restrictions on their gathering were principally opposed. In speech after speech, the popular enthusiasm for gathering wild flowers was sketched and applauded.

Some few thought the Bill was splendid as it stood, and, of these, the most enthusiastic was none other than Dr Ross (Member for Molong) who stands with Mr Clarke among the handful of individual petitioners pushing their own eccentric concerns in the 1897 Convention. 'If there is any class of people who will go to heaven', said Ross, 'I believe it is the lovers of flowers, plants, music, and the fine arts'. This is a touching, if in all probability meaningless, coincidence, for there is no evidence that the two men influenced or even met each other, except perhaps later in their shared final destiny as lovers of flowers and plants.

Without firm resolution, the Bill was finally sent to a select committee, where it languished, ultimately permanently, with the proroguing of parliament. As the process of selecting the committee took place, an interesting objection was raised to its proposed composition: 'If Scotch thistles were included in the schedule', said Mr Perry, 'I could understand these men being on the committee. [But] there is not a native proposed . . . except the member for Ryde'. Natives, the member implied, would appreciate the value of other natives, where non-natives could not be expected to do so. In committee, Mr Farnell made similar intimations, accusing an opponent of being 'a new chum' and declaring that he himself 'spoke with a knowledge of this colony, having been born in it, and he knew what he was talking about'.

Despite the Bill's dismal fate, it is striking to find the members in agreement on the beauty and value of the native flowers. Many displayed a detailed knowledge of varieties, as well as of the regional locations of species. The efforts of Joseph Maiden, Director of the Botanic Gardens, and Mr Baker, of Sydney's 'Australian' Museum, 'to disseminate a knowledge of the indigenous flora among the people of this colony', which were praised in another letter supporting Farnell's Bill,[41] may well have borne fruit.

In the press the public conveyed support and the 'hope that the wanton process of spoliation and destruction may some time or other be stayed by the repressive hand of the law'.[42] The writer of this particular letter explicitly made the association between native flora and the emerging sense of national identity:

Flowers elsewhere play a large part in the domestic sentiment of a people, but except for an accidental association of the Christmas bush and Christmas bells with that festival, perhaps, there is little link or tie between our native flora and the sentiment or life of the population . . . The sentimental associations of the earlier generations of Australian colonists clustered round the home-flowers of their childhood under other skies, and possibly the Australian generation proper has not sufficiently individualised itself yet to think for itself on such a matter. If that is really the explanation, Young Australia has no time to lose, for if the interesting process of sentimental development is too long delayed it may find Australian flora a thing of the past before it ripens into tardy maturity.

If the 'sentimental associations' were still not fully attached to the native flora, there is strong evidence (such as is found in the debate on Farnell's Bill) that this was emerging and Australians were indeed 'a flower-loving people'. Not only were armfuls of wild flowers regularly gathered for the home or for flower shows, a growing use of native iconography in decorative art can also be found in the Federation period, alongside the emergence of a distinctive Australian school of art in which the native bush was foregrounded. Like Farnell and Ross, Clarke evoked a duty to protect these icons for future generations. But to Clarke alone goes the honour of believing this sufficiently to be a national concern that its entrenchment in the new Constitution was necessary.

To Clarke, a 'people's' convention must have seemed a glorious new opportunity to begin with a virtually blank page and write on it a national commitment to the native environment. But the page was of

132   *To Constitute a Nation*

course not blank. On it were already sketched both the dominant values of the period, and the precondition of compromise and concession. Although protection of native flora was contemplated and a Bird Protection Act had already been passed in New South Wales in 1893, only what was minimally and necessarily national would be admitted in the Constitution, and in the 1890s this did not include the native flora, fauna and trees. The *Australian Federalist* thought Clarke's idea amusing: 'A man has been found who is going to vote against the Constitution because it does not provide for the protection of Australian flora! This is indeed a "floorer" for Federation'.[43] Since there was no concept of an interconnected, borderless environment (as we understand it now), the states, it was decided without debate, self-evidently were to have jurisdiction in this area.

Through these complex, interconnected associations with nativeness, the Australian Native had been redefined as a particular type of 'Coming Man', the robust, young colonial, whose mission included the forward movement of white men into 'uncivilised' frontiers,[44] but who was imbued also with a personal attachment to the environment, and a democratic sentiment of a particular type. In 1887 the *Bulletin* had infamously 'defined' the Australian as 'not those who have been merely born in Australia' but any man who leaves behind 'the memory of the class-distinctions and the religious differences of the old world . . . [who seeks] freedom of speech and right of personal liberty'. Not any man really: 'No nigger, no Chinaman, no lascar, no kanaka, no purveyor of cheap coloured labour is an Australian'.[45] The ANA's version was less crude, and ultimately more persuasive, for not only did it capture a certain commitment to English politeness, it also directed itself at ways for the Coming Man to arrive. Its version of nativeness was one that addressed the political organisation and processes by which a 'native' nation might be constructed.

When Alfred Deakin characterised the Australasian Federal Council as 'indigenous', like 'that extraordinary animal' the platypus, 'a perfectly original development compounded from familiar but previously unassociated types',[46] he might well have been speaking of the Constitution. A characteristic example of Australian 'improvisation', the Constitution was pieced together out of a commitment to British institutions and to the unwritten conventions of the British constitution, along with added bits and pieces from other models, within an American framework. Like the ANA, it both broke from and remained attached to the British model. It was both derivative and native at the same time.

This formula was written into the Constitution. A definition of the Australian is deeply inscribed in its sections: British legacy but an Australian design, room to move towards local adjustment and further

Australian modification, democracy and freedom, rough egalitarianism with differentiation according to states rather than any other principle—except whiteness. The Australian was a resident of a state, a democrat, even a participant, a domestic free trader, and white.

It was, wrote Andrew Inglis Clark in 1895, the now distinctive Australian character that impelled the colonies towards nationhood, the culmination of a natural tendency towards the evolution of a type, especially among isolated populations.

> [In] successive generations born on Australasian soil and nurtured under Australasian influence, [this] will become more and more emphatic, and will more clearly distinguish the native Australasian from his contemporaries in England and America; and it is this distinctively Australasian type of life and character which will be our contribution to the multiform civilisation of the world.

But, Clark concluded, to make it 'complete and perfect', to make it as much a privilege to say 'I am an Australasian' as it is to say 'I am an Englishman' or 'I am an American', Australia must have political union.[47] The Australian Native and the Australian Nation were now on the same course.

CHAPTER EIGHT

The People

> Then let the Federal spirit rise
> To quicken all our energies
> The glorious mission to fulfil
> By virtue of the peoples' will.[1]

If the natives were white, who then were 'the people'? Between 1893 and the completion of the Federation process at the immensely popular Inauguration ceremony less than eight years later, the concept of 'the people' was to acquire great significance. Although the term was in circulation, and the idea that there was a single 'people' across the colonies functioned as one of the strong arguments for Federation from the start, it was not until the Corowa Conference of 1893 that the idea of 'the people' as part—indeed as an essential part—of the formal process of federating began to emerge.

The Corowa Conference was the work of the Federation League branches on the New South Wales and Victorian borders. There, poised right at the intersection of conflicting colonial policy, right at the heart of what simultaneously propelled and obstructed the forward movement of Federation, right where Mr Service's 'lion'—the tariff—stood threateningly in the path, the desire for action had not faded, as elsewhere it seems to have done in the early years of the decade. The means was still sought of overcoming the problems and inconveniences created by intercolonial tariffs, of addressing the grievance felt in the Riverina at neglect by the New South Wales Government and the conviction that the region had ended up in the wrong colony. Federation became for many a beacon of hope.

When progress with the 1891 Constitution Bill stalled in the months and then years following the first Convention, the New South Wales Australasian Federation League and branches of the Australian Natives' Association, along with business representatives and members of the colonial parliaments, combined forces to ponder upon what might be done. For two days the Corowa Conference followed a predictable pattern, deliberating warmly, passing resolution after resolution on principles in support of Federation. It might have gone no further than this, and have slipped into history as one of the minor, even inconsequential, events of the decade.

At the very end, however, something happened. Cheers and congratulations greeted its conclusion. The Conference had 'really done something besides talk', Robert Garran wrote years later.[2] But, he added almost ingenuously, not everyone who attended knew exactly what it was they had just done. By the time of Federation, John Quick and Robert Garran were certain of what had happened. Their joint account in the great work of 1901 that bears their name[3] would enshrine Corowa as one of the key moments in the Federation process. Quick and Garran met in person for the first time at the Conference, and the younger Garran went on to become, in his own words, 'the junior partner of a steam roller'.[4] What it was they had done at Corowa was later explained by the two men in unambiguous terms. The Conference had passed the Corowa Plan.

The meaning of the Corowa Conference was, even as early as 1901, both a matter of actual lineage in the chain of events leading to Federation's conclusion and also a myth. Much else happened in 1893 and in every year leading up to 1901. Many events and processes were necessary to achieve Federation, and much debate about what was and what was not 'popular' about the Plan might be had. But in Corowa, a single moment and an apparently simple, and ultimately successful, idea coincided. It went on to become a symbol of what it was the Federalists most desired and needed in order to accomplish their goal: legitimacy. This was provided by the appeal, made at Corowa, to 'the people'.

Corowa represented, wrote Quick and Garran with the teleological confidence of the age, a turning-point where a stagnant Federalist movement regained momentum and forged a path culminating in Federation's ultimate success. The key to Corowa's triumph, the Corowa Plan, was at first nothing more than a motion. Moved towards the end of the Conference by the representative of the Bendigo Australian Natives' Association, Dr John Quick himself, it was received with much acclaim and passed unanimously:

That in the opinion of this Conference the Legislature of each Australasian colony should pass an Act providing for the election of representatives to attend a statutory convention or congress to consider and adopt a bill to establish a Federal Constitution for Australia and upon the adoption of such bill or measure it be submitted by some process of referendum to the verdict of each colony.

Although the term 'people' does not appear in the resolution, Quick and Garran were to summarise it soon after as if it did. The Plan, they said, was 'the best guarantee' of both interest and confidence in a Federal Constitution, because it ensured that 'the people should be asked to choose for themselves the men to whom the task was to be entrusted'.[5]

136   *To Constitute a Nation*

The story of the Plan's genesis goes like this. In the final session of the Conference, only minutes before the great resolution was moved, both Quick and Garran (on behalf of the Central Federal League) had separately moved other, predictable resolutions, amounting yet again to an affirmation of support for Federation and a commitment to working for its accomplishment.

But with the second (Quick's first) resolution, a debate ensued. Elated, no doubt, by two days of intense discussion and the enthusiastic reception of senior politicians and statesmen at Corowa, a desire for action had begun to grow in the participants. With it came a feeling of dissatisfaction that the Conference was to wind up with nothing but 'words, words, words!'. As Garran later described the scene, the reader may imagine one of those moments where the desire to avoid anti-climax leads on to bold initiative: 'the dramatic moment of change from routine to inspiration', Garran called it.[6] On the prompting of Mr Herbert Barnett, a small committee retired for some minutes, re-emerging, almost magically it seems in the telling, with Dr Quick's Motion—the Corowa Plan.

Although it matters only to literal history and not to the equally important myth, there remains in fact some doubt as to the original source of the proposal. Many years after the event, in a personal but colourless account, Quick says simply that he and others prepared the Plan 'in consultation'.[7] Together, however, Quick and Garran identify its origins more closely with Quick's authorship. Alfred Deakin's intimate account, *The Federal Story*, mentions, however, that Henry D'Esterre Taylor, Secretary of the Imperial Federation League, had suggested the popular convention and referendum to Quick in the train going up to the Conference. But, Deakin adds, 'the same idea had probably occurred independently' to Quick.[8]

Someone else, however, thought it worth reminding others that Quick was not the author. In early 1895, the 'Melbourne Correspondent' of the *Corowa Free Press* wrote: 'At the Corowa gathering, Dr Quick got the credit, but he is not entitled to it. The man who suggested the Federal Convention being elected by the people . . . was <u>Mr H. D'Esterre Taylor</u>. I am able to speak definitely on the matter'.[9] The correspondent had had, he told his readers, discussions with Mr Taylor beforehand, but found himself unable to travel up to Corowa with Taylor, who went early to 'work up a feeling in favour of his proposal'.

Might alternative travelling plans have made the course of the Conference, even the course of history, different? Might Taylor, rather than Quick, have received a knighthood for his services to Federation in the Queen's Honours on 1 January 1901? It seems unlikely. Whether Taylor's contribution, assuming it was such, was overlooked because of

The People 137

his own reticence, or because he was known as an Imperial Federationist rather than a national Federalist, or for any number of other reasons, the plan was henceforth always thought of as Dr Quick's Plan.

But why did it matter, and why did Mr Taylor's friend (indeed, perhaps it was Mr Taylor himself) want to lay claim to authorship? The most immediate reason for the rebuttal of Quick's claim in the press was the attention the Plan was receiving in early 1895, when the six colonial Premiers, meeting in Hobart, restructured the Corowa Plan into a draft Enabling Bill for each colony to move towards Federation. The broader reason lay in the ultimate ascendancy of the idea that the people should play a direct role in Federation, and the sense that this was not only the key to moving forward, but also a moment of historical significance, that the 'greatness' of the Plan made it likely that its author's name would be linked (as indeed it was) with its historical record in the future.

But the little mystery, with its restrained intimations of impropriety, need not have arisen even in 1895 if the real originality of the Corowa Plan had been properly recognised. Like the 'Melbourne Correspondent', historical memory has focused on the idea that the people (rather than the parliaments) should elect the Convention and that the Constitution should be submitted to a referendum. But the real genius of the plan was, as Quick and Garran themselves make clear (and Garran reaffirms in a later analysis of D'Esterre Taylor's claim), 'the idea of mapping out the whole process in advance by Acts of Parliament—of making statutory provision for the last step before the first step was taken'.[10] This meant that the colonial politicians were each able (if they wished) to set in train a precise and manageable process, one which rested upon a claim to popular support and was political without being obviously partisan. It is not, however, the sort of political achievement that is easy to recognise or admire. It lacks the simplicity and the clarity, it fails to capture the resounding appeal to democratic sentiment held in the single idea of popular participation.

The fact that the latter idea took off, rather than the more complex political accomplishment, is itself a guide to the political culture of the period. In the 1890s the ever familiar character of intransigent party rivalries and public disdain for politicians as a type were well entrenched. The federal movement of the early 1890s was a politicians' movement. It had begun with great promise and had produced two Conventions and a draft federal Constitution. This Constitution was to have been put before each colonial parliament for debate leading to adoption, but changes in the composition of governments, and obstruction and conflict between politicians (especially in New South Wales) had seen the draft lie abandoned and the movement sullied by 'politics'. 'The reception which the Bill of the 1891 Convention had received was sufficient

138   *To Constitute a Nation*

warning that no merely parliamentary authority would be held sufficient to prepare a Federal Constitution', wrote Alfred Deakin.[11]

For Federation to come about, it was certain that the parliamentary process would have to be avoided at least at the (new) beginning. This was, argues historian Stuart Macintyre, 'a calculated appeal to popular prejudice', an 'act of ventriloquism' whereby the disembodied people were called to rise above the local class and party loyalties displayed by politicians, and it involved a 'remarkably attenuated conception of citizenship and politics'.[12] But by the time of the movement's culmination in Federation many had embraced this conception. It was the democratic character of the Constitution—meaning its endorsement by the people and not the politicians—that was imagined, claimed and emphasised. Against this claim to democracy John Quick's name was readily and repeatedly mentioned.

If all that Quick had done was to move his (or another's) motion at Corowa in 1893, the attribution of achievement would certainly be misplaced. But a motion may remain no more than a motion. As Quick saw immediately, if anything were to come of it, more action had to be taken. The idea for the first step came, he tells us, from an editorial in the *Argus* soon after the Corowa Conference.[13] Who, the editor asked, would draft the Enabling Bills for the colonial parliaments? Quick, both a former politician and a lawyer, took this upon himself. By early 1894 he had presented to the Central Committee of the Australasian Federation League his 'Australian Federal Congress Bill'. It was adopted in a slightly modified version and Quick was to spend most of that year meeting with politicians and lobbying for his Bill. The Federation League in New South Wales took up the plan and they too lobbied enthusiastically. Particular headway was made with George Reid, elected Premier of New South Wales in August that year, who had hitherto been unenthusiastic about Federation to the point of obstructing its progress. This was significant progress because, as was well recognised at the time, the support of the 'Mother Colony' was crucial if Federation were ever to be achieved.

Neither Reid nor Henry Parkes had attended the Corowa Conference although they had been invited. Perhaps among their other reasons the desire to avoid each other may have figured in their minds. The two men loathed each other, and their public hostility had at the very least contributed towards Reid's reluctance to support the earlier Federation movement, so closely identified was it with Parkes. Quick's approach represented not only a new start for the movement, but also the chance for Reid to take it out of the hands of Henry Parkes at a time, said Alfred Deakin, 'when local reactions were rendering it possible for him to reappear as a popular leader'.[14] While the Corowa Conference met and then as Quick and the Federation League (and South Australian Premier,

The People   139

Charles Kingston) wooed Reid, Parkes made one final attempt to regain the leadership of the movement. But it was too late. The Corowa Plan was on the table.

It was to be the principal subject of the Premiers' Conference in Hobart, in 1895. On his way to Hobart, George Reid had stopped off in Melbourne, met up with the South Australian Premier, and together they had addressed a large meeting of the Victorian Federation League. There, in the Melbourne Town Hall, with the enthusiasm of a convert, Reid told his audience that the 'vital defect of the efforts of the great men of Australia during the past five years . . . was that they never quite came home to the hearts of the masses of the people. The first essential of a thoroughly successful federal movement is popular enthusiasm. (Cheers)'.[15]

On the actual agenda at the Premiers' Conference were in fact three alternative bases for achieving Federation: the first was the Federal Council 'as a complete organisation', then the 1891 draft Constitution as it stood, and thirdly, 'Dr Quick's popular proposal'.[16] It was Dr Quick's solution Reid and Kingston intended to carry. The others appeared on the list, it can be assumed, in order to avoid antagonising any more than necessary the Premiers of Queensland and Western Australia, those members least likely to co-operate if the conclusion seemed pre-empted. But it was Quick's Corowa Plan that immediately absorbed the bulk of their energies, and quickly became the Premiers' Plan.

Meanwhile, in the Federal Council, meeting down the road, the idea of the people playing a central role met with much scepticism. John Hackett from Western Australia feared that an elected Convention would not result in the best men being chosen, and that, 'while I have no theoretical horror of the referendum . . . [w]hat I dread is the application of it to a measure of the transcendent importance of Australian Federation'. It must be understood that under the Premiers' Plan, 'Parliament is for the nonce to be abolished'.[17]

Mr Hackett 'sets forth with great force all the difficulties he can imagine to be involved in the Premiers' proposal', replied Alfred Deakin, 'and I congratulate him on the wealth of imagination which he has displayed', but the 'great danger Mr Hackett [really] appears to see is that in adopting the constitution we shall be guilty of innovation'. The men elected to the Convention would be the best men in any case, argued Deakin, and while some groups might attempt to target the Convention for their own ends, 'I know no colony in which those sections can, to use an Australian phrase, come within coo-ee of the solid vote that would be cast by the serious-minded people of the country'.[18]

Queensland Councillor, Andrew Barlow, saw the original failure of the 1891 Constitution Bill as the result of a 'large party growing up [in other colonies] . . . which desires a complete severance from the United Kingdom' as well as the elimination of property, among other things. The Premiers' Plan would be supported only by this 'agitating and active portion of the various population', he said, and he hoped it would be defeated so that New South Wales would then have 'the opportunity' to enter the Federal Council. The result otherwise would be 'socialism in our time'.[19]

Victoria's James Patterson assured them that the question of Federation rose above the level of 'party passions' and that every 'lover of his country' would think in elevated terms. But Queensland's Attorney-General Thomas Byrnes had, for the moment, the last word: 'I say that if this federal constitution is going to be borne up by appeals to the masses of the people to rise up against this Federal Council, then I say that you are building up a Frankenstein that will devour the very constitution itself'. The new Constitution would have 'its origins in a source that is absolutely poisonous', in a movement for which the term 'revolutionary' was 'a mild epithet'.[20]

The conclusion of the Premiers' Conference, despite some stormy moments, was a clear resolution that each colony would pass Enabling Acts, so that ten delegates each could be chosen to meet in a Convention, a federal constitution would be drafted, then considered separately by each colonial parliament, the Convention would reconvene to consider proposed amendments, and the Constitution would be put to the people at a referendum before being submitted to the Crown.

This resolution followed the Corowa Plan almost exactly, departing only in two respects. First was the commitment to individual parliamentary scrutiny of the draft Constitution in the middle of the process. This extra step (borrowed from the Central Federation League of New South Wales) represented a stroke of further political ingenuity. Arguments that the original Corowa Plan did not allow the separate colonies to consider a proposed federal scheme in the light of their own distinctive interests could now be met. Despite the view of the rapidly fading federal leader, Henry Parkes, that it was 'preposterous to talk of a mob of people making a constitution',[21] the plan took off.

Even if he did not like the idea of an elected Convention, Parkes (so the Victorian Premier George Turner reminded members at the Federal Council meeting) had himself once suggested that direct popular involvement was a necessary precondition and that the parliaments could not decide the course of Federation.[22] Indeed, in his very first communications in 1889 with the New South Wales Governor, Lord Carrington, which set in train the 1890 Federation Conference in Melbourne, he had written that he hoped 'to move the Governments by wakening the People'.[23]

By 1895 the conviction was widely expressed (in four colonies at least) that it was both necessary and right for the people to choose the delegates to a new Convention. And although the *Brisbane Courier* raised the question of whether the ratifying authority for a constitution should be each parliament or 'the foreign expedient of a referendum', it soon decided that the referendum was not so foreign after all (it was found to have been used in 'other Anglo-Saxon countries') and was suited, it seemed, to the exceptional case such as this.[24]

In Hobart, upon the insistence of the Queensland and West Australian Premiers, the Corowa Plan was modified in a second way. Uncomfortable about the process, for a range of political reasons close to home, Queensland's Premier Sir Hugh Nelson extracted an agreement from the other Premiers that election of delegates to a new Convention would not be mandatory, and that each colony would be free to adopt whatever means of selection it chose. Sir John Forrest was at first unwilling even to attend the Premiers' Conference and then, having decided to come, did not stay to the end, but he remained throughout immovably opposed to the popular election of delegates.

These positions held by the Queensland and West Australian representatives translated into a slice of the Constitution's history. Queensland's Parliament, deadlocked over whether both Houses or just the Legislative Assembly (the Lower House) should choose the delegates for the Federal Convention (and with a substantial number of members supporting popular election instead), failed to pass the Enabling Bill their Premier had half-heartedly agreed upon in Hobart. Thus, rather ironically, since Sir Samuel Griffith (by then Chief Justice of Queensland) had been the principal drafter of the 1891 Constitution, that colony remained altogether unrepresented at the second Federal Convention.

But in this Convention the other delegates kept on hoping that Queensland's representatives would eventually turn up, and they kept in mind the colony's interests throughout their debates. Queensland was subsequently invited to take part in a special Premiers' Conference in 1899 (called the 'Secret' Premiers' Conference by the anti-Billites) where certain modifications to the new draft Constitution were accepted, including one designed for that colony's special dilemma.

Queensland had been deeply divided, regionally, for many years and was close to seeking separation into three parts (North, Centre and South) at times during the preceding decade. These regions also held different views on Federation, and neither the North nor the Centre believed the South (which had Brisbane, and the numbers) could represent their interests in either the Convention or the new Commonwealth Parliament.

Section 7 of the Constitution is now a trace of this history, providing that 'the State of Queensland . . . may make laws dividing the State into divisions and determining the number of senators to be chosen for each division'. Seemingly bland, even insignificant, this is one of those easily overlooked sections of the Constitution which, like a magical room, appears much smaller from the outside than it is, in fact, once entered. On its own, like so many others, this single paragraph of section 7 could be the subject of an entire history.

If Queensland held out until 1899 to have its referendum on the Constitution Bill, when four colonies had already held referendums the year before, it did at least hold it in the same year in which the others had their second go. But Western Australia had its referendum only at the last minute in 1900, after the British Parliament had already passed the Constitution Act. Western Australia too was experiencing significant regional tensions, with a large section of the colony outside the capital hostile to the incumbent parliamentarians, and a powerful 'Separation for Federation' movement active in the eastern goldfields. The Parliament took the extra precaution of specifying in its Enabling Bill that the Constitution Bill would only be submitted to the people if the Parliament approved it first. But, because they left it too late, Western Australia, unlike Queensland, was to be unsuccessful in having a similar provision to section 7 inserted in the Constitution. By 1900, the other colonies thought Western Australia should consider itself lucky to enter the Federation at all as an 'Original State', thereby gaining, among other things, a constitutional guarantee of equal representation in the Senate.

The West Australians had turned up to the Convention, but their Parliament alone had chosen its own delegates without reference to the people. In the event, however, concerns raised about the wisdom of an election in the other colonies were far from realised. The majority elected to the Convention were serving or former politicians, several of whom in fact were there in the Federal Council meeting where the Plan was rejected, and many of whom would have been chosen by their respective parliaments had this method of selection been adopted.

Politicians at that time were the frequent target of ridicule and criticism, mistrusted for their motives, often assumed to be ruled by self-interest. The 'degeneracy' of colonial parliaments was 'one of the most commonplace topics of Australian politics', said the then Prime Minister's brother, G. B. Barton, in the year of the Inauguration: when the division bell rang, Members 'come trooping in from the billiard room, the refreshment room, the hotel across the street, the ante-rooms, or other haunts to which they retire, in order to escape a debate'.[25] Women suffragists and temperance reformers deplored the spectacle of disorderly and vulgar parliamentary debate, anticipating its being softened and civilised with the entry of women into politics. The parliamentary 'bear-pit' was a frequent feature of reports of last century's politics.

The People 143

But alongside disgust there was much popular amusement at the antics of members of parliament, which suggests that for many people the disgust was a strategy for reminding the politicians not to get above those they represented, and there was a willingness on some politicians' part to play the clown. George Reid (later fourth Prime Minister and first Australian High Commissioner in London) was especially notorious for clowning and parading his obese body in front of an audience, and by all accounts he attracted both amusement and electoral support. In the days before radio and television, political campaigns were conducted from the public platform and speakers who could move their audience to laughter, who were quick with repartee and wit, drew large crowds and even correspondingly large numbers of votes.

But when it came to drafting a constitution, this image, for most people and for the politicians themselves, was set aside. The standing of elected delegates as experienced politicians and, in the majority of cases, also as lawyers, was seen by most (if not all) as an asset, indeed as a qualification for such a task. The New South Wales delegates were, the *Sydney Morning Herald* told its readers,

> admittedly the best ten men New South Wales could have sent forward for such a purpose . . . [They] were chosen for their legislative experience, their special training, and for the confidence reposed in them by the people who have neither the time nor the training to go into these intricate matters properly for themselves.[26]

If, among all these politicians, one labour representative alone was elected to the Convention, William Trenwith was not alone as a representative of progressive, even radical, views. Many colonial liberals found their way to the Convention, and the reasons for the failure of the other labour candidates are complex, arising to a significant degree from the immaturity of organisation and political skill of the Labor Party in the dying years of that century. If Federation was designed, as some writers have suggested,[27] to keep the emerging Labor Party from power, it failed. Despite the view of much of the labour movement that the Constitution should be written differently, the first national labour government in the world was soon formed under that Constitution, little more than two years after the colonial 'wedding' transformed all the little nineteenth-century parties into vulnerable players on a mass political stage.

Where, in the early years of the 1890s, opinion held that 'Among the people there is no desire for Federation, and, what is much more fatal, there is a positive distrust of it ever since the convention drew up its Commonwealth Bill, with its provisions for a Governor-General and

144 *To Constitute a Nation*

Senators at £500 a year, and other costly appurtenances',[28] the idea of 'the people' had, by 1895, a life of its own.

Still, it took some time for this to become the dominant theme in Federation culture. The Hobart Premiers' Conference, having come and gone, its efforts seemed for a while to go no further. Enabling Bills were passed in four colonies late in the year or early in 1896, but, while the parliaments waited for Queensland's Bill, and the Federalists waited for the parliaments, then waited for the announcement of the elections they had foreshadowed, the movement seemed once again to wane. Inaction from the parliaments, little noise from 'the people' whose interest was supposed to be excited by the new turn of events. Alfred Deakin, always inclined to pessimism, saw the situation in the bleakest terms:

> Unquestionably what all Federalists are striving against is the inexhaustible *vis inertiae* of our populace as a whole. We brace ourselves at times, seeking to lift the deadweight of apathy a little . . . But the load is too heavy for the strongest to sustain for more than a short time, and back the mass sinks again into its ruts of routine . . . When one Colony shakes off its indifference and takes a step forward, all the provincialists within its borders join in a chorus of contemptuous criticism. Knowing that the movement must fail unless it is taken up by several members of the group, they delay the response of their own Parliament by appeals to local emergencies, until the opportunity has passed, and they can pose once more as Federalists pining for an opportunity of action which neighbouring Colonies refuse to give them.[29]

More than two years were to pass before 'the people' were finally asked at an election in four out of the six colonies to choose their representatives to write their Constitution. The delay seemed, to those who waited, interminable. So 'gentlemen of Bathurst who ardently desired to see the Union of the Colonies brought about'[30] were moved to set up a Branch of the Federation League and, with the speed with which the organisation of events seems typically to have moved in those days, within six weeks to find themselves before a so-called *People's* Convention, ready to immortalise the Corowa process and the idea of 'the people'.

What did they mean by 'people' in this context? A commitment had already been made in four colonies to popular election of the delegates to the next Convention and for that Convention's work to be put before the people at a referendum. The idea of a Convention had already moved well beyond the models offered in 1891, when members of the first Convention were elected by the colonial parliaments.

The term 'people' seems to have been adopted at Bathurst in order to distinguish this Convention from the one (referred to as the 'Statutory Convention') the parliaments would organise. The choice of the name

The People 145

People was, therefore, partly a matter of finding a different title for their Convention, but also of indicating that theirs was the work of organisations outside of politics. The idea of 'the people' and the success of the concept were, as much as anything else, an expression of the essential scepticism towards politicians embedded in Australia's political culture. Get the people involved, appeal to the people and the politicians will be humbled. Members of parliament were meant, in the democratic tradition, to represent the people, but few people openly believed it.

For all this, the employment of parliamentary legislation was central to plans for reform and experiment in Australia, and by the 1890s seats in parliament were sought by groups, including the labour movement, in order to achieve their goals, even as they scorned the motives of parliamentarians. It is yet another enduring paradox of Australia's political culture that à readiness to use political resources to accomplish change, even a dependence upon government action, co-existed with mistrust and scepticism about political actors.

The Bathurst People's Federal Convention had, in fact, much greater representation of members of parliament and official sanction than the term People's Convention might now suggest. It began with the Mayor of Bathurst, Thomas Machattie, at the centre, in a circle of organising committees: procedure, finance, accommodation and transit, plus a ladies' subcommittee. The latter was, we may note here, in all probability the very first women's federal organisation, a harbinger of things to come. Then the Government of New South Wales offered a range of concessions and services: free railway passes for accredited delegates, discounts from steamship companies, the loan of Hansard reporters to cover the Convention's proceedings (with Labor leader, Billy Hughes, protesting in Parliament about the use of Hansard staff for a privately arranged Convention and announcing that he would ask for similar privileges at the forthcoming Labour League Conference). Victoria and South Australia got in on the act, offering railway reductions for travellers to Bathurst. The provisions of the mistrusted parliaments were welcome.

Two hundred delegates, a mixture of invited and locally nominated representatives from a range of organisations, turned up in Bathurst on 16 November 1896. They took the 1891 Convention Bill as their point of departure, debating each of the sections, recommending changes, 'assisting' the future Statutory Convention.[31] The 'people' who went to Bathurst were men from a broad group of associations, by far the majority of them from New South Wales: other Federation Leagues, the Australian Natives' Association, Municipal Councils, Chambers of Manufactures, Commercial Travellers' Associations, one Labour League representative, one delegate from the Social Democratic League, one from the

146   *To Constitute a Nation*

Single Tax League, another (the notorious editor of *Truth*, John Norton) from the National Republican Union of New South Wales. Members of the Victorian and New South Wales Parliaments, as well as distinguished others, like the Catholic Cardinal Moran and, of course, Quick and Garran, came as invited guests.

The Convention was, wrote Robert Garran many years later, a 'picturesque episode' (by which, we assume, he intended approbation rather than irony). 'Practically everyone was welcome who could present credentials from any league or society whatever'; it was 'thoroughly representative—there were lawyers, doctors, clergymen, farmers, pastoralists, merchants, shopkeepers, members of parliament, journalists, professors, civil servants, and even an undertaker'. The Convention represented 'every shade of political and social belief', wrote Quick and Garran together.[32] They all went home, said Garran, 'more Australian and less provincial in outlook'.[33]

If we smile now at Garran's idea of 'thoroughly representative', the intention of being 'representative' was itself significant. The necessity for a 'representative' Convention was repeatedly emphasised by Premier George Reid in his speech to the Bathurst Convention; by the term he seems to have meant, primarily, elected. Partly offering an indirect account of why he had not been more active in promoting Federation himself (a politician's convenient, retrospective account of inaction), Reid explained that he personally had long recognised the need for representative processes:

> I felt that Federation should not come until the people themselves . . . could make the national Convention representative of themselves and their principles . . . that Federation should not come till the people themselves were prepared to bring it into existence. Not to bring it into existence after their destiny had been framed; not to put simply a formal seal upon the Constitution; but to send into a national Convention, as representative of themselves and their principles men who were to frame a Constitution.[34]

His opponent, Opposition Leader William Lyne, also emphasised the representative nature of the Convention. This lay, he said, in its being 'composed of representatives of all shades of political belief . . . [T]here were Conservatives, Liberals, ultra-Radicals, and even Republicans present'.[35] Edmund Barton, meditating in his speech upon the basis of American Federation and the disaster of the doctrine (that the union was dissoluble) that had led to the Civil War, asked rhetorically whether surrenders and sacrifices were required in entering a union. 'It is not', he said, 'a surrender or a concession that which you give up to the Federation. You give to the Australian people'. And 'who', he added. 'are

The People 147

the people? You. You get the benefit. When viewed from a fair standpoint it is not a real concession, surrender or sacrifice merely to transfer certain things from the people acting in one capacity to the people, acting in another'. His vision, he concluded, was a Constitution 'of solid strength, of perfect justice, and a tender humanity'.[36] The audience cheered.

But the idea of the people was a broad one, also amenable to opposing both the Federation movement and the Constitution. The *Bulletin* called the Bathurst meeting the 'Toy Convention', the 'amateur Federal Convention which has been amusing itself with the manufacture of a toy constitution': the Federalists' flag, its cartoonist suggested, should read: 'One People, One Debt'.[37] Labour and socialist anti-Billites used the concept of the people to refer to the whole population of Australia, in other words, in opposition to states' rights principles, which promoted a divided model of the people. This latter criticism in particular was to become the enduring focus of labour criticism.

The labour movement began with the argument, shared indeed at the Bathurst Convention, that the 1891 draft Constitution was essentially undemocratic (in its inclusion of an unelected Senate, and its omission of a guarantee against plural voting, for example). Later, these demands having been met in the 1898 draft, its opposition was most particularly directed against the election of equal numbers of senators from each state. Numerically, this was considered 'undemocratic', since it gave the population of the small states considerably greater representation per head in the Senate than those of the larger states.

Labour Member of the New South Wales Legislative Assembly, Chris Watson, however, objected less to the idea of equal Senate numbers for each colony, since this might be needed to induce them to join, than to equal representation at the elected Convention in the first place. In his speech on the Enabling Bill in the House in October 1895, he endorsed the referendum and disparaged critics of the Bill who suggested that the people were unable to judge a constitution, but he rejected as undemocratic the proposed Convention. It was 'out of all reason', he said, that the small colonies should have equal power in determining the basis of Federation, with New South Wales and Victoria 'containing a million and a quarter of people'. 'Everyone', Watson asserted in response to an intervention, 'claims to be democratic; but when it comes to be a question of granting the people effectively—not merely in theory, as at present—an opportunity of carrying out their wishes, only comparatively few . . . are willing to support such a proposal'.[38]

Socialist and labour leaders also used the concept of the people in the abstract ethical sense meaning specifically the working class. This referred not only to the greatest number or proportion, but also to those

148   *To Constitute a Nation*

representing the working part of the population. The working class was held up as the people, not just as the numerical majority, but also the productive foundation of society. In an anti-Billite speech before the first referendum, the British socialist leader Ben Tillett told an audience in Melbourne that the Australian Constitution was a 'snare laid for' the working class 'by a pack of unscrupulous lawyers', and an 'arrangement of shopkeepers to protect their own petty interests one against the other'. Federation, he argued, 'must spring from the hearts and the homes of the people, and have its roots deep down in democratic principles'.[39]

Although the concept of the people has changed since Federation, one significant remnant of the prevailing notion of popular can still be found firmly in the Constitution. In that simple mythical sense, it is attributable to the Corowa Plan. It was the referendum. Although the Corowa Plan advocated a referendum on the Constitution Bill and did not mention the referendum as the permanent means of constitutional amendment, the latter was most probably advanced in the delegates' minds once they had been popularly elected to the Convention, with the knowledge that their product—the whole Constitution—would be put to referendum.

The idea of the referendum was not the product of the genius of Corowa's delegates. It was in the air during the decade and had been put into practice on more than one occasion in South Australia.[40] In 1891, however, the idea of the people as the source of legitimacy for Federation had not yet taken hold. While Charles Kingston's draft Constitution included the referendum and Andrew Inglis Clark's raised it for consideration, the majority of the first Convention's delegates concluded, in the words of Victoria's Duncan Gillies, that 'You will never carry a constitution with that proposal in it!'.[41]

The means of altering the Constitution adopted in its first draft Bill was to be based on the American method: proposals would pass first through the Commonwealth Parliament, then be submitted for ratification to elected conventions in each of the states. But, by 1897, the device of state conventions had been dropped, and a direct vote of the people would be taken. Who, then, were the people?

The term used in section 128 of the Constitution is 'electors' rather than 'people'.[42] This might seem straightforwardly to settle the question of definition. There was a problem, however, and delegates at the second Federal Convention were exercised in pursuit of its resolution. 'How are you to reckon the people of the States?', asked Neil Lewis. 'Is it to be on a population basis, men, women and children?'[43] But if you confined your reckoning to electors, the national picture was uneven. South Australian women had the vote, and 'the double voting power in that colony', said Deakin, 'would be certainly unfair to the remaining

States'. Perhaps, some suggested, different coloured ballot papers or different ballot boxes for men and women might be employed (effectively in order to eliminate the women's vote without preventing them from voting in the first place), but were polling officials to be expected to ask whether a voter was or was not a man?[44] The Convention settled this dilemma by agreeing to Frederick Holder's proposal to halve the votes in colonies where the female suffrage existed, until the franchise was uniform throughout the Commonwealth.[45]

But, this was not the only problem. In the days before compulsory voting, the prospect existed (at least in the minds of delegates) that a large state, where voters did not turn out in number at a referendum, could on its own defeat a proposal, since the numbers in the Commonwealth might for this reason alone fall short of a majority. The problem hinged on the difference between the people and the electors: 'you are not getting a majority of the people, only a majority of those who vote—a quarter of the people may vote', said Josiah Symon. 'What is the objection to taking the total population of the States?', asked William Trenwith.[46] The objection, it seemed, was that the smaller states together could override the larger ones, just as the abstention of the voters in one large state might do.

Despite an apparently simple resolution at first, the problem of the South Australian women would not go away either, and while everyone seemed to agree that their state should not have a double numerical advantage, Premier Charles Kingston pointed out that South Australia was making sacrifices for the sake of the other states. It was the final substantive debate at the Adelaide session of the Convention. For a moment it appeared that a count of the women's vote would be defended. 'They sacrifice their women', said Trenwith, and Henry Higgins added that 'Anyone in favour of woman suffrage would support an inducement to put themselves on an equality with South Australia'.[47] But it was too late, and too little political will seems to have been left to carry this thinking through. Although Kingston continued to protest a little, pointing out that the Yes and the No votes of extra voters would effectively cancel each other out, Holder's proposal for halving the vote was accepted as 'a rough and ready way of dealing with the difficulty which we ought to accept'. The problems associated with counting the people seem to have exhausted any further ingenuity on the delegates' part. The tone of weariness was only lifted with the Chairman's motion that he 'report the [Constitution] Bill with amendments. (Loud cheers)'.

But section 128 was far from finally resolved. It came up again in the third session of the Convention, at Melbourne, this time with more energy, but with less concern about who the people were and more focus on the justification for resorting to the people. In the attempt to

150   *To Constitute a Nation*

marry the Westminster Parliamentary system (with its emphasis on government in the Lower House) and the American Federal system (in which powers of the two Houses are effectively equal, and sovereignty is dispersed), it was crucial to resolve the matter of a potential deadlock over a Bill between the Houses. Recourse to a referendum in order to break the deadlock had been raised and rejected. In a debate that concentrated on the question of whether there should be a dissolution of both Houses following a deadlock or just of the House of Representatives, the referendum was again proposed (as its supporters made clear) as an alternative to a double dissolution. If a double dissolution could not be won the referendum might be used to counter-balance equal state representation in the Senate.

There was relatively little attention paid to the concept of the referendum itself, with South Australia's Sir John Downer almost alone protesting against it in principle. The referendum was, he said, 'a return to barbarism', to 'the haunts of our early ancestors with very little on, and mostly under trees'. 'The people we hear so much about', he added more soberly, were not good judges on complex political matters, 'and there could be no more miserably inefficient means of deciding the truth than to appeal to them on subjects which involve, not one question but thousands'.[48] But even Downer, despite the alarming image he evoked, agreed that he would 'submit' to the deadlock referendum if it were necessary in order to accomplish Federation.

Later, still in Melbourne, Downer was joined by Bernhard Wise who launched a passionate and almost equally colourful attack on the introduction 'in any form whatever of this pernicious principle'. The British model, Wise insisted, was 'altogether incompatible with that power of direct legislation which is the essence of the referendum'. The people were a 'vague and immaterial mass', and the referendum a 'subtle poison, which before long will destroy the vitality of Parliament'.[49]

But, for the Constitution Bill's ratification and for future constitutional amendment, the referendum was largely accepted without protest. William Trenwith, speaking with a tone of sarcasm, alone noted something of a contradiction in having the referendum for amendment, but opposing it for resolving deadlocks on ordinary legislation, since, 'when parliamentary government has exercised all its ingenuity on a proposed alteration of the Constitution, then the masses—the ill-informed ignorant people—are to be asked to say if they will agree to the proposal'.[50] In an earlier debate, which focused on the question of whether a referendum should be allowed when one House alone had passed a proposal for constitutional change, Isaac Isaacs emphasised that this

> did not raise the much-debated question whether it is right or wrong to refer to the final determination of the people the decisions of their Legislature as to

amendments of the Constitution. That position is conceded on all hands. It is agreed already, by the wording of the clause and by its spirit, that although the trusted representatives of the people in both Houses agree . . . to a proposed law for the alteration of the Constitution, yet notwithstanding that, and notwithstanding all the benefits of representative government, the proposed law in such a case shall not receive any validity until it has been sanctioned by the people who are behind the Legislature.[51]

'Then what is the use of having a Parliament'?, asked Sir William Zeal. 'Not much sometimes', said Isaacs, 'and it is worse than useless if they stand in the way of the will of the people'. Arguing that it should be possible to hold a referendum even where one House *opposed* constitutional alteration, Isaacs declared that this 'is no attempt to gain, by a mass vote, any change of the Constitution to the detriment of the states. The only point of difference between us is—Shall the people be consulted only when the Houses agree, or in precisely the same way when the Houses disagree?'.[52] Isaacs emphatically raised his particular fear that Australia's Constitution might be virtually unchangeable, as America's was, and while 'We may make mistakes in other parts; this is our means of correcting those mistakes'. He went on,

> I only ask in the interests of the whole Federation, for some outlet for ill-feeling that might otherwise arise . . . for some ultimate means of preventing catastrophe. I only ask those honorable members who say 'Trust the Federal Parliament' to go further and meet the inevitable by trusting the people who are behind the Federal Parliament. Let us trust the people whose interests are all in all to us, who have to pay the taxes, whose life, whose liberty, and whose property are at stake.[53]

Sir John Downer (who at this stage had not yet associated the referendum with 'savages') suggested that Isaacs was assuming 'that the Houses of Parliament will not represent the people':

> I look upon this proposition, that on a vote of either House the voice of the people shall be taken immediately and directly, as an absolute invasion of the first principles on which this Federation is established. Of course, the people's voice will rule . . . The people it is who elect the Senate; the people it is who elect the House of Representatives, but they are not the same people; that is to say, they have a different basis of representation . . . the very theory with which we require two Houses, with different terms of office, [is for them] to be a check on each other, and to prevent the voice of the people, which, in the long run, must rule, not of necessity ruling too quickly.[54]

Patrick Glynn also objected that the referendum 'undermines the principle of representative government' and put it 'that Mr Isaacs wishes to refer matters of great complexity and difficulty to the uninstructed wisdom of the populace in all cases, although many of the matters . . . would be amendments of the Constitution involving far-reaching consequences'.[55] Glynn suggested as an alternative that amendment might be effected instead by parliament, voting with specified strict majorities, but 'without any reference to the people'. He did not mind the referendum for ratifying the Constitution in the first place, but objected that the principle of representative government—which he referred to as the result of 'the wisdom of centuries, operated upon by the law of the survival of the fittest'—would be undermined by the referendum for constitutional amendment.

Glynn was, by this stage, certainly in a minority. Isaacs in response used the ultimate trump card of political debate of the time, assuring the delegates that the proposal had in fact the stamp of Britishness, that 'a sure shifting of power from the Parliament to the people' was an irresistible tendency in Britain itself. The Australians, he added, 'should not be afraid, as a learned writer has said, to tear a parchment more or less in the interests of the people'.[56] Isaacs too was in a minority in taking the principle so far, but other delegates were satisfied that no threat existed, so long as a referendum proposal was first passed through the parliament, in Dr Cockburn's words, 'after due enlightenment of the people by means of a discussion in Parliament'.[57]

Throughout the Convention members freely and readily declared in their arguments that acceptance or rejection of this or that particular measure would mean that the people would be inclined or disinclined to accept the Constitution. The referendum clause, Bernhard Wise (who in the debate on deadlocks might appear to have represented altogether the opposing view) pointed out, 'is an affirmance of the principle that the people have the right, by a direct vote, to determine what shall be the limits of representative government under the Constitution. They are the only persons who can say under what Constitution they will live'.[58]

The people had become the legitimating force behind Federation. Through the Corowa Plan and the concept captured at the Bathurst People's Federal Convention, through election of delegates and the referendum process for ratifying the Constitution, and now for amending it, the people were recognised, or deferred to as the sovereign agent. Acting through their representatives in parliament was not enough.

After the loss in the 1898 referendum, when a New South Wales vote of 71 412 was defeated by 65 954 voices because the statutory minimum of 80 000 decided for this referendum by the New South Wales Parliament had not been reached, some suggested that the act of voting itself was not enough, that 'the people' must mean, literally, the majority of heads. 'If democracy means anything at all', said the Australasian

Review of Reviews, 'or if in Australian politics the popular will is the final argument, the Bill is carried, and Australian Federation is assured. But this is not the case'.[59] The case made by later historians, that the Constitution Bill was not carried by 'the people' because the percentage of Yes votes in a number of colonies did not represent an absolute majority of all eligible voters, suggests a similar view.

The pattern of the 1898 referendum (with voting non-compulsory) was one of relatively low voter turnout, providing an overall positive result. In no colony did more than 50 per cent of those eligible cast a vote. Majorities in favour among those who did were, however, substantial in Tasmania, Victoria and South Australia, but narrow in New South Wales, insufficient to be counted as a statutory Yes.[60] In 1899, turnout increased dramatically in almost all colonies, and Queensland joined in, although adding only a slim majority (38 488 for, to 30 996 against) to the picture. West Australians, on the other hand, recorded a significant majority (44 800 to 19 691) when their colony got around to its referendum in 1900.

But, despite the 'overwhelming majority' across the country, 'it is easy to over-estimate the popular interest in federation', L. F. Crisp has argued, placing much greater emphasis on the voter turnout (60 per cent overall, in 1899, and around 45 per cent in 1898) than on the Yes votes.[61] W. G. McMinn concludes that in 1898, 'the vision of a nation for a continent had seized the imaginations of no more than about a quarter of the people of New South Wales and South Australia, and less than 40 per cent of those even of Victoria', and even in 1899 the rate of voter abstention could only mean 'that a considerable majority of the people remained deeply sceptical' in New South Wales, and opponents in the other colonies had given up.[62]

But which is more significant: the rate of turnout, or the rate of approval? By which should the people be measured? It is impossible to know now why individuals failed to vote.[63] Any number of explanations, some mutually incompatible, may be advanced: difficulties attached to voting (such as the need to take out a special elector's right); apathy; hostility; complacency; even acceptance or approval. But to claim that Federation was a popular movement is not the same as to claim it was a mass movement. The vast majority of governments elected in Australia, even since the introduction of compulsory voting, could not claim such popularity. But there are other ways of being 'popular'.

Federation was, by the second half of the 1890s, a popular process, to begin with because its formal procedures (the election of Convention delegates, and the referendums) were now to be conducted according to a mechanism which *required* popular involvement. Neither the British authorities nor the colonial parliaments could proceed without the

154   *To Constitute a Nation*

approval of the voters. Seeking that approval demanded and generated public participation: public meetings, petitions, press commentary. The decision of some key urban newspapers greatly to increase their print-run at the time of the referendums is an indicator of the level of public involvement, as were the great crowds gathered outside the newspaper offices waiting for the referendum results to come in. Federation was also popular by being 'in the air', a matter on which almost everyone had an opinion, something discussed popularly, even if individuals were not mobilised or actively politicised by it. As we have seen, the imagined nation generated much poetry and commentary; even in a journal otherwise almost totally silent on the subject, we read in 1899 that at 'the present time one hears of scarcely anything but Federation'.[64]

However they were counted, the people had become the body which alone could contract to form a nation, the body to which politicians, whether sincere or not, had at least to appear to defer. The concept, while it did not have the scope it would later assume, was none the less sincerely promoted. It was well and truly in circulation in the political culture of the time, partly because of growing claims of hitherto non-enfranchised groups (working men and women) to participate fully as citizens, and partly because of the emergence of political actors and agents (seen in the rise of big party politics soon after Federation) beyond individuals. No doubt other factors played a part, including the technologies that were beginning at that time to facilitate communication between people on a mass scale, allowing them to become familiar with communities beyond their local or provincial sphere. The concept of the people resulted not only in the employment of mechanisms for ratifying and amending the Constitution, but also in a general democratisation of its provisions (like directly electing the Senate and ruling out plural voting) beforehand, in part on the grounds that the people would not be disposed to accept the Bill otherwise.

But the concept did not entail a notion of the people as the originating force. The power of Initiative (now known as the Citizen Initiated Referendum) in constitutional change, while it was recognised in the otherwise almost consistently favourable Swiss example, was not to be granted. Tasmania's Henry Dobson, for example, objected that allowing the referendum when a proposal had passed only through one House would be 'giving us a popular initiative' when, on many matters, the question

> is not ripe to be submitted to the foremost men of their colony . . . The people of Victoria, like the people of New Zealand, are engaged in experiments in reference to factory and social legislation, and it will be monstrous that, the moment disagreement arises between the two Houses of Parliament, we

should provide that they must go back to the people to make up their minds about the question at issue, when even the more intelligent men in Parliament have not been able to do so.[65]

But no one seriously proposed that the Initiative should be part of the Constitution, nor did the people themselves demand it. Their demand, embedded in the culture of the period, was to be consulted, to ratify or to veto. Politicians, untrustworthy creatures though they may have been, should none the less get on with the job of forming policy and putting structure to the expression of desire for change.

The overriding reason for this was that the people, in addition to being adjudicators in the last instance, were not just one people. 'The people it is who elect the Senate; the people it is who elect the House of Representatives, but they are not the same people', Sir John Downer had said.[66] Those, like Isaacs and Higgins and Kingston, who argued in favour of a referendum where the Houses disagreed, were assumed (although they denied it) to be asserting the Lower House's rights over the Senate's. This meant, in the context of political debate of the time, the assertion of the principle of a national majority over that of states' rights. The lines along which delegates divided on this issue meant the difference between seeing Federation essentially as the creation of a nation, and seeing it as the assemblage of pre-existing states. The majority saw it as a bit of both, and many could not decide which one they wanted most.

To devise a referendum, where votes were counted both in terms of majorities of the states and majorities of the whole, allowed for the dual imperatives of the people as Australians and the people as members of a state to be satisfied. At least one could specify what 'the people' would be doing. But, when it came to a deeper conceptual approach to the question of who the people were, the result was, for almost all parties, confusion. The paradoxes and ambiguities in what Federalists were trying to achieve were expressed nowhere more clearly than in the debate over the meaning of 'citizenship'.

CHAPTER NINE

Citizens

Section 117 of the Australian Constitution now reads:

A subject of the Queen, resident in any State, shall not be subject in any other State to any disability or discrimination which would not be equally applicable to him if he were a subject of the Queen resident in such other State.

But the section once contained the word 'citizen' and behind this otherwise bland final wording lies a long and tortured debate over the use of that term.

At the time of Federation Australian citizenship was not a matter of law. Legally, Australians—either native-born or naturalised—were British subjects and they remained subjects after Federation (indeed, until 1949). A person became a subject simply by being born 'within the King's allegiance', in any of the British colonies or dominions. Subject status was, furthermore (until the First World War), inalienable, like having a particular set of parents whom one can never give up or lose.

Prior to 1901, naturalisation of foreign residents as subjects was performed by the individual colonies, according to their individual Naturalisation Acts. In contrast to birth, subject status by naturalisation was alienable. It was, importantly, not 'portable'. Like snow carried down from a mountain to sea level, it melted away when naturalised persons left their home colony. In a case in 1888 in Sydney, for example, where a Chinese man, naturalised as a subject in Victoria, attempted to leave his boat without paying the Chinese poll tax, the New South Wales Court held against his claim for a writ (absolute) of habeas corpus that, 'letters of naturalization issued in a colony have no extra-territorial validity'.[1]

But the loss of subject status meant little, in fact, for naturalised white subjects, since, as it was not a requirement to carry identity papers, officials would not necessarily recognise a traveller as a likely alien. It is striking to read in the very same debate in which South Australia passed its Coloured Immigration Restriction Act in 1896, that the question of

156

whether the Member of Parliament King O'Malley was a Canadian or an American was speculated upon, with much irony and ambiguity, including by O'Malley himself, there in the very Chamber.[2] No one demanded to know, as a corollary, whether Mr O'Malley was a naturalised subject, and whether his rights to travel as a subject, indeed his right to be a member of parliament, were implicated.

Chinese people, on the other hand, needed to carry papers in anticipation of being harassed by officials who were likely, in recognising them as different, to want to know their status. This applied in practice not just to certificates of naturalisation, but even where British subject status was held by birth. The New South Wales Chinese Influx Restriction Act of 1881, for example, specified that a certificate of the Governor of a British colony or that of a British consul would serve as sufficient evidence of British subject status. If they wished to avoid paying the poll tax or being subject to the restrictions placed on numbers of Chinese allowed to enter per tonnage of ships, the Chinese British subjects needed their papers.

The main provisions of the colonial law around the time of Federation were drawn from the British Naturalisation Act of 1870, which the Australian colonies copied, at least in principle. The status of aliens—all those, in British law, born outside Britain and its dominions—also came under naturalisation law. Among other things the British Act had introduced a much greater liberalisation of property rights for aliens.[3] But several matters, as might be anticipated, complicated the issue for the Australian colonies feeling their way towards nationhood. In respect of certain types of alien, even of certain types of subject, the Australians, as we have seen, desired greater restriction rather than greater liberalisation of rights. The imperative for a distinctive Australian approach and for national uniformity linked both the desire to restrict 'citizenship' and the desire to have a citizenship in common.

But 'citizenship' was something beyond legal definition. Despite the desire for uniform national naturalisation law (one of the secondary issues of Federation), the concept of citizenship was only indirectly related to the issue of naturalisation policy. Powers over 'naturalization and aliens' (as found in the American and Canadian Constitutions) were included on the list of Commonwealth powers, at section 51 (xix), without debate. But defining Australian citizens (if there were to be such a thing) would prove a much more complex, and ultimately impossible task. A citizen would be a type of person found within the larger category of British subject, but having extra characteristics or qualifications. None of the Constitution's framers, however, could say precisely what these qualifications and their limitations should be—what it meant to be a citizen—although they tried at length.

158   *To Constitute a Nation*

In a simple, formal sense, the term 'citizen' was not employed in a monarchy. Citizens were the members of a republic. Since Australia remained a monarchy at Federation, Australians remained subjects. But, informally, the term citizen had been used loosely and widely in the pre-Federation years. Sometimes it referred to people in an active civic role, in, for example, accounts of public meetings, where it was common for participants to be referred to as citizens. At other times the term was used positively or assertively, as an act of declaration, by persons claiming a right or claiming recognition: for example, in their campaign for the suffrage, women (who were, legally, subjects) argued for the right to vote on the grounds that they were 'patriotic, and law-abiding citizens'. They argued for the vote, not in order to become citizens, but because they already were citizens. By this they meant, and they pointed this out, that they were already making a civic contribution, 'taking an equal part in the religious and moral development of the people, and doing more than half of the educational, charitable and philanthropic work of society as at present constituted'.[4]

The political rights we most readily associate now with citizenship were, in this rhetoric, not what defined a citizen but what followed from being a citizen. Although nothing strictly speaking changed with Federation—except that (white) women gained the vote for Commonwealth elections, thus completing the formal political entitlements of citizenship at the national level—there was an attempt to make sense of what it meant now to be a member of the new Commonwealth, a national citizen, as well as a member of an individual state and a member of the Empire.

In the second Convention, Dr Quick, for whom the concept of an Australian people was a central factor in federating, argued vehemently that the new status of Australians as members of the one nation needed to have constitutional recognition. He moved, at the Melbourne session in 1898, that 'citizen' should be defined in the Constitution, or, if this were not agreed to, that a new Commonwealth head of power over citizenship should be included in what is now section 51. But, for reasons both varied and complicated, he failed ultimately to see either achieved.

Throughout the long, tortuous debate on these motions (which resulted eventually in section 117), the delegates, most of whom were not hostile at all to the idea as such, attempted a series of definitions of the citizen. Edmund Barton began: 'I take it that a citizen is either a natural-born or a naturalized person possessing the ordinary political privileges of the Commonwealth or of a state'.[5] Then Sir John Forrest immediately articulated the concern that would remain the major stumbling-block throughout: that 'coloured persons who have become British subjects' might in this definition be considered citizens. A concept of citizenship should not be allowed to rule out discriminatory legislation against, in particular, the Chinese.

In Western Australia at that time, Forrest told the Convention, 'an alien can hold land in just the same way as he could if he were a British subject . . . and he would probably think himself a citizen, whatever nationality he belonged to'. Isaac Isaacs joined Forrest in emphasising that Chinese residents should not be allowed to think of themselves as citizens, as had happened in America where in one case, a 'Chinaman' had successfully sued for the same right to hold a laundry licence as a white man.

Richard O'Connor then suggested a definition: 'Surely every person who has the suffrage . . . within the Commonwealth—and who lives within the Commonwealth, is a citizen of the Commonwealth'. All citizens, he added, should 'have the guarantee of liberty and safety in regard to the processes of law . . . whatever their colour'.[6] 'We want to go further than that', said Mr Isaacs, to provide that citizens—'by virtue of their citizenship'—would be entitled to common privileges and immunities: 'In other words, there is to be an equal citizenship'.[7]

But, the whole purpose of this Constitution, objected Josiah Symon shortly after, 'is to secure a dual citizenship': states, he said, must be free to impose whatever conditions or disabilities they thought fit. What was necessary was to ensure that 'an alien, not admitted to the citizenship here' would not be given the same privileges and immunities as a citizen. Then, his Premier, Charles Kingston, added: 'I say we are creating a Commonwealth in which I hope there will be federal citizenship, and I shall be glad indeed to see the powers of the Federal Parliament enlarged to enable that body to legislate, not only with reference to . . . aliens, but also with reference to the rights and privileges of federal citizenship'. He was followed by 'an Honourable Member' with what became a plaintive refrain: 'What is the meaning of citizenship?'.[8]

With no progress on the question of definition, Dr Quick reactivated the question almost three weeks later: 'We are creating a new political organisation, entirely different from that of the states and from that of the even wider political organisation—the empire'. The Constitution would be incomplete without a provision for Commonwealth citizenship.[9] He was himself inclined, he said, towards a definition 'to the effect that all persons resident in the Commonwealth, being natural-born or naturalized subjects of the Queen, and not under any disability imposed by the Federal Parliament, should be citizens of the Commonwealth'. It was, he felt, a definition that would capture their opposition to 'all races, black or white, or aliens, [being] considered members of this new political community'.

Tasmania's Henry Dobson tried to return to the simplest definition: 'Would not every voter be a citizen?'. 'Exactly', replied Mr O'Connor, 'there are no other rights I know of as yet'. Some days later, however,

Mr Symon pointed out that while some thought that making people citizens of the Commonwealth meant conferring the franchise on them, we 'are doing nothing of the kind. [We are] merely giving the persons resident in the Commonwealth . . . the rights of free men'. The expression 'citizen' does not mean only persons exercising the franchise, he added: 'it includes infants and lunatics, if you like. Every one who is recognised as an inhabitant, and is under the laws, is a citizen. Women in most of the colonies except South Australia do not exercise the franchise, but no one can say that they are not citizens'.[10]

For a while longer, the members tried out the idea that citizenship might mean equal access to the protection of the law. Equal protection of all citizens was imperative, Mr Kingston insisted, otherwise inequalities would undermine the democratic culture of the new nation. But this approach failed to convince, partly because no one could think of a case where this might be disputed, except for coloured persons for whom many (if not all) did not want equal protection in the first place.

But to make citizenship too narrow also had problems: 'It would be simply monstrous', said Kingston, 'that those who are born in England should in any way be subjected to the slightest disabilities . . . but, on the other hand, we must not forget that there are other native-born British subjects whom we are far from desiring to see come here in any considerable numbers'. Gradually, then, the debate turned away from definition and onto the addition of a Commonwealth power as an alternative. Supporting this approach, Mr Higgins told fellow delegates not to 'jump before we come to the stile': 'We can leave citizenship to be settled afterwards by the Federal Parliament'.

But, if the term was to be used at all, the need for a definition could not be avoided. O'Connor, for example, pointed out that Quick's proposal was to give power in regard 'to a matter which is not mentioned [in] the Constitution. The word "citizen" is not used from beginning to end in this Constitution, and it is now proposed to give power to legislate regarding citizenship . . . when we really do not know at present what is meant by a citizen'.

A small digression is necessary here: Mr O'Connor was mistaken. The term citizen does appear in the Constitution and had been there since 1891. In what is now section 44 (i), 'a subject or a citizen of a foreign power' is listed among the types of person ineligible to stand for parliament. This whole section came dramatically into the public eye in 1992, with a High Court ruling against three of the candidates (including the successful one) in a by-election in Melbourne for a House of Representatives seat.[11] Two of the unsuccessful candidates held dual Australian–European nationality and were deemed thus to be 'citizens of a foreign power', ineligible to stand.

In their lengthy reflection on classical forms of citizenship, Quick and Garran explain that the term was used in this section simply to describe non-subjects, since citizen was what people were called in a republic. In the course of the brief Adelaide Convention debate, it appears clear that the delegates' main concern, for which this section was a remedy, was the possibility of divided loyalties among members of parliament in time of war. 'A man', said Edmund Barton, 'might have to go out of our Parliament to serve against us'. Then Joseph Carruthers from New South Wales evoked the spectre of the recent Anglo-Japanese treaty, whereby a British subject travelling in Japan enjoyed 'practically the same rights and privileges as he would enjoy as a citizen of his own country'. The Convention had to be sure that this section did not apply in such a case: 'Our Members of Parliament who are hard-working take their summer trips, and it may be that some of them may come back and find they have lost their seats as a result of this clause'.[12] The delegates concluded that there was little danger, and that the section would apply, it seems, only to cases where a person actively asserted or declared his loyalty to a 'foreign power'. The use of the term citizen meant little here for Australian citizenship, so little indeed that O'Connor had forgotten its inclusion less than a year later.

In Melbourne, debating Quick's motion, doubts were finally raised about using the term at all and these would quickly prove decisive, although Quick protested to the last. 'We have provided in this Constitution for the exercise of the rights of citizenship, so far as the choice of representatives is concerned', Mr Barton said, 'and we have given various safeguards to individual liberty in the Constitution'. 'Each citizen of the state is a Commonwealth citizen', he went on, 'if there is such a term as citizenship to be applied to a subject of the empire. I must admit, after looking at a standard authority—Stroud's Judicial Dictionary—that I cannot find any definition of citizenship as applied to a British subject'.

'We are subjects in our constitutional relations to the empire', concluded Barton (who did not seem to have noticed that 'subject' is not listed in Stroud either[13]), not citizens. Why not use the term subject? It would be 'far better not to import the term "citizen" here if we can deal with it by a term well known in the constitutional relations of the empire between the Queen and her subjects'.[14] As the feeling of the Convention now moved away from attempting a definition, O'Connor declared that 'All we mean now is a member of the community or of the nation, and the accurate description of a member of the community under our circumstances is "a subject of the Queen resident within the Commonwealth"'. They settled, at last, for 'subject'.

The debate (of which the above is merely a small précis) had been divided essentially between those wanting a simple pragmatic, legal

162   *To Constitute a Nation*

approach, and those with a vision of a national identity, a shared allegiance to a national community, captured in an idea of national citizenship. If anything at all was agreed and inscribed in the final formula for this section, it was that Australians were to have 'dual citizenship', to be both members of a state and members of the nation at the same time, but at neither level would the term lend itself to definition.

If there was to be no definition of citizen, might the Constitution include instead a list of inalienable citizen rights? A major constraint to such an approach lay in the general reserve about directly including policy in the Constitution, instead of powers subsequently to enact policy. Specifically, the British legal tradition (in which in fact the ideas of freedom and 'fair play', far from being overlooked, were thought central) largely relied upon the common law, rather than statute or constitutional provision to define and protect individual rights and liberties. This approach was adopted for the most part by the Australians in constitution-making. It explains in large degree the shortage (as it is now perceived) of explicit statements of ideals and guarantees of rights, and of descriptions of essential human or national attributes.

Granting a government the power to make laws in respect of a range of matters, as in the Australian Constitution, does not sound especially permanent or inspirational. Even the great scholar of the Constitution's history, J. A. La Nauze, wrote of the 'anaemic' wording of section 117, in contrast to 'the resounding phrases of the Fourteenth Amendment' of the United States Constitution.[15] In the beginning of the debate on what became section 117 it was suggested in fact that the section should be directly modelled on the Fourteenth Amendment. But the Fourteenth Amendment 'protects Chinamen, too, I suppose, as well as negroes?', asked Mr Higgins. If so, added Mr Isaacs, Victoria's discriminatory factory legislation would be void. How, then, could the members 'expect to get for this Constitution the support of the workers?'.[16]

But there was an additional, more persuasive argument for leaving out a positive protection of rights. Opposing the inclusion in the Constitution of a provision prohibiting the deprivation of rights without due legal process, Dr Cockburn insisted that such deprivation was simply unthinkable. Its inclusion would be a 'reflection on our civilization', as if it were necessary to have a written provision in order to prevent injustice. Such a thing was, he added, only 'necessary in a savage race'.[17]

For all this, freedoms and rights are not altogether absent from the final Constitution. In his 'Message to the Australian People' on the day of the Commonwealth's Inauguration, Edmund Barton, the freshly anointed first Prime Minister, described what he considered to be 'the main principle of the Commonwealth' expressed in its Constitution: 'Its representation in one House bespeaks justice to the individual; its

Citizens 163

representation in the other bespeaks equal justice to each State. It will, and must be, the aim of the Government of the Commonwealth to give complete effect to both those principles'.[18]

The people, as citizens of their states, had gained certain things and had imagined even more in agreeing to federate. But what did the individual gain? While in the future High Court judgments[19] may open up this field, it is unusual to regard the Constitution as addressing the individual at all. Where did 'justice to the individual' lie? What, if any, rights and freedoms were offered as part of a national citizenship?

By the conclusion of the 1890s, it was common to emphasise the free character of the Federation processes and the freedoms built into the Constitution. In contrast to America, Dr Quick said in his Inauguration message on 1 January 1901, where British parliamentary corruption and royal madness had forced its people into independence, the Australian people, in 'times of peace, without pressure or coercion . . . of their own free will and through their own chosen representatives, whose work they ratified, have settled the terms of their constitutional partnership and entered into an indissoluble union under the Crown'.[20] The *Sydney Morning Herald* spoke of a 'nation dawning of its own volition—riding free on a foundation of freedom, not adopting a constitution under any form or semblance, coercion or suspicion of actual threatening danger'.[21]

It is difficult now to imagine what people meant in 1901 when they spoke of freedom in these terms. For the most part, they referred broadly to the democratic character of the Constitution, which provides for direct election of representatives for both Houses, rules out plural voting, requires popular approval for amendment. At that time, no other constitution in the world was as 'free'. But in the abstract, 'freedom' is such a slippery concept that no one can say with confidence exactly what it amounts to, and the dominant notions of freedom become immediately dated, even unrecognisable, the moment they cease to circulate. If other freedoms and rights are indicated in the Constitution, they must be read through the eyes of the past, in places in between the lines, since a precise, separate statement of such things is not there.

For Australians in the midst of the construction of new institutions, abstract statements of rights were, it seems, a distraction. In 1895, recognising this, the first issue of the Victorian Social Democratic journal, the *Champion*, announced that the journal would give expression to the 'great deal of loose democratic sentiment floating in this community', but would not indulge in 'windy disquisitions upon the Rights of Man'. Papers that contain 'that kind of thing', it added, 'are not read'.[22]

The rights and freedoms of the 1890s lived in a conceptual universe that was both familiar and different from the one we know one hundred years later. We are used to the view that the Constitution is virtually silent

164   *To Constitute a Nation*

on such matters, even, in the eyes of some, wilfully neglectful. The unhappy petitioner from Kyneton, who appealed to the 1897 Convention in the hope that they would include in the Constitution 'some means of preventing conspiracies, perjuries, vindictive and malicious persecutions for private vendettas by the Police', must in his disappointment have shared this view. Still there are several ways in which freedom is expressed in the Constitution.

Two sections directly use the word 'free'. The first, section 92, guarantees that 'trade, commerce, and intercourse among the States . . . shall be absolutely free'. The intercolonial tariff question, which this section was designed to solve, has such a routine, even tedious place in accounts of Federation, that it is difficult to see it as anything other than a predictable, colourless guarantee. How can 'absolutely free' trade between the states arouse emotion?

It is especially hard to appreciate this section if we think of rights and freedoms only in terms of individuals. The guarantee of absolute freedom appears exclusively to be made to the states, and even more precisely to concern the free movement of capital. But the problem for which section 92 was formulated also entailed a more recognisable form of individual freedom, the freedom of movement. The customs houses on state borders were the major immediate experience of the absence of nationhood for many people before Federation. Being stopped at the border and subjected to questioning, and even the search of a person's luggage, was both inconvenient and alienating. Interstate travellers, Victoria's Premier James Patterson told his audience at the Corowa Conference in 1893, were treated like smugglers or foreigners, 'liable to be stuck up by policemen or customs officers',[23] rather than welcomed as members of a shared national community. This was not just an irritation for the leisurely tourist: simply crossing a bridge over the Murray River, or seeking one's fortunes in the West Australian goldfields, or droving stock over the Queensland–Northern Territory border, might subject the traveller to a search or the payment of duty.

In some cases, the customs houses were used to harass literal aliens, as we have seen, such as the Chinese residents of New South Wales who hoped that Federation would allow them to move and trade freely without such humiliations. Seen in this light, section 92 offered more to personal freedom than might be imagined. At times, Federalists even had to remind each other in respect of such hopes that Federation was not only 'a matter of sentiment'; it was also 'a matter of money', an 'indispensable means to the attainment of freedom of trade within the colonies'.[24]

Section 92 was of course primarily concerned with trade, rather than individual movement. But, in the dominant political culture of the time, freedom of trade itself was regarded as a genuine freedom. Although

Citizens   165

socialist ideas were evolving, the commitment to socialisation or nationalisation of industry had not yet become central to the labour party programmes in either Britain or Australia. While Marxist theory was finding expression in the programmes of socialist leagues, the major labour parties did not adopt a socialisation policy until after the First World War, in the case of the Australian Labor Party, 1921. Australian labour demands at the turn of the century were principally directed towards a combination of industrial regulation (which was largely gained in section 51 (xxxv) of the Constitution), protection of 'white' wages, and protection of Australian industry against cheap imports. The latter required internal free trade, and a tariff against the rest of the world. In the popular arguments for interstate free trade, the merging of economic argument with argument about the quality of life of individuals and families appears.

Except in industries dependent upon localised protection, section 92 was especially thought to promise improved wages and lower prices in formerly protectionist states. In addition, it proffered greater freedom of movement among workers looking for employment. It would help women specifically ('they are the real heads' of households), some argued, in making the housekeeping cheaper: 'Federation will by degree . . . cheapen all articles of food and other necessaries'. Fruit, for example, 'so necessary to health in this trying climate, is above the reach of all who are not well off. This is made so because . . . a heavy duty is imposed so as to keep fruit from coming in from other colonies'.[25] It would also, many thought, assist the employers, who would pay less for their primary material. Many individuals made a very personal reading of this section and believed (whether mistakenly or not) that the guarantee of absolute freedom of trade contained within it an enhanced freedom and well-being for themselves personally.

Those who argued against the financial provisions of the Constitution focused very little on the principle of free trade as such, and a great deal on the formula (called by its opponents the 'Braddon Blot') whereby the surplus of revenue collected by the Commonwealth would be redistributed, one which, on all calculations, would find the large colonies effectively subsidising the small. It is not, said one New South Wales anti-Billite, 'in human nature to consent to a surrender of its own interests'.[26] Such opponents saw themselves getting a particularly unfavourable deal out of the federal agreement; ultimately they failed, however, to convince the majority that the likelihood of loss was greater than the likelihood of gain.

A second way in which freedom is captured directly in the Constitution is in section 116 which prohibits the Commonwealth from making 'any law for establishing any religion, or for imposing any

166   *To Constitute a Nation*

religious observance, or for prohibiting the free exercise of any religion', or imposing a religious test for Commonwealth public office. This section must be read with an awareness of the reference in the Constitution's Preamble (discussed in chapter eleven) to 'Almighty God'. To the dismay of some who believed that 'righteousness exalteth the nation', God's blessing, and not His agreement, was 'humbly' sought. The Constitution's framers had taken pains to guarantee the Australian people's freedom from having to ask for God's agreement.

Section 116 is easier to appreciate now as an expression of freedom and rights than is section 92, since it addresses the rights of individual conscience. The Constitution guarantees freedom of religion against the Commonwealth, but the states remained constitutionally free to regulate religious observance, to establish a religion or require a religious test for state public office, as they chose. Although the 1891 draft of the Constitution included such a prohibition specifically upon the state parliaments, even Quick and Garran, with their extraordinary combination of direct experience and capacity to find a positive explanation for almost everything in the Constitution, found it 'difficult to conjecture' how such a clause 'crept in' to the Bill. It was immediately abandoned in the second Convention (although its legacy remains in the anomalous retention of section 116 in the chapter called 'The States'). The states' right to legislate freely on religion was preferred to the 'human' right of free conscience and worship.

None the less, the framers must have had something in mind that went further than simply the division of jurisdictions in a Federation. They might have said nothing at all on the matter. The technical reasons for the reappearance of section 116 in the Constitution can be stated fairly briefly. During the 1897 Convention delegates were effectively inundated with petitions from Church organisations and religious communities in which the recognition of God in the Constitution was demanded. The petitions, organised nationally (a specially printed form of the petition was circulated), asked for the recognition of God as the supreme ruler of the universe; for the declaration of national prayers and national days of thanksgiving and 'humiliation'. But, the essence of their petition was that the Constitution should include a statement of spiritual—specifically Christian—identity for the new nation.

So persistent were the petitions and private lobbying as well, that it was felt these could not be ignored. Many members of the Convention were themselves observant, and independently supported the principle, anyway. Finding a form of wording to capture this principle without alienating any particular group or sect presented something of a difficulty, but in the end the Constitution's Preamble had the simple words added, 'humbly relying on the blessing of Almighty God'. The *Worker* declared that this had been done to get the support of 'the unthinking goody-goody folk', promoted by hypocritical parsons.[27] But the 'parsons' had not got all they had asked for, and the argument for this particular formulation, and its sequel, is itself of interest in the issue of individual rights and freedom.

Once the Preamble had embraced the Almighty, the question of prohibiting religious tests or religious establishment or restrictions on the free exercise of religion was reactivated. The original prohibition on state parliaments had been dropped, but Victoria's Henry Higgins led the move to reinsert something similar at the Commonwealth level. He persuaded the majority of delegates that the words 'humbly relying on the blessing of Almighty God' would give the Commonwealth the power—by implication—to make laws in regard to the nation's religion. These words would go, he suggested, even further than the American Constitution, which had been defined by the United States Supreme Court as recently as 1892 as establishing a Christian nation.

The American decision had, it appeared, allowed the Congress to make religious laws for the whole of the nation. Higgins hinted that such an intention could be found among the organisers of the Australian petitions: the recognition of the Almighty was not, he argued, 'proposed merely out of reverence', but for 'distinct political purposes', of 'which the signatories should have been informed'.[28] He also warned against the 'recrudescence of religious strife' brought about in the United States, where supporters and opponents of a compulsory sabbath had clashed with each other. Although he was willing to agree to the inclusion of God in the Preamble in order to get the support of a large part of the community for the Constitution, there remained, he insisted, the need for a safeguard and also for reassuring those whose support would be lost by the pious inclusion.

The feelings of the large number of other petitioners who opposed the inclusion of reference to God in the Constitution had also to be weighed up. In Higgins's own colony alone their numbers (including Seventh-day Adventists, alarmed at the prospect of the imposition of Sunday worship) amounted to 38 000. Conceding this, some suggested that the restriction could satisfactorily be limited to prohibiting a religious test for Commonwealth office alone. But, in the end, section 116 went in, more or less as proposed by Higgins, prohibiting not only the religious test, but the making of 'any law for establishing any religion, or for imposing any religious observance, or for prohibiting the free exercise of any religion'. The Christian community was not altogether convinced they had gained a victory in seeing 'Almighty God' merely mentioned in the Preamble, if the disclaimer represented by section 116 was also to be included. But, for the most part, the balance between the two sets of

168   *To Constitute a Nation*

interests and the opposing fears they represented was considered to be a happy one.

This controversy and the processes involved have been discussed in detail in another work.[29] Our concern here is the way freedom was conceptualised, as a clue to understanding its status in the culture of the 1890s. In the first debate on the proposed section, Higgins in fact made a connection between our two types of freedom:

> There is a tendency in these days to interfere more and more with a man's actions in all sorts of directions, to have rules of all kinds with regard to his economical relations. Well, it is not at all clear as to where the line will be drawn. If we interfere with a man's actions in his economical relations, it will be very hard to draw the line and say that he is not bound to act in a certain way with regard to religious observances.[30]

The connection between these freedoms may no longer be immediately obvious. No one challenged it in the Convention debate. But nor did they demand that these be absolute freedoms. Just as the right to free economic activity was to be restricted in the case of coloured people (especially the Chinese), 'repugnant' religious practices would not come under this guarantee of freedom. During the course of Convention debate, Tasmania's Premier, Sir Edward Braddon, suggested an amendment specifying that the state 'shall prevent the performance of any such religious rites as are of a cruel or demoralising character or contrary to the law of the Commonwealth'.[31] He had in mind, he said, cruel, barbarous and murderous practices such as the 'Hindoo' rites of the 'suttee' and the 'curruck'. The delegates were confident that the several existing powers to deal with aliens could be employed against such practices, but they never really explored whether in fact the freedoms guaranteed in section 116 might prevail.

The views of those colonial liberals who drafted the Constitution were, for the most part, representative of the liberal utilitarianism associated with the ideas of John Stuart Mill, adapted over several decades to a particular, Australian setting.[32] They believed that the free pursuit of material happiness should be mixed with the social advancement wrought by public education and the evolution of democratic opportunities and institutions. Conservatives counter-balanced the liberals in numbers, but, lacking a coherent philosophy, most fell back on a blank assertion of states' rights. In doing so, they found themselves at times defending progressive policy. In the area of human rights, the majority, including most conservatives, took the Millsian approach, seeking the restriction of belief and action only in so far as their free expression harmed others.

The tendency, then, was to respect rights and freedoms, to protect them negatively from interference, but not to declare them positively. To write something positively, in a 'resounding' way, is, in any case, not the only way to achieve resounding results, nor does it guarantee such results. Equally important are the matters over which constitutional power was to be exercised. The delegates thought the exercise of many of these powers would achieve inspirational things. Many of the Commonwealth's new powers were unremarkable; some powers (such as arbitration, pensions, divorce, and custody of children thereof, among others) were, if limited, extremely progressive for their time, and held out a promise of a unique national polity. In their closing speeches in the last session of the second Federal Convention, the delegates spoke again and again of such promise and such hope. Even allowing for the florid rhetoric of the age, the sentiment is striking. The Commonwealth, said Josiah Symon,

> will be a union with strong foundations set deep in justice, a union which will endure from age to age, a bulwark against aggression and a perpetual security for the peace, freedom, and progress of the people of Australia, giving to them and to their children and to their children's children through all generations the priceless heritage of a happy and united land.[33]

If the promise was not altogether fulfilled, this tells us nothing more than does the fact that the promises of America's Bill of Rights did not always turn out as hoped. And if we look back now with regret at the absence of resounding and universal sentiments written into Australia's Constitution, it is well to remember that one of the first 'self-evident' principles the delegates would have wanted to inscribe in the Constitution—had this approach been adopted—would have been a white nation.

Outside the Conventions, the idea of freedom and rights, and claims to citizenship circulated freely. Even the delegates allowed themselves to use the term loosely. In his New Year message on 1 January 1901, Alfred Deakin told 'fellow Australians' that they would wake on that day to find themselves 'for the first time in our history the possessors of a common political citizenship'. Sir Samuel Griffith also told the Queensland readers that 'henceforth, every Australian is a citizen of the new-born Commonwealth, itself an integral part of the British Empire'. This is not, he added,

> a mere question of words. When we are dealing with abstract ideas, such as citizenship, liberty, status, or equality, words are not mere counters, but stand for the facts which without them cannot be conceived as existing, and the accurate use of words is in such matters essential to intelligent thought or action.[34]

One might imagine that the delegates who had struggled to reach a definition of citizen, and had given up because its 'accurate use' kept slipping from their grasp, would have read such declarations with scepticism or bemusement. But if Alfred Deakin, that most precise of men, permitted himself such imprecision, the others, too, it is most likely, were happy to fall back on the general, cultural use of the term. Citizens were members of the community whose attributes and comportment gave them the right to claim the title without derision. There were citizens and subjects, there were aliens and people.

A citizen was an individual member of the people, someone who was a political subject, responsible, respectable, sober enough to participate. The citizen could not be defined any more clearly than the people, but there were things that the people could be legally allowed or even required to do. For the time, at least, the people had the upper hand.

CHAPTER TEN

Half the Nation

> Unless Australia is federated in the interest
> of women as well as men, our national life will
> be one-sided, inharmonious and dwarfed.[1]

The majority of women 'believe that the laws for the people should be made according to the voice of all the people (and women are people)', wrote Elizabeth Ward, New South Wales Superintendent of the Woman's Christian Temperance Union's Franchise Department, early in the Federation decade.[2] Later, anticipating the 1897 Convention, Annie Golding, Secretary of the Newtown Branch of the Womanhood Suffrage League, lamented the neglect of women by candidates for the Convention. Some, she said, had mentioned manhood suffrage, but ignored women. Others mentioned the people but only as 'represented by men'. 'Are women of the people?', Golding asked. 'Are they not half the people, and are their claims not to be considered?'[3]

If women were people, where, then, did they fit into a model of participation and legitimation based on an idea of the people? At the time of the 1891 Convention no Australian women had the right to vote and none sat in parliament or occupied positions of formal power. No woman represented the people: except, that is, in the most prominent and notionally powerful position of all.

At the centre of the Empire, as Head of State of Britain and all the colonies, Head of the future Australian nation, stood (or rather, sat) a woman: Queen Victoria. But the paradox, it seems, was not apparent—paradoxically—until women themselves began to campaign in their own right for their right to be counted among the people. Then, they and their male supporters commented regularly on the Monarch's gender and its significance in representing the capacity of all womanhood to play a political role. 'England', said Elizabeth Nicholls, National President of the Woman's Christian Temperance Union, 'has been greatest in the reigns of its queens, and if Victoria may wield imperial power, surely good women less exalted, but equally worthy, may exercise wise and beneficent influence in our Legislative Halls'.[4]

Until the early 1880s, women's organisations do not appear to have existed in the Australian colonies. Women played a significant role in philanthropic and charitable societies, although most of these, up to the

171

172   *To Constitute a Nation*

1880s, were dominated by men. By the 1880s, women in New South Wales had begun to manage, even exclusively run, such societies.[5] In the early years of that decade the WCTU and the first women's suffrage and literary societies were also formed. What was distinctive about these new organisations was that the women themselves initiated and then ran them. The emerging political groups in addition assumed a common interest among women beyond domestic matters, as well as a capacity for informed opinion on social and political issues. By the start of the 1890s, still tentative but growing in legitimacy and respectability, women's groups were recognised sufficiently, at least in New South Wales, for that exemplary citizen, Quong Tart, ever aware of the importance of new social and political movements, to provide a women's meeting room, with magazines and writing implements, in his famous George Street tea-rooms.

With the new decade came the 'New Woman'. She had, or took, freedoms unavailable to her mother. She worked, cycled, smoked, wore 'rational' dress, had opinions, wrote, agitated for women's rights. She wanted the vote. She was *modern*, part of the 'age of progress and enlightenment'; her male opponents, in contrast, were representative of an 'amazing dullness of intellect in this *fin de siècle*'.[6]

The idea of the new woman captured the abandonment of Victorian lifestyle and values as the Victorian era came (literally) rapidly to its end. While the *Champion*, for example, used the term 'new woman' uncritically in its 'World of Woman' column in the middle years of the decade, the *Bulletin*'s use involved caricature and mockery, depictions of masculine, overbearing spinsters with hard faces and thin legs, or domineering married women with henpecked husbands.[7]

The idea or model (if not the caricature) was based in significant reality. In Australia in the 1890s, women did enter paid employment in unprecedented numbers, and the rate of marriage and the number of births declined, sufficiently indeed for an official enquiry into the 'problem'.[8] For unmarried, middle-class women, getting around without a chaperone was now acceptable. Female education levels increased, and male bastions, such as medicine and law, were breached for the very first time. It was an 'efflorescent Age', wrote the Reverend Langdon Parsons in his contemplation of 'Women as Citizens', 'in which so much that seemed intended to endure has been swept away for ever . . . in which universal and technical education, the new conditions of life, and the increased severity of the struggle for existence, have wooed and forced women out of their old retirement'.[9]

Women gained the vote in South Australia in 1894, and increasingly agitated for it in other colonies throughout the decade, succeeding a second time, in Western Australia, before the turn of the century. Although the changes overall were incremental and the numbers of women who could take advantage of these changes constituted in most cases a small minority, their cultural impact was at least potentially revolutionary. Satire and criticism, depictions of new women as strident, manly, even unhinged, were reflections of the alarm experienced by some as they confronted real change.

Throughout the 1890s, women's societies also grew in number. By the mid-1890s, all colonies except Tasmania had suffrage leagues, and in every colony the WCTU organised its members into 'Education', 'Hygiene' and 'Franchise' departments. Tasmania had a women's discussion group, the 'Itinerants', and in Western Australia in 1894, the Karrakatta Club, the first women's group devoted specifically to social and political discussion, was formed. Its first secretary, Edith Cowan, would go on to become, nearly thirty years later, Australia's first female member of parliament.

In 1895, following Margaret Windeyer's first-hand experience of the American model, many of these societies, as well as women's philanthropic organisations, joined as affiliates to a New South Wales National Council of Women. Formed by Miss Windeyer with Maybanke Wolstenholme, it was copied in 1899 in Tasmania, and both Councils affiliated to the International Council of Women. Australian women went as delegates to the international women's meetings in London and America before the decade, which had begun with almost no female political organisation at all, was over.

With these societies, a number of women's journals appeared: *Australian Woman*, *Woman's Voice*, *Woman's World*, *Woman's Suffrage Journal*, *Australian Woman's Sphere*, *Dawn*. Like the majority of all journals of the period, most were short-lived, but *Dawn*, edited by Louisa Lawson, persisted until well into the twentieth century. Its unusual success was most likely due, in part at least, to the broad range of topics the magazine covered, including many regular items on traditional women's domestic activities, advice on child-rearing, sewing patterns, household tips, and serialised stories. Unlike many other 'reforming' journals of the day, it did not confine itself to the serious discussion of social and political issues, and no doubt it attracted many readers who would not have otherwise been exposed to these issues.

During the referendum campaigns of 1898, the Australasian Federation League journal adopted a similar formula with a woman's column in which folksy little stories, fashion news and household tips combined with gentle admonitions to women to become more involved in political matters. Unlike *Dawn*, however, as a general Federalist paper, it did not offer something specifically to women, nor could it serve as a voice for the overriding political goal held by the female activists of the time: the suffrage.

174   *To Constitute a Nation*

Suffrage was the common goal, often the binding thread through women's political organisations, writings, and activism in the Federation period. Although the suggestion by Maybanke Wolstenholme early in the 1890s that suffrage be discussed in the New South Wales Women's Literary Society raised a cry of protest from 'an energetic and much-esteemed member . . . [who] hoped we should never discuss such a disgraceful matter'[10] (and this led to Wolstenholme's leaving to establish the separate Womanhood Suffrage League of New South Wales), by the last years of the decade, suffrage was embraced in the most respectable circles and, as a result of the work of the intervening years, considered to be an appropriate subject for debate in any group.

The Women's Literary Society, established in 1889, had involved, in the eyes of Wolstenholme, 'almost every [New South Wales] woman who in the years that followed worked for education or reform . . . Our little society was a training school'.[11] Mrs Nicholls also described the experience of women in South Australia, as they worked to gain the suffrage: it should be known, she said,

> how they lobbied the members, how they interviewed some and argued with others and stimulated a third; how they deluged the press with letters; how they attended the House in throngs at all hours of the night to see fair play; how they used every means in their power to secure their end . . . [and how] at last they triumphed.[12]

It is only when we realise that women did not so much as attend public 'banquets', even as wives of politicians, until the end of the 1890s (and then only rarely) that we can begin to appreciate the magnitude of the step they took in entering public debate and eventually—for our story—playing a role in the shaping of Federation and its Constitution. Men, in the élite circles of parliament, business and law, sat together in evening dress, eating, telling jokes, listening to political speeches, drinking, 'subsiding below the mahogany', smoking and always at some point toasting the Queen.

When women did begin to attend functions, the novelty was not taken so far as to invite them to speak or even to imagine that they might do so. But a number of prominent American and English women, including Jessie Ackerman, Annie Besant and Beatrice Webb, had toured Australia in the 1880s and 1890s, reinforcing a growing notion that women could hold political views, that they could participate in public debate, even lead. Australian women, like Vida Goldstein and Catherine Helen Spence, in turn went as lecturers on international tours. But in social circles, the cultural change was slow. In her Australian diary, Mrs Webb noted (as usual with scorn) that at a Sydney City Council lunch in

Half the Nation   175

1898, she had 'completely dumbfounded the company . . . by rising to answer on my own behalf' a toast proposed in her honour.[13]

To break into such male reserves, to contemplate 'having to run the gauntlet of the louts and hangers-on who congregate about the polling places',[14] took great courage on the part of individuals, as well as a major adjustment in the political culture of the time. When New South Wales suffragist Rose Scott spoke publicly on Federation late in the decade, she was greeted as a novel spectacle, even by a female journalist:

> I had never heard a lady speak before . . . on a political platform on a political question, and in my mind's eye I saw a large, florid, tall, aggressive, not to say vinegary, person, with a loud voice, and ultra-offensive assertive manner, and spectacles . . . Instead of which I saw a very nice lady, not too large, with demure, not to say quakerish ways.[15]

Women's emergence into the Federation campaigns of the late 1890s is a measure of the scale of the adjustment. The New Woman was to be part of the New Nation.

'The movement in favour of woman's enfranchisement is like a rising tide all over the world', said Mrs Nicholls. To gain the vote, she stressed,

> is not simply the privilege of voting on election day, but in the fact that a woman with a vote has her wants considered, and is not either politely or roughly ignored when she chooses to give expression to them. Her outlook is widened and her intelligence is aroused, for she realises that she has a duty to discharge and must find out how to do it.[16]

Great expectations were attached to the goal of the suffrage. Women confidently predicted improvement in the culture of parliament, 'change in the character of the debates . . . for the better. "Scenes" will then be things of an inglorious past',[17] the wife-beater and the drunkard would find no place in parliaments, the welfare of children and the infirm would finally get proper attention. 'Those of our women', wrote another,

> who give any attention to political matters at all must deplore the low level to which discussions in our Parliaments frequently sink. The lack of sincerity, the obvious talking to please a party or an electorate, without regard to the question of right or wrong . . . are all only too evident. The advocates of adult suffrage hope that this state of things will be improved, when, by the influence of woman's vote, men with higher aims and loftier conduct are returned from the poll . . . Even those who have no wish to see the existing franchise enlarged will agree as to the ennobling influence women may have on political discussions.[18]

176   *To Constitute a Nation*

In short, the nation would be 'civilised' by the influence, even the presence, of women in politics. A new nation seemed to many a new opportunity for such a transformation. Advertisers, always ready to seize on an emerging idea, picked it up: 'Pears' Soap', said an advertisement in *Australian Woman*, as early as 1893, 'will assist the Ladies in Cleaning Australian Politics'.

When the Federation movement first began to grow and to flourish (if only in fits and starts), in the very first years of the 1890s, there was little chance for women to be involved directly in nation-building even had they the desire and the confidence to do so. The success in achieving the suffrage in the first colony was still several years away, and effectively all women's political energies went into this campaign. Elsewhere, women continued with the charitable and educational work that absorbed many, but was not yet identified as *political*. Some were also occupied in the emerging union movement and socialist circles. Others, like Mary Cameron, among the most forceful individual women in Australia, left for Paraguay with William Lane's Utopian exodus, one year before South Australian women achieved the vote.

The early Federation movement was a politicians' movement. There were no female politicians. When, after two years of relative neglect following the 1891 Convention, groups outside the parliaments took up the baton, the movement was then dominated for a time by the Australian Natives' Association. But the ANA did not admit women. By the middle of the decade, few opportunities presented themselves for interested women to become involved in Federation. The large majority of men were not. The movement was in the doldrums. Then 'the people' took over.

By 1896, when Enabling Bills had been passed in four colonies to set in train the election of delegates to a Convention, and a commitment had been made to a referendum on the product of the Convention, women in South Australia had the vote and had already exercised it at a general election that year, and numbers of women in all colonies had gained experience in political organisation, speaking, lobbying and expressing political opinions.

The broader significance of the Premiers' Plan was that popular involvement by way of election and referendum not only allowed South Australian women to vote for delegates, indeed to stand for election, and West Australian women to join them in casting an opinion on the Constitution Bill after its completion, but also opened up Federation to public debate. Whatever politicians thought of popular participation, after 1895 they were forced to endure, perhaps even take notice of, the expression of popular opinion. Speeches, letters to the press and questions at public meetings took on a centrality and legitimacy they could not have assumed had Federation remained in the hands of the parliaments.

Women could contribute through public commentary. They could anticipate their imminent enfranchisement, and the politicians would have been foolish, at least in New South Wales and Victoria (where adult franchise Bills had passed the Lower House already several times), to rule this out before the completion of Federation. Women became, albeit often weakly, a distinctive constituency. By the time of the first election following South Australian women's enfranchisement, candidates for 'political honors [found] it necessary to study politics from the woman's point of view as well as the man's'.[19] Women in other colonies could begin to ask themselves, and then others, questions about why they had not been invited further into the Federation movement, and about why they too were not recognised as 'people'.

In South Australia the women's claim to belong to the people was substantive. Just how far their membership went was at times debated, but no one could henceforth deny that women had the right to be involved in a movement that officially revolved around the electors. By the time the elections for Convention delegates were organised, two years after the Hobart Premiers' Conference, not only had South Australian women had the experience of voting but some of them had campaigned in the 1896 general election. One of this latter group, South Australia's 'grand old lady', Catherine Helen Spence, was herself persuaded to stand for the Convention and, in doing so, to become Australia's first female political candidate.

Some raised doubts about Spence's eligibility, as they would do again six years later when the first women candidates for Commonwealth office announced themselves. The right to vote did not, it was argued, carry with it the right to sit in parliament. But the claim did not go as far as a legal challenge, as it had done in Britain. There, in 1889 (while the principle that 'he embraces she' in statutes passed after 1850 had been established), Lady Sandhurst, a successful female candidate for municipal election, was none the less ruled ineligible.[20] Some uncertainty may have surrounded the application of this case to Australian politics, but legal opinion (indeed Quick and Garran) seems to have accepted a positive construction of it for Australian women. Whatever the outcome of a legal challenge might have been, there was none, and Spence (like subsequent female candidates) 'got away with' standing, thereby as much as anything else affirming women's right to do so.

In the South Australian campaign for the Convention, the WCTU endorsed Spence as an advocate of female suffrage, even though she was not a temperance advocate as such. No party or newspaper included her on their ticket, although one liberal organisation listed her among its

178 *To Constitute a Nation*

'ten best men'.[21] In the event, Spence was not successful, being placed twenty-second on a list of thirty-three candidates out of whom ten were to be chosen. According to WCTU calculations, if all women had voted as their membership had, she would have been elected.[22] At the 1897 Convention Simon Fraser, a Victorian delegate, thought the failure counted as a blow against all suffragists: 'A lady presented herself—a very estimable and eligible candidate stood for the Convention—but the people of South Australia did not elect her. Her own sex voted against her, probably'. 'Well?', interjected South Australia's Mr Kingston.[23]

Spence had stood as an advocate of 'Effective Voting', the Hare Clark electoral system of proportional representation, which she and others campaigned to have adopted by the new Commonwealth. She had already been prominent among the protesters against the block vote for the very Convention elections for which she stood, and a member of the unsuccessful delegation to the Acting Premier of South Australia, Frederick Holder, to ask for the Hare Clark system for this election.[24] We cannot know whether Spence's supporters were attracted by her policy or by her sex, whether voters declined to lend support to 'Effective Voting' because its advocate was female or whether the reverse was true. One paper at least thought her chances had been 'more or less damaged from the unfortunate fact that uncertainty exists as to whether, if she were one of the chosen ten, she could legally take a seat'.[25]

Spence continued her campaign for proportional representation after the Convention election, including publicising her calculations that a different result would have been effected had this system been adopted, and petitioning the South Australian delegates to advocate its inclusion in the Constitution.[26] But she did not go on to campaign actively in the Federation movement once the Constitution Bill was written and in the hands of the people. Unlike any other unsuccessful candidate, however, Spence had a presence in the Convention to which she had not been elected. More than one delegate found her example instructive, and Tasmania's Adye Douglas went so far as to imagine her there, in their midst, as an advocate of female suffrage. Spence's failure, he assented, indicated that few women wanted the franchise: 'No doubt had we a lady here to advocate this cause it would be agreed to; but unfortunately the people excluded her'.[27]

During the campaign, other candidates, at least in Victoria, had been canvassed by suffragists over their position on the inclusion of women's suffrage in the Constitution. Alfred Deakin replied to a survey conducted by the *Champion* that he would not give any pledges of any kind, while the unsuccessful John West opposed its inclusion on the grounds of flexibility, pointing out (not unreasonably) that since voting rights were exclusively male in 1891, had the franchise been entrenched then, and the 1891 Bill adopted, it would have been necessary to amend the Constitution for South Australian women to gain the Commonwealth vote in 1894.[28]

Once the Convention began sitting, women's groups were among its many petitioners; they asked in particular for women to be included in the Commonwealth suffrage and for this to be written into the Constitution. Through the WCTU and other temperance organisations, women also demanded that the states should retain the right to control the importation and sale of alcohol and opium (this was achieved, and is now entrenched in section 113) and they featured in the numerous petitions asking for the recognition of the Almighty in the Preamble to the Constitution.

The very first petition presented to the Convention, sitting in its second day in Adelaide, on 23 March 1897, was a women's petition. It came from the central committee of the WCTU and urged, on behalf of its estimated 8000 Australian members, that the Constitution should include the provision 'that all voting by electors for Federal Parliaments be upon the basis of equal voting rights for both sexes'. Further pro-suffrage petitions came from the Womanhood Suffrage League of New South Wales and from Tasmania. A telegram from Mr George Maxwell in Melbourne informed the Convention that 'at a large and influential meeting' in Prahran the previous night it was 'unanimously carried that this meeting strongly urges the Federal Convention to embody the principle of womanhood suffrage in the Federal Constitution Bill'.[29]

The Womanhood Suffrage League petition, presented by New South Wales delegate James Brunker, made the point that women were taxpayers, and that they were 'patriotic, and law-abiding citizens'. The right to vote, the petition concluded, should be 'possessed by women' as well as men 'so that United Australia may become a true democracy resting upon the will of the whole and not half the people'.[30]

Petitions also appeared from the National Defence League of South Australia and from 'citizens of Tasmania' opposing the grant of adult suffrage and arguing, in the latter case, that the women of Tasmania 'do not desire political responsibility to be thrust upon them', their interests being guarded well enough by men in parliament. 'How many signatures has it?', asked Dr Quick. 'Ninety-six', said the clerk. 'From the whole of Tasmania!', replied Quick.[31]

The representatives of such small minorities, sitting in conservative and unreformed colonial Upper Houses, could still hold up the progress of women's suffrage by rejecting Bills passed in the Lower Houses, and they did so several times in the 1890s in New South Wales, Victoria and Tasmania.[32] But they could not stem the steady, if slowly moving, tide that would lead in the end, if not to the entrenchment of adult suffrage

180   *To Constitute a Nation*

in the Constitution, at least to an irreversible commitment to the granting of Commonwealth female franchise in the first national electoral Act.

It was South Australia's determination not to deny its enfranchised women the national vote, combined with the support given by progressive delegates from other colonies (especially Victoria), that resulted in this commitment. Suffrage organisations had lobbied hard in the lead up to the Convention. In New South Wales one newspaper found the pressure too much:

> Pray Lovely Woman, cease to tease
> The Candidates with tearful pleas
> About your suffrage matter.
> Give us a chance, pray, if you please
> To Federate the colonies,
> Without your endless chatter.[33]

But, once the people are invited into the process, all sorts of chatter must be endured. The result of the suffragists' chatter is section 41 of the Constitution:

No adult person who has or acquires a right to vote at elections for the more numerous House of the Parliament of a State shall, while the right continues, be prevented by any law of the Commonwealth from voting at elections for either House of the Parliament of the Commonwealth.

Long, convoluted arguments across the three Convention sittings and the continuous rewording and reworking of this section were undergone before the present formulation was reached. In the course of the debate the delegates were often forced to touch upon matters they normally avoided. As they grappled to find the right words for this section, so that South Australian women would not be disenfranchised while the other states would not be forced to grant their women the vote (and at the same time to ensure that neither 'Chinamen' nor 'infants of sixteen' could be enfranchised), they argued about the nature of rights, the experimental character of Federation, the identity of the new Australian citizen and the nature of representation.

A number of the South Australian delegates sought, as the women petitioners did, to have a uniform franchise enshrined in the Constitution at the start. They presented arguments to the Convention very similar to those found in Suffrage League manifestos: that women were taxpayers, that they were bound by law and that they contributed equally to the country. They repeated the point, so often made by female suffragists, that the Queen was herself a woman, at the head of a great empire,

Half the Nation 181

representative of the potential of all women to participate politically. It is 'most fitting', argued Frederick Holder, who reminded his fellow South Australian delegates that they had been elected to the Convention by women as well as men, 'that when Federation comes into effect it will come . . . broad-based, not only on the will of the male electors, but upon the will of the adults throughout Australia'.[34]

Opponents argued less against the principle of female suffrage than along states' rights lines. The states, they asserted, should retain the right to decide this matter for their own elections and the Constitution should not be used 'to venture upon an experiment'. A few, it seems, struggled to couch their obvious disapproval of women voting at all in terms of states' rights and general caution. New South Wales delegate, Bernhard Wise claimed that female suffrage was dangerous, since in America it would have led to 'a complete disruption of the Union' with women supporting the abolition of slavery without having the physical strength to fight for it. Mr Douglas reported that he had read in an Adelaide newspaper an account of a domestic row caused by a woman's participation in election campaigning. Victoria's Mr Fraser added that he knew of a town in New Zealand with a Lady Mayoress, and he did not think there would be another Lady Mayoress in New Zealand. Charles Grant from Tasmania thought women more 'subject to emotional or hysterical influences' than men (as had been observed, he added, in their determination to hold on longer than men in industrial strikes), more 'moved by impulse', and lacking the self-control that men, 'from being continually associated with each other, are compelled to exercise'. These facts, he concluded, suggested caution and hesitation before 'attempting to force upon the new Commonwealth woman suffrage'.[35]

But almost no one, it seemed, wanted to admit to outright opposition. Albeit with some scorn, Mr Wise conceded that the cause, if it 'is as good as its advocates insist that it is—and we do not hear a great deal in opposition to it, because I do not think the opposition to it has been seriously expressed yet— . . . [it] will make its own way'.[36] To his example, Mr Fraser added the assurance that he was far from intending to disparage 'womankind' but was only 'speaking now what is the opinion of all', and Mr Grant felt constrained to let fellow delegates know that he had always been in favour of female suffrage (because it was 'the strongest conservative element') indeed since 'before many members of the Convention were born'.[37] Both the South Australian example, by which it could be shown (and suffragists in other colonies frequently employed this strategy) that women in practice valued the right to vote, and, furthermore, that they exercised it in a calm and informed manner, along with what appears to have been an unspoken understanding that reasonable people did not condemn the suffrage outright, led to a

182   *To Constitute a Nation*

willingness to seek and tolerate a compromise through which, finally, supporters of the franchise would get to win the day.

Section 41 says effectively that every person already holding the right to vote in their colony would gain the suffrage for Commonwealth elections. South Australian women would therefore have to have the Commonwealth vote and since the Commonwealth, it was agreed, must have a uniform franchise (at least for all white adults), all white Australian women would get the vote in the first Franchise Act.

The compromise allowed women in some states to vote at the Commonwealth level, but not for state elections. States' rights advocates were reassured, believing that the vote in their state could be granted, if at all, at their leisure. But most were sufficiently experienced to know that the leisure must be largely illusory, that the pressure for uniformity would be irresistible. In the event, although some states held out for several years after the Commonwealth franchise was granted in 1902 (Victoria, the longest, until 1908), the reality of politics and the imperative towards consistency meant that women gained the vote everywhere before the end of the first decade of the century.

Section 41 also met the concerns of those, like Victorian unionist William Trenwith, who supported female suffrage but did not want it in the Constitution, 'good as [it] is, equitable as it is, little dangerous as it is', because its inclusion might create difficulties for achieving Federation, given the 'considerable number' of opponents to be found in some states. If Federation was obstructed, Trenwith added, 'the cause of woman suffrage' would not be advanced.[38]

For the most part, women suffragists themselves seemed to have been satisfied with the virtual guarantee supplied by this section. But the confident tone of the New South Wales petition gives no indication that the Convention's worth and that of the whole Constitution Bill were matters of some considerable dispute among the membership of the Womanhood Suffrage League. In its annual report for 1897, the League's Executive regretted that, along with Premier Reid's absence in England at the Queen's Jubilee, the 'holding of the Federal Convention . . . had greatly retarded their progress this year'.[39] Behind this lay a growing division over the terms of Federation generally and the value of these terms to women in New South Wales in particular. In 1898, with the completed Bill before the people, public campaigns saw the members of the Womanhood Suffrage League emerge both as opponents and supporters.

Rose Scott, at that time the League's Secretary, waged a fierce campaign of opposition, becoming in the process one of the most prominent anti-Billites in her colony during the two referendums. Speaking frequently on general platforms with other anti-Billites, as well as to meetings specifically organised for women, and writing often to the press on

Half the Nation 183

the matter, Scott advanced both the conservative states' rights and the radical labour case: that Federation would be a disaster for New South Wales in particular, since it would lead to the sharing of that colony's greater wealth with the smaller, poorer states at a time when economic circumstances were not favourable even in the Mother Colony, and that the freedoms of the people of New South Wales would be compromised by equal representation in the Senate for the small and large states.

Scott anticipated economic adversity for her colony. Women, who were 'experts' in making ends meet, had recognised, she said, that the financial provisions of the Bill would prove disastrous (unless the Federal Treasurer was a woman).[40] Men were 'not born to manage money matters, any more than they were to manage the baby'.[41] She foresaw, since the states were to be 'reckoned as human entities and . . . people are merely massed in the States', the loss of fundamental personal freedoms, even the likelihood of civil war, as had happened in the United States where the many differences found in a large territory had led to conflict.

The value of freedom, the lure of 'false sentiment' and 'the gambling spirit of the age', where 'the man-politician . . . will even speculate with the interests of his country and gamble away the freedom of the people for a handful of capital', were Scott's distinctive themes in the debate. Unrepresented, she warned, women were being overlooked, and the Constitution was designed so that it would 'lay its hands upon all laws concerning "Marriage, Divorce, Parental Rights, and the custody and guardianship of Infants"! Matters upon which, you would think that men with their usual sense of justice would feel ashamed that Woman had no representation'.[42]

Scott was deeply sceptical furthermore of the promise of female franchise. 'When we are told that Women will have a chance to get their rights, when a "uniform Franchise" is adopted by the Federal Parliament, we reply we don't want any "ifs" upon a matter, in which our absolute rights are concerned!'[43] Joining Scott in her anti-Billite campaign, Newtown Branch WSL members, Belle and Annie Golding, both assumed the task of public speaking and letter writing. For Belle Golding the Bill was just

> another instance of acres before men . . . Remember, this union is indissoluble—a union for all time . . . Electors, you have no right, in the sight of God or man, to rivet chains on generations yet unborn, chains that will gall, chains that will drag them down, but never, never break. Pause before you commit this outrage on the liberties of those who are to follow you.[44]

Other New South Wales women, including Miss May Hickman, Mrs Dickie, and Mrs Jane Darvell, a prominent resident of Ryde, active in

184   *To Constitute a Nation*

local politics (who died in early 1899), and Miss Nellie Martel, are recorded with the anti-Billites, as was suffragist leader in Victoria, Vida Goldstein. The anti-Billite *Daily Telegraph* in particular promoted their point of view, with reports of Rose Scott's speeches in detail, and stories such as 'Women as Critics of the Secret Bill', in which it was argued that women were not dazzled by 'the prospective glamour of . . . full nationhood', being more practical, with necessarily 'more knowledge of domestic economy and the management of the household and family than of poetical abstractions'. 'This wisdom in material everyday things', it added, 'is not to be underrated, or its promptings belittled'.[45]

Among the other women opponents around the country were the remarkable Mrs Bateson and Mrs Tracey in Western Australia. Mrs Tracey preached her rambling anti-Federation cause in the Perth Town Hall and 'on the Esplanade', and Mrs Bateson hired the Town Hall during the referendum campaign of July 1900, where she treated her capacity audience to a hilarious speech in which she variously accused the WCTU of hypocrisy and of serving 'stale buns and long-standing tea', the public men of the colony of having 'skeletons not only in their cupboards, but in their cradles', and the West Australian Convention delegate, lawyer Walter James—'a shining light in the woman's franchise movement'—of meanness and unkindness to poor women ('At the convention he took the prize . . . for beauty. What could the others have been like?'). She warned that under Federation West Australian women would lose the power they had gained through the franchise, that the Senate would be a lawyers' house (with Walter James in it) and that Western Australia would be thrown 'back for twenty years into poverty and distress'. She concluded by advising them 'to keep Federation out as well as rabbits'.[46] Thanks to the wonderful reporting custom of the era of noting audience response in parentheses, we know that the Perth Town Hall shook with laughter that night.

But, although the historical records are in other respects scanty, and although Rose Scott asserted that 'many women think as I do',[47] it seems clear that female opponents were a minority. What divided the Womanhood Suffrage League of New South Wales, among other things, was not just Federation itself, but the fear held by some that Rose Scott's anti-Billite position would be taken as representative of the whole membership. On more than one occasion other members of the League wrote to the press emphasising that Scott's views were her own, and Scott also chose (or perhaps was asked) publicly to make this point herself. Two letters to the *Australian Star* pointed out that Rose Scott's position was not representative of the WSL membership (and that she was in fact not President of the League as had been reported), with one claiming that 'seven out of every ten women who attend the suffrage meetings are in favour of Federation'.[48]

Scott herself replied by conceding that the WSL 'as a league has no opinion upon' Federation, but allowed herself none the less to conclude with the claim that 'the most democratic members . . . are, with myself, bitterly opposed to the Convention Bill'. Belle Golding was prepared to go even further and announced at one WSL meeting, during the vote of thanks to the visiting speaker, that the Newtown Branch of the League did have a position on the Bill: opposition. Called to order by the Chair, WSL Vice-President, Mrs Palmer, Golding was undaunted, and repeated that the Newtown Branch had a position and 'what little they could do they would do to defeat the Bill'.[49]

But the numbers, as far as we can tell, were with Federation. The *Evening News*, in Sydney, for example, ran articles on 'What Women Think' over two issues, canvassing women prominent in a variety of fields, including Mrs Armitage, Honorary Secretary of the National Council of Women, Miss Edwards, Secretary of the Working and Factory Girls' Club, Miss Frances Levvy, Honorary Secretary of the Women's Society for Prevention of Cruelty to Animals, and Mme Juliette Henry, known for her 'keen interest in foreign politics' but 'equally sympathetic regarding the welfare of the country of her adoption'. They, and almost all others who were asked, supported Federation. Most gave as their main reason the promotion through Federation of co-operation, harmony and combination for greater strength. Rose Scott, as expected, declared herself 'entirely opposed', reminding readers that 'it is unwise to legislate in advance of the people'. Federation was, she argued, clearly in advance: 'How can it be otherwise in what is at present a huge and sparsely-populated continent, whose separate divisions are only just learning to govern themselves, and to understand what it is they really do want?'.[50]

It may well have been the fear of Scott's high profile creating an impression that suffragists generally opposed Federation and/or the Bill that led to the establishment of the first formal Women's Federal League in the colonies. The Bathurst People's Convention of 1896 included a women's organising committee, which may perhaps be counted as the first ever women's pro-federal organisation. Bingara's women had a presence at Bathurst, too, with their presentation of two embroidered flags, the first to the citizens of Bathurst and the second, a day later, to the People's Convention itself. The 'power of womanly sympathy in a great national movement', said one (male) speaker on the occasion, 'was simply unspeakable'.[51]

But the first group specifically formed to involve women in the overall campaign appears to be that established in Sydney in early 1898 in preparation for the constitutional referendum held in June that year. This organisation—the Women's Federal League—was established from within the Australasian Federation League (effectively the men's organisation)

186   *To Constitute a Nation*

by the WSL's immediate past President, Maybanke Wolstenholme. In a colony where women did not have the vote, the goal of the Women's Federal League was principally to canvass for men's Yes votes in the referendum by arguing for the virtues of Federation and by encouraging 'Men who are indifferent or hostile to the Bill, to at least give it serious consideration'. 'Let us look to the near future', urged the Women's Federal League, 'when Australia, the new-born nation, may proudly take her stand among her Elders, helped to her great position by the slender hands, but staunch, true hearts, of our countrywomen! Women of New South Wales, YOU may turn the scale!'.[52]

Women, the League declared, should make an effort to understand the Constitution Bill and its debates, to set up WFL branches, to organise small groups of canvassers, and obtain promises from male voters of support for the Bill. They would be sent copies of the *Australian Federalist*, the organ of the AFL in which around this time a 'Women's World' column had begun to appear.[53] Women were prompted to invite others to their homes, to map out districts for canvassing, to visit these districts and 'try to obtain the promise of votes' from men. The benefits of Federation would be defence security, national laws and financial schemes, intercolonial free trade, uniform railways, as well as the elevation of noble sentiment and love of country. The Bill's acceptance, argued Wolstenholme, rested upon one question: 'Shall our children be Australians and of one family, or shall they be colonists and rivals? It is a woman's question, for from the home the national life must spring'.[54] Working from an office in the Equitable Buildings, George Street, the first WFL produced leaflets and contributions to the AFL's paper, and Wolstenholme spoke on several occasions on platforms with other Bill supporters, including Edmund Barton.

But the League did not thrive. Wolstenholme herself was experiencing deep personal difficulties at that time,[55] and the defeat of the 1898 referendum in New South Wales must have, for a while at least, opened up the prospect of an interminable campaign stretching into an uncertain future. Writing as 'Euphrosene' in the *Australian Federalist*, Wolstenholme lamented the lack of commitment of women to the cause, when the 'political world is just now in a ferment'. There were, she wrote, women in Sydney 'with great qualities, but who find the sacrifices too great' and while there is 'clamour for the suffrage' women leaders are lacking in other fields.[56] Wolstenholme's earlier writings in her own women's journal, the *Woman's Voice*, suggest also a theme for future disillusionment. Federation, she wrote, would occur, but 'federation of the heart' must come first and could not be achieved 'by parchment and red tape. Imaginary borders are much more easy to erase than the jealousy they typify', but, she warned, 'Public Men' seemed rarely to recognise this.[57]

Half the Nation 187

In another contribution to the *Woman's Voice* Wolstenholme had commented:

> When we have achieved Federation, and decided on free-trade and floated another loan, and built a few more grand public buildings, perhaps some of our great men will begin to think of the immortal nature of our little children, and the necessity of educating them so that we may become a nation united in unselfish brotherhood, and not a struggling community of selfish grab-alls.[58]

It seems clear also (although not whether this contributed to Wolstenholme's 'retirement') that relations with fellow suffragist Rose Scott were damaged. In one of her speeches Scott referred to 'an appeal to the Women of New South Wales by the Women's Federal League . . . signed by a lady who once appeared to be democratic'. She described the idea that women should obtain 'promises of votes' as 'descend[ing] to the pernicious system of canvassing'.[59] The following year, when a second Sydney WFL was established in anticipation of the second referendum, Scott and the Golding sisters renewed their attack.

This League was the creation of middle-class women, including a significant number of wives of prominent Federalist politicians: Mrs Barton, Mrs Reid, Mrs Wise and others. At a women's anti-Billite meeting in Balmain just before the 1899 referendum, in front of an audience of three hundred ('despite the inclement weather') Belle Golding described the new WFL as a 'Ladies Federal League', 'composed of society ladies with whom they had nothing in common . . . [and] formed, like Mr Reid's Secret Conference Bill, in private . . . The members were the wives of political leaders, who had their own ends to serve'.[60]

The second WFL advocated the Bill, among other reasons, because it would 'provide honest work for those willing to work' (and 'The salvation of man is work'); it would 'build up industries and encourage intercolonial commerce'; would 'assure' the position of civil servants; and would create a great national power. They too held meetings, including one at Paddington Town Hall where, with a little creative interpretation, if not stretching of the literal truth of the formula agreed to in section 41, Edmund Barton presented the promise of uniform Commonwealth suffrage as a guarantee of state suffrage, 'just as the women in South Australia (Loud applause)'.[61]

If the new Women's Federal Leagues were the successors to the old, they took their inspiration, it seems, from a more remote, if temporally immediate model, the Women's Federal League of Hay in the Riverina. This League was established in mid-May 1899 on the initiative of the Hay Federal Association whose Vice-President, local department store owner, Mr Maclure, declared himself 'a great believer in woman's influence . . .

188   *To Constitute a Nation*

[who] would like to see a meeting called of the women of Hay'.[62] It would be necessary, he said, to encourage every Yes vote possible in the impending referendum.

The people of the Riverina, on the border with Victoria, far from Sydney, suffering from prolonged drought and convinced that they had been neglected by the New South Wales Government, wanted Federation. Anxiety that the second referendum might also be defeated was high. The women of Hay—and there had been 'no more interested listeners' at Federal Association meetings[63]—responded immediately, and in less than a week found themselves at the Athenaeum at a meeting of which the attendance 'was the largest of the kind ever seen in Hay'.[64] There the men's Association Vice-President, Dr Broinowski, told them that it was 'specially befitting that the women of the country should be called upon to assist in the making of a nation', and Mr Maclure, delighted at the attendance, declared he would 'be prepared to support any movement to give ladies a vote after that occasion'.[65] After advising the women present that they should decide for themselves what direction to take, the men let the women take the Chair. Mayoress Mrs Anna Miller —'received with long-continued applause'—expressed her pleasure (mixed, we must assume) that the gentlemen 'had taken her little speech away, and had left her very little to say'. She then asked the men to leave, and without even reporters present the women formed their own League, with fifty-three signing up. Mrs Miller was chosen as President, Mrs Kennedy, Vice-President, Mrs Wheeler, Secretary, and Mrs Maclure, Treasurer, with a committee of twelve others.

Many of these women had been active already in the local WCTU Branch and the Benevolent Society. They were members of the town's little middle class, the type the *Bulletin* and papers like the *People and Collectivist* liked to mock as wowsers, puritans and patronisers, the sort Belle Golding despised. They were none the less remarkable. Their experience of charitable and temperance work no doubt had contributed to their capacity to think of themselves politically, but they had much to overcome in the culture of the period in doing so. 'There were cynics who would not have anything to do with the ladies taking such an interest in a matter of this kind', said the Reverend Colwell at the first Hay WFL function, although he himself 'did not know what they would do without them'.[66]

Above all, movements like this, small and transient though they proved to be, were signs of the modernising processes under way in both the nation and its population. The Hay League was also an exemplar of the tendency, perhaps even the rule, that political motivation follows experience and interest. If Maybanke Wolstenholme found the enthusiasm of Sydney women focused on the suffrage at the expense of

Federation, the women of the Riverina had a more immediate and personal investment in Federation, given the experience in that region of the direct daily impact of colonial separation, and they made this the priority in their campaign.

At their first meeting the Hay Women's Federal League pledged themselves to advancing the cause of Federation and, in the immediate term, to designing and selling a League badge. 'So far as I have been able to observe', wrote one local journalist, this was 'the first meeting of the kind held in the colony. Even the great-grandmother of journalism . . . the "Herald" commends it to the people as an example worthy to be followed'.[67] If he was mistaken about its uniqueness, he was not about the example. Within three weeks, the local press was reporting the establishment of the (second) Sydney WFL, of which, 'of course', 'the great metropolis' would never have thought 'if Hay had not set the example'.[68] The Hay WFL had already prepared its first function, a popular type of musical supper known as a 'Conversazione'. It was, by all accounts, a great success: bunting, flowers, pot-plants, a federal flag and smaller flags of nations decorated the tables and 'Federal badges were much in evidence, and so anxious were the gentlemen to wear one of the badges of the women's league that the stock was speedily sold out'.[69] Money was raised and passed on to the men's League, for further campaigning. Soon after, the Women's Federal League sent a telegram wishing success to the new Sydney League, and received one in return.

They were attracting attention around the country. It was, no doubt, in part the novelty, in part the respectable profile of these women (the Mayor's wife, the doctor's wife, the wife of the major department store owner), but perhaps also in large part the colourful, entertaining approach they adopted, all of which gave the women of Hay a profile Wolstenholme's more serious and taxing programme of door-to-door canvassing could not achieve. On the great day of the referendum itself, the streets of Hay as well as the 'fair federalists' themselves were decorated with WFL colours, with ribbons and badges and banners. It was a festive approach, the type of thing Australians in that era seemed to prefer in their politics, whatever the issue, to the sombre and cerebral debate or sermon.

Having witnessed a successful outcome to their efforts, the combined male and female Leagues of Hay decided on a grand celebration. Federalist leader, Edmund Barton, and Sydney WFL executive member, Mrs Barton, would be the guests. At the lavish dinner at Tattersalls Hotel, under the federal flag and the Women's Federal League banner, Mr Barton toasted the 'loyalty of this district, and also the good work of the Women's Federal League', their great service to the cause and their role as an example for all women of New South Wales. He also praised his

190   *To Constitute a Nation*

own wife's work and, thanking the women for presenting her with a bouquet, assured them that she would not herself like to speak. He dismissed Maybanke Wolstenholme's Federal League as 'a weak sort of Woman's League' and he joked that there was no cause 'in which women held such unanimous views—even with husbands'.[70] Mr Barton too was a product of his era.

The second half of the decade—the 'people's' years—had given groups hitherto outside the political framework the right to speak and organise. Federal activity for women took different forms across the colonies, with addresses on Federation to already existing women's groups, discussions and meetings, as well as petitioning and lobbying taking place. But, as far as we know now, actual federal leagues or committees of women were confined to New South Wales and Western Australia. What these colonies had in common, if nothing else, was their unpredictability in the referendum vote. New South Wales had rejected the Bill in the first referendum, and although technically the other colonies (at least three of them together) might have gone ahead without the Mother Colony, this was in reality unthinkable.

The urgency of attracting a higher number of Yes votes in the second referendum led to unprecedented pro-Federation activity in that colony. Western Australia, for its part, participated in the referendum processes considerably later than the other colonies, literally at the last minute, in July 1900. In a colony so distant from the rest of the country, where responsible government had been gained only ten years earlier, the advantage of joining a Federation under a national, but remote government was appraised with very mixed sentiment and the colony's hesitation on the brink reflected the resulting division of opinion.

As in New South Wales, women became directly involved in the campaign. The big difference for West Australian women was the passage of the colony's Constitution Amendment Act, in which women gained the suffrage, in 1899. The government's procrastination over the referendum had the indirect result of allowing women in that colony the chance to record their opinion on Federation. The female franchise gave women not only a direct interest in the referendum (as in South Australia) but also, because of the apparent precariousness of support for Federation, a sense of real potential to influence the outcome. Much effort was expended by both the Federalists and the anti-Billites to attract women to meetings, to address women's issues and concerns and, especially by the women themselves, to educate each other in enrolling and voting. Provision was made for women not already on the electoral roll to take out elector's rights specifically for the referendum. The efforts bore fruit, or perhaps the vote was less precarious than had been imagined, for the West Australian result was substantially in favour of

Federation, and, indeed, a majority would have been reached even without the overwhelming support of the (male-dominated) goldfields.[71]

The grant of one right so often leads to the demand for another, and thus as an evolutionary consequence of this concession, the WCTU soon afterward petitioned the Premier to allow those who had been on the electoral roll for less than six months to vote in the following Federal election, pointing out that they must be included as 'electors' since they voted in the referendum, and that such encouragement was needed as 'women have long been dissuaded from taking an interest in electoral matters [and] it cannot be expected that they will all at once become enthusiastic'.[72]

In the goldfields, where the numbers of women were small compared to the men, the campaign also involved canvassing of men's votes. As well as a Committee in Fremantle, Women's Federal Committees were established in Kalgoorlie, Boulder, Menzies and Coolgardie. The *Kalgoorlie Miner* reported, for example, a meeting of around two hundred women at the Boulder Mechanics' Institute, where a Committee was appointed to canvass the mines and the streets, as well as a 'very large meeting of the ladies' Federal Committee' in Kalgoorlie, where 'arrangements were made for a number of ladies to attend each of the polling booths at stated times, in order to advise the fair sex how to record their votes'.[73] Seven women's district committees were subsequently formed in Kalgoorlie. As much as anything this campaign must have been directed at encouraging men and women to enrol for the referendum rather than simply to register a Yes vote, since the mining electorates were already strongly in favour of Federation, to the point of having convincingly threatened separation from the rest of the colony, if necessary, in order to join the rest of Australia in federating.

A good many of the women who found themselves in Western Australia in the 1890s had come from South Australia and the eastern colonies. Life on the 'frontier' has long been thought of as a likely factor in making men more 'Australian-minded', less protective of states' rights and boundaries, as a 'melting-pot' mixing men from different colonies.[74] The literal kinship with family members in other colonies, and the experience of isolation must have struck the women even more forcefully than the majority of 'immigrant' men, and reinforced the desire for political and symbolic bonds of 'kinship' with the rest of the nation. The bond of kinship and community was indeed one of the major themes employed by women who supported Federation. This was mingled with the view that women had special qualities which fitted them particularly for participation in national political life, and that Federation would (by promising the franchise) create an opportunity to exercise these qualities. One letter to the press, purporting to come from a 'puzzled'

192   *To Constitute a Nation*

husband, spelled out these reasons in his wife's 'complaint' against not having the suffrage: 'Women represent homes, and a "State" is but a collection of homes', its author wrote;

> the women's vote would represent a genuine force . . . [and] Women would be far more likely to select good representatives . . . because their gift of curiosity alone would compel them to become acquainted with the principles and capacities of the candidates. Men would vote as machines, without knowledge or discrimination . . . As federation itself is a particularly bold experiment, it will be no objection that a women's constituency would be an experiment . . . [since] the average woman is by instinct a Conservative.[75]

We know now that women in most colonies did not directly get a chance to be a 'genuine force' in shaping Federation, and that the interests closest to the experience and values of most active women in that period—matters of social welfare, health, education, and protection of children—did not for the most part get included in the sphere of 'things properly federal'. But many attempts were made by women to have this chance, and the impact of their attempts was felt both in the political culture of the time and specifically in a limited number of provisions in the Constitution.

If, by and large, the Constitution was not 'feminine', it was less of a specifically 'masculine' document by the end of the decade than it had been at the beginning. That is to say, it was much more gender-neutral than its first draft allowed, in large part because the 1891 draft gave a greater role to the parliaments (in selecting the Senate members, and in shaping the proposed Conventions for constitutional change) and because it did not anticipate uniform suffrage. That provision in the final draft would ultimately create the opportunity for women's issues to be drawn into the political and constitutional landscape.

Just how much Australian women took an interest in Federation was the subject of a small, but interesting debate in the period immediately before its completion. 'An English-Woman', writing in the new journal *United Australia*, commented on 'the very limited interest I have found women taking in the extraordinary and unique political changes imminent in your magnificent country'. Apart from Catherine Helen Spence, the writer found that unlike in England, women who had the chance, 'to learn so much at first hand . . . seem to despise their opportunities, and to consider politics out of fashion and supremely boring . . . [even] at this moment, when your country stands on the threshold of nation-hood'.[76]

'An Australian Woman' in response complained that the English-woman 'had not had the educative advantage of being in New South Wales during the taking of the Federal Referendum' before making her 'sweeping charge' of apathy against women. Many women attended meetings, 'eager, interested, mostly work-a-day faces', and seats were reserved for women. Women should not be judged by 'the less serious-minded of the female leisured class . . . With the same degree of fairness one might judge masculine interest by the men who lounge around Clubs . . . or by the man who avails himself of the holiday granted for voting purposes, by mounting his bicycle, and riding many miles away from the ballot-box'. The growing 'earnestness and ambition of many of our young Australian women to strike out . . . must be provocative of an earnest desire for the right to exercise their judgment in assisting to form the conditions under which they work'. In the past, the writer concluded, the study of politics had had little significance for women, but 'feminine interest' is quickly adapting itself.[77]

In the next issue, 'An Anglo-Australian Woman' responded to both letters:

> I cannot help thinking that, even if [the Englishwoman] had attended Federal meetings, she would not very greatly have modified her views; for although a good number of women were seen at meetings, it was my fate in a drawing-room, during the thick of the fight, to be asked by a well-educated and very intelligent girl: 'What *is* Federation?'

When one speaks of the 'women' of any given country, surely all classes of women are included, she commented. Like most English people, 'an Englishwoman' was struck by the indifference of the class that could, if it wished, 'calmly and dispassionately ponder on the greatest good for the greatest number', but fails to do so, because, as a class, it has no 'axe to grind'. The 'work-a-day' character of the women's faces at Federal meetings showed that 'politics have of late found favour only amongst the less educated classes'. Upper-class women, the writer concluded, must take more interest and support men of their own class in politics: let them 'even make politics "fashionable"—it would be a more sensible fashion than the "Novel" or "Play" tea mentioned by "Australian Woman" as the absorbing fashion of the hour'.[78]

In these contributions we see much that characterised the political culture of the day, the competing issues and values as these were being subjected to new movements and forces of the time: the combination of loyalty and resentment in Australian–British relations, the emergence of labour politics, the tension between apathy and enthusiasm, and above all the issue of women's entry into the political arena. Had Federation occurred ten years earlier, the combination of these elements would have been quite different, and women would not with confidence have engaged in such a debate.

194   *To Constitute a Nation*

Although it cannot be claimed that women played a role in the formal processes of Federation on the same scale as the men, their struggle for the suffrage, their attempt to have the domestic recognised in the political sphere, their expectations of change in the culture of politics once women had a political presence, all played their part in building a modern nation. Whether Elizabeth Nicholls's hopes that Australia would be federated 'in the interest of women as well as men' were fulfilled remains still to be judged.

At the very end of the decade, the presence of women on public occasions, if less unfamiliar, was still greeted as 'an innovation', 'approved' by one Governor who hoped, he said, to see more of them at banquets in the future.[79] But even then, if they were permitted to attend at all, women often sat apart. At the official banquet for the Inauguration of the Commonwealth, in Sydney on 1 January 1901, despite the role women had directly played in those last years of nation-building, the female guests were placed, as usual, upstairs in the Town Hall Gallery, as if they were spectators in the public gallery of a parliament, looking down (so it must have seemed) on the real centre of power. The irony of this did not go unnoticed. It has been much (although much less openly) commented upon during the Inauguration celebrations, wrote 'A Country Visitor', that

> little or no provision has been made for entertaining the women, who were certainly as much interested in the question as the men could be. It is true that we were on two or three occasions invited to sit in the gallery and watch the men feasting below us, and listen to their speeches . . . but . . . as we women will have to help pay the bill, it would only have been common justice to have given us a fair share of the amusements.[80]

But, looking down on the men eating, toasting and speech-making, the women could be confident at least that the nation from its beginning was to number them, formally, among its citizens. The optimism of this moment embraced a vision of gains for women, of their growing significance and of the modernising trends transforming their lives. West Australian Karrakatta Club member, Madeleine Onslow, wrote:

> The approaching end to the long and weary dispute as to woman's proper place in the scheme of life is one of the culminations of which we are now watching the progress in Australia; and . . . the movement, known as that for 'Woman's Rights,' having successfully run the gauntlet of opprobrium, scorn, and ridicule, incidental to the march of all progressive measures, it is in the nature of things that the last stage before the goal is reached should prove a short one . . . It is in order that woman should give of her best to the nation

Half the Nation 195

and the home, and that she should maintain her authority in the latter, that I would claim for her from the Commonwealth her enfranchisement and the gift of equality of opportunity with man.[81]

Looking back, we must allow such women this optimism. It is the optimism of new beginnings, of fresh starts, of the culmination of years of vision, imagination and pragmatism. It is the optimism of those who had seen what they struggled for achieved in their own lifetime.

CHAPTER ELEVEN

The Federal Compact

> Whereas the people of New South Wales, Victoria, South Australia, Queensland, and Tasmania, humbly relying on the blessing of Almighty God, have agreed to unite in one indissoluble Federal Commonwealth under the Crown of the United Kingdom of Great Britain and Ireland, and under the Constitution hereby established . . . Be it therefore enacted . . .

A Constitution's Preamble is a singular thing. It carries the burden of mixed expectations. It should be inspirational as well as precise. It must serve as a type of national desideratum and as a stepping-stone into the body of the text. It should sum up, in one passage, the hopes and aspirations of the parties involved and list them at the same time.

Australia's Preamble describes four types of party: the people, the states (at least five of them), the Almighty, and the Crown (in perhaps both its senses, Monarch and Parliament). It tells us that the agreement was voluntary, that it is 'Federal' and 'indissoluble' and that it is founded in hope. For what did the parties (at least those who saw themselves as gaining by Federation) hope? What type of agreement did they see themselves concluding?

If the individual had a secondary, but still a greater part in the Constitution than might have been thought, what then of the whole people and of the states as parties to an agreement? How did their varied interests balance in the complex equation of terms offered and consent given? The rhetoric of the referendums in 1898, 1899 and in Western Australia in 1900 captures much of what was thought to be agreed.

Although successful in four states, the 1898 referendum was lost, because New South Wales failed to obtain the special majority of 80 000 votes upon which its Parliament had insisted. The second referendum, a year later, saw the Constitution Bill accepted in all the colonies. Certain amendments had been made at a special Premiers' Conference in early 1899, concessions (such as the provision that the federal capital would be in New South Wales) designed to make New South Wales voters more favourably disposed to the Bill, and the special majority requirement was subsequently dropped for the next referendum.

In both years, the campaign was intense, with vast amounts of literature produced and circulated, so much so that the New South Wales Deputy Postmaster-General complained about the quantity and weight of newspapers being posted.[1] The appeal to voters for and against the Bill varied to an extent from colony to colony and regionally within the colonies. But overall, two common themes emerged: the first concerned the business side of the union (whether individual states or regions would gain or lose out in federating) and the second (which increased in prominence as the campaign went on) focused on the 'sentimental' question: would Australians agree to cement their brotherhood? Would common kinship, 'blood', and 'racial destiny' be recognised? Would Australians rise to the challenge to create a great nation, one that might achieve far more than the individual colonies could achieve separately?

By the time of the referendums, almost no one in Australia could be found declaring themselves opponents of Federation as such. Most agreed that the colonies would and should federate eventually. The question was not, would it happen, but, upon what terms? Critics acquired the generic name of anti-Billites since most pitched their criticism against the particular Constitution Bill, commonly on the grounds that it would be materially injurious to individual colonies or regions. Its supporters on the other hand were simply Federalists (rarely Billites), successful in their claim that the whole issue of Federation, rather than the specific Bill, was really at stake. Opponents of the Bill maintained that they recognised the nation's destiny and were not opposed to Federation as such, but they were, no doubt, increasingly exasperated by the constant conflation of the two issues and by the overwhelming impression created that the referendum was on the subject of Federation rather than on a particular Bill.

The *Adelaide Advertiser*, for example, a moderately anti-Billite newspaper, argued on the eve of the referendum of 1898 that the disadvantageous financial clauses of the Bill had given rise to distrust and jealousies among the colonies, and was therefore preventing the achievement of Australia's common destiny. If South Australia accepted the Bill, its rather tortured logic concluded, this would entail such a sacrifice as to give 'a complete proof of the sincerity and intensity of her attachment to the Federal cause'.[2]

The challenge for supporters was to demonstrate both that the particular interests of their colony or region would be protected, even improved, and that the great Australian nation could be created at the same time. The threat of a particular region's separating or seceding from a colony was heard more than once, most notably in the eastern goldfields of Western Australia, where a powerful 'Separation for Federation' movement emerged. There a mass petition of almost 28 000 signatures praying for the region to be formed as a separate colony so that it might join the others in federating was collected and sent to Britain. The petition complained of harsh, unjust and discriminatory treatment from

198   *To Constitute a Nation*

the West Australian Government, and of the refusal of the colonial parliament to pass the Constitution Bill, thus by its 'arbitrary action' preventing the goldfields population 'from realising our intense desire to join the Federal Union and participate in the moral and material advantages of Australian National life'.[3]

Warnings such as these served both to alarm advocates of colonial independence and/or states' rights about their material prospects if they were abandoned by significant sections of their population, and to indicate that the experience of kinship with the rest of Australia was part of the desire for Federation. The idea of kinship captured the conviction that the fortunes of particular regions would be better served in a united Australia than in a separate colony.

A good deal of energy went into arguing about whether material interests or sentiment should be uppermost in deciding on the Bill. The *Adelaide Advertiser* warned against an 'emotional eclipse of the critical faculty' in the campaigns,[4] and Rose Scott argued that Federation should be treated with less sentimentality, like a business undertaking, where each party determined its own destiny,[5] while a meeting of the Western Australian Federal League was told that the issue depended on 'the power of sentiment' and it was impossible to understand why in 'some quarters it was common to pooh-pooh sentiment'.[6] Maybanke Wolstenholme suggested that Federation as a 'business contract' was indeed necessary, but this itself was not the reason for wanting Federation:

> when brothers enter into partnership or when man and woman join in the still closer partnership of marriage, they make, if they are wise, the clearest possible arrangements as to money and property . . . but these arrangements do not constitute the union. He would be mad, indeed, who would expect a lasting partnership or a happy union to grow upon such dry, dead bones.[7]

During the campaign, Federation was quite frequently referred to as a union, a partnership, a marriage, sometimes a charter, but most commonly as a 'federal compact'. Sometimes the various terms appeared together in virtually the same breath. A federation is not dissoluble, said Edmund Barton at Bathurst: 'One might as well be told that you could put an end to the compact of marriage . . . When the States have taken security in the Federal compact against wrong and oppression that contract [*sic*] must be sacred'.[8] But the term 'contract' was used only rarely, no doubt principally because the Australian founders knew that the claim that the American states had made a contract with each other had proved deeply divisive in the early history of the United States Constitution. They were perhaps also influenced by their knowledge that 'social contract' theory had fallen out of favour by the end of the nineteenth century as it was ridiculed by the dominant utilitarian theory of the age.[9]

But the idea or imagery of contract was readily evoked. A contract, such as the southern American states at the time of the Civil War claimed they had originally entered, implied effectively a voluntary, reversible 'business' agreement made by already sovereign agents.[10] Alongside such discussions of the material terms of Federation, organic metaphors of nationhood played a very large part in the campaign. If the parties to the Federation debates had been more precise in their use of words, they might have reserved the term compact for such an organic union, one which is permanent, affective, even 'spiritual', as much as or more than material, and applied the term contract to the reversible, 'business' type agreement. But since they were not, we must now take pains to unravel the imagery behind the generic term of the period—compact—to find in it a range of imagined unions between the colonies.

The nature of an agreement is captured significantly in the terms that are accepted for its alteration. Whether the agreement can be ended or can never be broken, whether it is to be easily altered or only with great difficulty, whether it requires an extraordinary or a routine procedure to effect change, all go towards indicating what type of undertaking it is. Whoever can make the change is sovereign.

One of the keys to what was imagined as the nature of the Australian federal union lies in the means that was settled on for amending the Constitution. In the 1891 draft, following the American model, this was to be a series of elected state conventions, voting separately on the proposed amendment. By 1898, following the Swiss model, section 128 as we know it now had emerged: a direct referendum of the electors. In both, the Commonwealth Parliament had first to pass the proposal, and the subsequent vote was to be counted twice, with majorities in both the states and in the Australian population required for its success.

In the Convention debates on this matter, it is clear that some delegates regarded Federation as a contract (in the 'business' sense) to which the parties were the colonies. In Sydney in 1891, Duncan Gillies from Victoria argued that the future states should have the greater power in voting on constitutional amendments, 'as they had made a bargain, entered into . . . a written agreement without which they would not have entered the federation at all—[and] no part of that agreement ought to be lightly set aside'. But, he added, 'no state ought to be compelled to submit to an amendment of the constitution when it has not a right to withdraw from that constitution'.[11] The issue of separation was subsequently to be of great importance; what is interesting here is the idea of an unbreakable contract. The bargain must be a really good one, Gillies suggested, if it could never be rescinded. This is already a

200   *To Constitute a Nation*

peculiar type of contract, as the West Australians were to find in the 1930s.

Alfred Deakin, anxious that the Constitution should not be too binding or too difficult to change in the first place, said: 'I take it that one of the first principles of the Constitution is that we present it to the several colonies, not as a complete constitution, but as one which they can make complete . . . which they can themselves adapt to [their] needs and desires'.[12] New Zealand's representative at the 1891 Convention, the grand old counterpart to Henry Parkes, Sir George Grey, argued passionately and repeatedly on the other hand, that the people alone must have the power to amend the Constitution because elected members, as everyone knew, were not their representatives; they represented only capital, land, 'the bare soil of the earth', 'the dry and senseless soil', not people, not 'individual living men, not individual interests of families, of wives, and of children'.[13] The people of the states, he implied, not the states themselves, must be the sovereign body.

Some contemporary commentators, it may be added, thought the act of federating itself such a momentous, 'revolutionary' act, a 'complete alteration of the conditions under which the people are now governed', as John Cockburn argued at the 1891 Convention, that this meant that the people must have 'the right to speak directly' on it.[14]

In Sydney in 1891, the argument centred less on the respective merits of convention or referendum than on the principle of the 'double majority': should the votes of state conventions alone be sufficient for amendment, or should all the people of the states be counted as one body? Which party, in other words, had agreed to the union and might now alter it: the colonies or the people? This would become the overriding question of the next nine years. Was it a Federation of otherwise separate states and nothing more that was contemplated, or a union of all the people into one nation? A contract of the states, or a compact of the people? Or both?

Quick and Garran's account of section 128 describes the Constitution as an 'organic' compact: 'A Constitution is a charter; it is a deed of trust, containing covenants between the sovereign community and its individual units . . . [It] may be compared to a living organism', which must be allowed to grow and change.

> The Constitution of a nation is the outward and visible manifestation of its national life, to the pulsations of which it necessarily responds . . . [But where] a community is founded on a political compact, it is only fair and reasonable that the compact should be protected, not only against the designs of those who wish to disturb it by introducing revolutionary projects, but also against the risk of thoughtless tinkering and theoretical experiments.[15]

But the compact, for all that, must have something of a contract in it, terms that can be weighed up before joining, something concrete it offers its parties beyond the mere honour of membership. Some commentators thought that interested parties were too focused on attempting to get specific 'terms' out of Federation: one press comment, for example, suggested that the anti-Billites were just like the anti-smokers, anti-vaccinationists, total abolitionists, 'and the great and glorious army of faddists recruited from everywhere'. Why not weld them together to oppose the Bill, it asked, because it doesn't give them some guarantee about their particular cause?[16]

But the Australian Constitution does offer special terms. With the exception of making mention of the Almighty in the Preamble, and including section 113, which was ardently sought by temperance groups (and which allows the states to restrict the trade in liquor and intoxicants, regardless of section 92), special enticements are offered to the states, more than to individual interest groups. Apart from the general appeal of a unified defence force and the undertaking to protect every state against invasion and (if asked) against 'domestic violence', the guarantee of free trade, commerce and intercourse between the states, powers to make all Australia 'white' and a uniform postal and other like services, special provisions were also made for individual states to entice them to sign. Western Australia alone was permitted to retain tariffs on imports from other states for the first five years of Federation (section 95). Queensland alone might 'make laws dividing the State into divisions and determining the number of senators to be chosen for each division' (section 7). South Australia had the promise that it would be relieved of the burden of the Northern Territory, and section 111 anticipated this 'surrender'.

In addition certain guarantees were given that, subject to the Constitution, the states would retain sovereignty over their own territory, so that it could not be altered without their consent (section 128), and that their own state constitutions would continue 'as at the establishment of the Commonwealth' (section 106). Certain others, such as the transcontinental railway, were imagined, with many West Australians speaking of Federation as if the railway were directly inscribed in the Constitution itself.

Critics, like Rose Scott, thought that states' interests had received far too much attention. In the Constitution the states were represented as 'Human Entities', she said; it was the very 'defect [that] caused a civil war in America!'. Like 'Aladdin exchanging the magic and precious lamp of Freedom for the shoddy legal Political lamp of Federation', she concluded, the people were to give up their freedom.[17]

Striking a balance between the freedom of the majority and the freedom of minorities, as political theorists and politicians know only too

202   *To Constitute a Nation*

well, is almost the central dilemma of democracies. One group's freedoms are another group's constraints. If Scott was right, she was right for the large states, and much less so for the smaller. If the states were spoken of as entities with 'rights', and given a guarantee of equal representation in the Senate regardless of population size, the attempt was also made to reach a balance, with representation of 'real' people (in the sense of population) upheld in the House of Representatives.

If the two Houses were granted almost identical powers, the exclusive right of the House of Representatives to initiate money Bills (section 53) is a guarantee of the right of that House to form the government, in the British Westminster tradition. But the powers of the Senate to block (if not amend) money Bills (as is known from the dismissal of the government in 1975) may erode that right. So the balance of powers and freedoms swings back and forth. No one can say that the compromise reached in 1901 was entirely satisfactory. What is certain is that Federation would not have proceeded without it. Rose Scott, whose imagined nation was New South Wales, evolving (like New Zealand) on its own, would have argued that it should therefore not have proceeded. Like S. A. Rosa and William Lane, she foresaw civil war as the result. But in this respect at least, the critics were confounded.

In the final years of the decade, an examination of the 'terms' offered to individual colonies was repeatedly made both informally and in official reports on the financial aspects of Federation produced by Commissions in New South Wales, Tasmania and Western Australia. The reports in each case found the terms more or less unfavourable. One commentator, Tasmanian James Backhouse Walker, summed up the contractual imagery captured in this process in his personal diary. Explaining why he had come around to advocating Federation, despite the official report that the financial provisions would be injurious to Tasmania, Walker described his recognition that there were similar complaints in each colony. This, he concluded, 'seemed a strong argument for the Bill. Where each partner declared he was getting the worst of the bargain, it might reasonably be inferred, that the arrangement was fairly equitable all round'.[18]

But various differences between the draft Constitutions of 1891 and 1898 suggest that the idea of contract between the states was stronger in the earlier years, and that the agreement of the people to form a compact grew over the intervening years, to have at least co-equal claim by the end of the decade. Among other things, the Preamble of 1891 does not describe the Australian Commonwealth as 'indissoluble'. 'Indissoluble' was added, Quick and Garran wrote in 1901, to avoid the 'political heresy' that 'the Union was merely a compact among the States . . . and that the States had the right to resist any breach of the compact'. It was

The Federal Compact 203

this view, they said, that had led to the American Civil War. In addition, in 1891, as we saw, constitutional amendment was to be effected by State Conventions. Members of the Senate were to be chosen by state parliaments, rather than directly elected, as the 1898 draft has it.

In 1891 the Preamble began: 'Whereas the Australasian Colonies . . . have agreed to unite', where it now reads 'Whereas the People of New South Wales, Victoria, South Australia, Queensland, and Tasmania . . . have agreed to unite', adding that Western Australia may join, 'if Her Majesty is satisfied that the people of Western Australia have agreed thereto'. The change reflects the decision in the intervening years to seek the people's agreement directly, at a referendum, on the union they were about to enter.

But could a compact between the people create a nation? Could the colonies, even if only as colonies, themselves contract together to form a Federation? Some later commentators have suggested that they could not, that the pre-eminent party to the agreement had necessarily to be the Imperial Parliament, that the referendums on the Constitution Bill were only 'an agreement that the Constitution . . . should be submitted to the Imperial Parliament . . . [and] that the Commonwealth Constitution derives its force from the fact that it is a statute which was enacted by a legislature which had power to make laws for Australia'.[19] More recently, this view has been challenged, and the alternative view, that 'the real basis of the Australian Constitution was the consent of the people', has been persuasively made.[20]

The evidence for this latter claim lies not only in the procedures of electing delegates to a Convention, and voting Yes in the referendum. It is suggested in the fact that there was a much weaker interest in Federation on Britain's behalf than might have been expected if the Imperial Parliament was a major party in the compact, and if all the Australian people could agree to do was to submit the Constitution Bill to it. Other than in protecting its interests in Australia by retaining the right of appeal to the Privy Council, British concerns about the Australian Constitution focused almost exclusively on external matters. Having failed to persuade the colonies to conclude a defence treaty (which would have established a central Australian command and ultimate control by the British authorities), the Colonial Office was keen to encourage full Federation as an alternative.[21] But they knew the initiative must come from Australia or the Australians might typically get their backs up. They also cared little about the internal arrangement the colonies might make with each other, whether this was unification or a Canadian-style Confederation, or an American-style Federation.

The constitutional relationship between Britain and Australia had mostly been already settled well before and independently of the issue

204   *To Constitute a Nation*

of Federation. The Colonial Laws Validity Act of 1865 had limited Britain's powers of intervening to the test of 'repugnancy', that is to say, to cases where British law and domestic colonial law directly clashed. By the time of Federation, the British desire for uniformity of standards around the Empire had been eroded (Britain had given way on variable tariffs, variable immigration requirements, and variable divorce laws, among other things) and it had been established that British powers over its colonies were confined to external matters. So long as the Australian Constitution stuck to domestic matters, Britain had no real reason to treat it as other than the expression of a purely national agreement, and to enact it accordingly.

But what did Britain get out of this agreement? Did the British authorities have any reason to care one way or another? There *was* a type of contract between Britain and the new Australian nation (one the British were concluding with their other self-governing colonies around the world); in essence it was for Britain to supply a naval defence of Australian waters in return for the use of Australian soldiers to defend the Empire. On the eve of Federation, Australian soldiers went off with alacrity to fight against the Boers in the South African war, attracting little public criticism and without the official ambivalence of the previous decade when the New South Wales Government had hastily sent troops upon a fruitless military venture in the Soudan. The South African commitment was a very significant sign of the restored relationship between the Australian colonies and Britain.

In his speech to open the first Federal Parliament on 9 May 1901 (three and a half months after the death of Queen Victoria), the Duke of York told his audience that the King had only consented to a separation from his son at such a painful time because he was 'moved by his sense of the loyalty and devotion which prompted the generous aid afforded by all the colonies in the South African War'.[22] Australia's part in the contract had been willingly demonstrated. The domestic details of Federation concerned only the Australians themselves.

What then of the statement in the Preamble that the Federal agreement is 'under the Crown'? The legal meaning of 'the Crown' was of course the British Parliament, the real 'sovereign', not Her Majesty in person. The British Parliament passed the Constitution as an Act and, on 9 July 1900, the Act then received the signature of Queen Victoria, who acted, as the British constitution required she must, upon the advice of her ministers. The Australian colonies had effectively two options for bringing about Federation: one was a declaration of independence (with the risk of conflict), the other was enactment in Britain. They opted for the latter, not because they did not seek independence, but because they had no good reason to rupture the genuine sentimental attachment to

Britain shared by the majority of Australians. In addition they did not want war, either with Britain itself (as had happened in America) or with another power to which they might become vulnerable without Britain's support. They congratulated themselves, quite justifiably, on achieving nationhood without bloodshed. To regard this approach as evidence that the people of the Australian colonies did not have the power to constitute a government is to suggest that the evidence of conflict alone would suffice.

Unlike the Canadians in the 1860s, the Australians chose to draft their own Constitution. The Colonial Office offered advice and assistance and, perhaps because this was not readily accepted, it did attempt at one point (largely unsuccessfully as it happened) to influence certain sections of the Constitution by indirect means.[23] The question of whether the passage of the Constitution as an Act of British Parliament shifted the legal foundation from the people to the parliament may be tested by the resolve shown by the Australian delegates who went to London in early 1900 to help the Constitution in its passage. They went determined to protect the Constitution as it stood, unchanged, regardless of what the British thought.

The story has been told at length in Alfred Deakin's personal account of Federation. There he relates the conflict that arose between the delegates (he was one) and the Colonial Secretary, Joseph Chamberlain, over one particular section of the Constitution. The British did care about external relations, and they cared in particular about protecting Britain's investments in its colonies. Britain was, Chamberlain said, 'anxious to see the Bill passed', but remained 'duty bound' to protect Imperial interests as well as rendering to the colonies the services of a tribunal of appeal 'with regard to which there could not be even a suspicion of pre-possession'.[24] The as yet unformed Australian High Court could not be, it seemed, above suspicion of partisanship or conflict of interest. A deadlock thus arose over section 74, which, as it stood after the 1899 referendum, effectively ruled out appeals in all constitutional matters to the transcendent tribunal, the 'Queen in Council', that is to say, the Privy Council.

As Deakin describes 'The Struggle with Chamberlain', we find the majority of delegates determined to retain the Constitution, unamended (and succeeding with certain other, lesser alterations, which the Colonial Office had sought). Edmund Barton argued that 'it was not competent for delegates to consent to an amendment of a measure twice adopted after prolonged discussions by the whole body of the electors'; Charles Kingston 'followed with the firm declaration that he was not prepared either to ask or accept further authority from the colonial Ministries', and he reminded Chamberlain, among other things, 'that they had to deal

206   *To Constitute a Nation*

with the whole body of the electors'; Deakin declared that 'inasmuch as [section 74] was never challenged by the Colonial Office before the first Referendum on the Bill, nor when the Premiers were afterwards sitting in Conference . . . before the second Referendum, they were entitled to conclude that it was accepted as sufficient and that therefore the time was now gone by for altering it'.[25]

The situation may have led to a stalemate, but concluded happily with a compromise. Once the Australian people and the Australian press, following the delegates' progress, had expressed their approval of some alteration in this section, the delegates (who had joined hands and danced with delight around the table in the British Attorney-General's Office at the recognition that the Colonial Office would give ground) agreed to a compromise. It was suggested, fittingly, by Sir Samuel Griffith, the main drafter of the 1891 Constitution Bill upon which, through all the stages, over all the years, Federalists had effectively worked, and Deakin called it 'the golden bridge over which the delegates passed to union'. Griffith's compromise allowed general appeals to the Privy Council, but ruled out any appeal in *inter se* cases (that is to say, matters concerning disputes over jurisdiction, the bread-and-butter, as it turned out, of constitutional cases), except by special leave of the High Court itself. It kept intact the essential independence of the Australian Constitution.

The people of the various states had agreed to this Constitution. There is no evidence that the British Parliament could have forced through an alternative version or even amended the Constitution as if it were their own Act, in anything other than a purely formal sense, without the Australian people's approval. Once passed, the power to amend lay outside British hands since, by enacting the Constitution, the Parliament agreed to section 128 and, from that time on, to the principle that only the Australian people could alter the Act.[26]

Despite the legal necessity of British enactment of the Australian Constitution Bill, there is a surprising absence of reference to Britain throughout the Convention debates and the referendum campaigns. Over and over again, 'the people' were invited to make their minds up, to express their will, to play their part in bringing about the nation. States' rights advocates subjected the Bill to scrutiny according to its impact on their individual colony. Almost no one publicly raised the question of whether or not the Bill would be acceptable to the British.

This lack was picked up, almost in passing, towards the very end of the process. A pamphlet by Victorian George Caldwell, 'The Commonwealth Bill: Will the Imperial Parliament Enact it?', suggested that the answer was no. The Bill, Caldwell argued, gave the states power over their own boundaries, 'thus making each State a Sovereign Power'. But the Crown alone was sovereign. A presumption, likely to prove unacceptable to the British, 'appears to run through the Bill, that the Constitution shall be alterable by the people of Australia without the necessity for a special Act of the Imperial Parliament'.[27]

One newspaper at least took Caldwell's warning seriously. The future relationship of the new Commonwealth to the Imperial Parliament 'has received scant notice', the *West Australian* commented; how many people 'realise fully . . . what the break will be which will be made not indeed in the Imperial connection so much as in the exercise of the Imperial Power in directions in which the Imperial government has been hitherto supreme'? The Bill was described as 'indissoluble' and its Act would 'bind the Crown'—a 'new and most significant phrase', the newspaper added (it was later dropped). Once passed, there would be practically no powers to stop the Commonwealth.[28] But the moment of alarm faded and the processes continued unchanged, perhaps because of a failure to think the matter through properly, more probably because the British Parliament was, if necessary to the Federation process, neither sufficient nor fundamental.

If the compact was not, at least not essentially, between the colonies and the Imperial Parliament, was there another, literal, sense of 'the Crown' at work? Was the compact one between the Australian subjects and the Monarch? Was the binding agreement expressed in the Constitution's Preamble between Australians and their Queen?

Queen Victoria's Diamond Jubilee occurred in 1897, three months after the first meeting of the elected Convention in which the Australian Constitution was completed. The Premiers of the Australian colonies had gone almost directly from the Adelaide session of the Convention to London, to join other members of the Imperial family at the Jubilee. While there they took advantage of the opportunity to discuss at length the fruits of their work with the Colonial Secretary and others. On their return, they went back to the Convention, sitting in Sydney and then Melbourne. Exactly one year after the Jubilee, the first national referendum on the draft Constitution took place. We might expect to find expressions of bond or compact between the people and the Monarch on such an occasion, if this were the case.

There were virtually no such expressions. There were numerous jibes at republicans and references to their thinness on the ground during the Jubilee celebrations. The Australian celebrations were themselves sumptuous and extravagant, the fireworks alone outdoing anything we might consider spectacular these days. And Australian newspapers expressed satisfaction that the fact of the sun's rising in that part of the world while everyone in Britain still slept meant that Australians could be first in the Empire (New Zealand was left to make its own claim) to start the celebration of the Record Reign.

208   *To Constitute a Nation*

Where ten years before, during the Golden Jubilee, a significant level of republican sentiment had been in the air and a now famous resolution of disloyalty was passed at a meeting in the Sydney Town Hall,[29] and even a little grumbling was heard from those most normally loyal, almost everyone had decided by 1897 that the Queen deserved recognition. Even the 'most embittered Socialist', suggested one paper, 'must have ta'en the infection' of the Jubilee celebration.[40]

The once hostile *Bulletin,* while declaring that loyalty 'is fashionable, therefore every sheep-like person who lives in a groove is loyal', grudgingly admitted on the occasion, that while there was nothing especially admirable about this 'stout, rather cross looking old lady dressed in rusty black', that Victoria 'supplies as good an excuse as anybody else' for a celebration.[31] Processions, concerts, fireworks, illuminations and much sentimentality and philosophising on the part of the press were indulged in. Australia's material and political progress, Australia's part in the Empire, the development of technology were held up for reflection and praise. Not all commentary was flattering—the Melbourne *Argus,* for example, reminded readers that the Queen's reign had been marked by 'the red thread of war[s] . . . numerous and costly and bloody to a degree we all find it convenient to forget' and it deplored the amount of 'twaddle' written about a woman who had personally done nothing great[32]—but most was eulogistic. Victoria's virtue and duty and philanthropy were praised repeatedly. The Jubilee was a family gathering around a virtuous mother.

While the unity of the Empire and the 'common blood' of Britons and Australians were proclaimed again and again, almost nothing was said about the contemporaneous movement to unite the separate colonies of Australia itself. Some long-drawn parallels were made between the accomplished years of youth and maturity of both the Queen and the colonies, and some papers took the opportunity to comment separately about the progress of Federation. But, despite endless recitation of Victoria's virtues, including her combination of constitutional reserve and influence, nothing was said to indicate that Australians saw themselves as going through a process which involved the Monarch as a party.

In Western Australia alone (and in the course of subsequent developments) this relationship appears to have played a part. Despite the warning in the *West Australian* that the Constitution would 'bind the Crown' and that the Commonwealth's powers would prove unstoppable, the people of that colony persuaded themselves that Federation involved a dissoluble contract. Premier Sir John Forrest gave fellow West Australians to believe that the state could withdraw through Act of British Parliament, if Federation did not turn out well. The important thing, Forrest argued, was to come into the Commonwealth as an original state, to secure, among other things, equal representation in the Senate.

Within five years of Federation the West Australian Parliament had decided that 'the time has arrived for placing before the people the question of withdrawal from the union'. Commenting on this resolution, John Quick in Victoria had no doubts. Such 'menaces and fulminations are absolutely useless . . . doomed to be abortive' and to appear ridiculous, he wrote. Western Australia 'freely and voluntarily joined the Commonwealth in the full knowledge that it is not a mere compact or partnership, dissoluble at will . . . but that it is an indissoluble Federal Commonwealth'.[33]

The movement in 1906 did not get far, but the issue never died. In 1934, following a mass positive referendum vote on the subject, Western Australia appealed to Britain to grant it secession from the Commonwealth. The ensuing conflict throws much light on the issue of the nature of the original federal compact. Delegates again went to London, this time from the West Australian Government, taking their petition in a specially carved native timber box. There they argued, among other things, that Western Australia had been forced into Federation, that the terms offered were unfair to that colony, that it had never actually consented, and that since that time it had suffered materially from the arrangement.[34]

'Indissoluble', one secessionist argued, meant the Crown was indissoluble, not the Federation. The Federation must be dissoluble because to claim it was not, was to say that the Imperial Parliament had lost its sovereignty in Australia. A parliament could not bind its successors and the Imperial Parliament could not itself have created an indissoluble Federation. The prospect of civil war, evoked by opponents of secession, was unthinkable, 'indeed impossible, so long as we are under the Crown'.

The West Australians were to be disappointed in both their hopes and their anticipation of what followed from the view that it was the Imperial Parliament that had 'created' the Federation in the first place. But, although the Imperial Parliament declared that it did in fact have the power to grant secession, it declined even to receive their petition. Such a petition, it argued, could only be accepted if it came from the Commonwealth Government, not from an individual state, whose constitutional tie was with the Commonwealth, not Britain. The secessionists had failed to see, one commentator has suggested, that 'the sovereign with which they had [now] to deal was not the British sovereign, but the new sovereign which had emerged in its place . . . namely the Australian people'.[35]

Despite their confidence about the permanency of the union, Quick and Garran add that 'the indissolubility of the Commonwealth is not

210   *To Constitute a Nation*

affirmed by any clause in the Imperial Act, [but] it is recited as an accepted principle in the preamble'. The only reason for this they can think of, they write, is that because

> the people have a general power to amend the Constitution . . . it may have been considered wise and prudent that, coupled with a right so great and important, there should be a reminder placed in the forefront of the deed of political partnership between the federating colonies that the union . . . was intended by the contracting parties to be a lasting one.[36]

It is unlikely that the British would have agreed to West Australian secession prior to this campaign, even had it been asked before 1931 when the Statute of Westminster was passed, in which the Colonial Laws Validity Act was finally revoked and the independence of the self-governing colonies (by then called the Dominions) was affirmed. They had turned down Nova Scotia's appeal for secession in 1868, even though the Imperial Parliament had express powers over the Canadian Constitution at that time. In the Australian case, section 128 sat firmly there on the Constitution's last page, serving to remind any parliament from the start that only the people and the states together could alter the Constitution.

Australians had 'dual nationality'. They were Victorians or Tasmanians or Queenslanders or South Australians or West Australians or men and women of New South Wales. They were also Australians. They were 'citizens' of both state and nation. Their Constitution had been written to reflect their dual identity, and to attempt to keep it in balance. They had agreed, in effect, to both a contract and a compact.

Australia came into being with a paradoxical Constitution; on the one hand still providing, at least in theory, for British disallowance of Commonwealth laws[37] (although this was never used); on the other hand with life breathed into it by the will of the Australian people. The nature of the federal union—whether it was a contract, or a compact, or an uneasy compromise—remains a vexed question in Australia, both in constitutional law and in wider issues about Australian national identity. The Constitution's Preamble remains a riddle, in a type of legal no man's land. It is actually the Preamble to the Covering Clauses of the Act of British Parliament which brought the Constitution into legal being, yet it refers to the manner in which the Bill was consented to prior to this Act of Parliament, as if this were the constituting power of the Act itself. It is probably not justiciable (that is, able to be judged in a court of law), but opinion is now divided over whether or not it may be changed through a referendum.

The six colonies had agreed to federate. They had agreed to form an 'indissoluble Federal Commonwealth', and they had anticipated both spiritual greatness and material security from their imagined nation. They had also agreed to turn their colonies into states, and in doing so to give up a little of their local freedom in return for their share in the greater whole of which they would now be parts. They had recognised that they were a people. But what exactly had they agreed to? All we can say with confidence is that there is no uniform position now, and, beyond the metaphor of marriage, nor was there in 1901.

Of all the parties to this agreement, first on the list, the people, in the end had the edge. Although at the time of Federation they were a particular type of people—white, 'native' and British at the same time—nothing except the retention of the Queen as Head of State committed them to remaining any one of these things, and their control of the Constitution through section 128, which in the last analysis made it a people's compact, allows them to change this designation if and when they choose. No state could secede without the agreement of all the Australian people. It was unthinkable that the Crown would alter or rescind the Constitution without prior agreement of the people. And Almighty God, for the whole of the Constitution's history, has remained silent on the matter.

When the Inauguration of the Commonwealth was celebrated on the first day of the new century, many things were elevated to the status of national icon. But, above all else, the people celebrated their optimism and their imagination, and in doing so they celebrated themselves.

Conclusion

The timing of Federation is one of the enduring mysteries of Australian history. Federal schemes were suggested again and again from the 1840s onward; why then did Federation occur when it did, and not before? Part of history's appeal is that no one can say for certain why something happened at a particular time rather than another. But historians still try. The intention of this book has been to show, as far as possible, how the circumstances of the last two decades of the nineteenth century, both negative and positive, came together and joined up, as it were, with the strange, almost surreal optimism that accompanies the end of one century and the anticipation of another. As with other great temporal milestones (meaning nothing in themselves, but symbolically highly charged), a new century is experienced by many as a time when change is both possible and expected, when the routine and predictable may be set aside. Although the *fin de siècle* was not the cause of Federation as such (there was no single cause), it encouraged the will to achieve Federation to emerge. Along with faith in progress and the complex modernising processes shared by all 'Western' nations in this period, it allowed people to set aside the doubts and the suspicions that might otherwise have cautioned against change.

The late 1880s and the early 1890s in Australia were, it has been argued, a 'Utopian moment', a time of both optimism and dismay, of disillusionment with old constitutional relations and of confidence in the local ability to forge new ones. Utopian is not a matter of pipe-dreaming, of wildly unrealistic or unrealisable fantasy. The vast majority of Utopian writings over their five-century history have, indeed, been meticulously planned and detailed, careful and precise. Many have imagined things now thought commonplace. Even though a good number employ fantasy techniques, such as dream or time travel (or, in the case of Edward Bellamy's immensely popular *Looking Backward*, the protagonist's one hundred year long sleep) these have been devices to transport the reader into serious social commentary, into the alternative social blueprint that follows, more than key components of the work.

What makes a work Utopian is the belief that a whole system can be written down, constructed from a single set of principles.

To describe the seedbed of Federation as Utopian and to argue that the Constitution drew from the Utopian moment immediately preceding its completion is to challenge fundamentally a number of earlier interpretations of Federation. The major challenge is to the view that Federation was primarily caused by economic interests. There are three ways in which this view has been expressed: the first maintains that class interests galvanised the Federalists; the second that specific regional economic concerns can be traced in patterns of support and opposition to Federation; and the third that the motives behind Federation were purely materialist, self-interested and utilitarian.

On the first, the question of timing is central: Federation occurred when it did, some critics argue, because conservatives suddenly recognised the growing power of the political labour movement (which indeed had made dramatic inroads into colonial parliaments in that decade, holding and exercising the balance of power on significant occasions), and they realised that they would lose control of the processes if they waited. Some have argued specifically that Federation was a 'means of preventing one or other Colonies from jumping over to extreme socialism',[1] while more generally it has been commonplace to point out that Federation occurred 'without participation by a great section of the electorate, the labour section, which had almost no representation in either of the constitutional conventions . . . and, in the mass, did not even vote' in the referendums.[2]

The claim that there was, effectively, a conscious conservative strategy, even conspiracy, has been subjected to scrutiny by more than one writer, without corroboration. The fact that almost no direct evidence exists of conservative opinion or advice along such lines, and that many among the most conservative also opposed Federation have been among those arguments advanced in support of a conclusion against a conservative ploy.[3] It is true, however, that many Federalists were irritated with the demands of labour, and that labour was almost entirely unrepresented in the formal Federation processes. But the argument that this was a rational conservative strategy does not hold water. Rather than repressing labour, Federation created a national polity in which the Colonial Labor Parties could federate, and a national Parliament through which Labor policy could be implemented.

Constitutional problems experienced by the Australian Labor Party, as its policy was obstructed by High Court judgments, mostly came some decades later, after the 'Blackburn resolution' on socialisation of industry was passed at the 1921 Labor Party National Conference. The most famous of these, the Bank Nationalisation case of 1948, occurred during

214   *To Constitute a Nation*

the second term of a once popular and successful Labor government, which had overseen major constitutional changes, including the successful referendum of 1946 where a wide range of social welfare powers were transferred to the Commonwealth Parliament, and, most significantly, uniform income tax-collecting powers were gained, giving the Commonwealth the potential for a degree of control not at all envisaged in the original constitutional settlement.

The labour movement in the large colonies in the 1890s had great difficulty accepting the principle of equal state representation in the Senate on majoritarian democratic grounds and because of the almost co-equal powers given to the Senate. It was feared in particular that the small, conservative states would use their numbers, combined with the Senate's powers, to thwart progressive policy coming from the larger states. But, while states' rights arguments have been frequently conservative, they were also used (in particular by South Australia) to protect progressive policy and the flexibility to experiment free of Commonwealth control. Despite a long- (although no longer) held Labor Party policy of abolishing the Senate, no Labor government in power at either the state or the Commonwealth level attempted to pursue it.

The second claim, of regional economic interests, was famously aired in a debate in the post-Second World War years between R. S. Parker and Geoffrey Blainey. Parker had claimed that regional voting patterns in the Constitution Bill referendums followed particular economic interests, and that the power of local interests could be recognised in the decision to pursue a federal rather than unificationist national model.[4] Geoffrey Blainey, whose conclusions were subsequently supported by studies of referendum results in Western Australia and south-eastern New South Wales,[5] pointed out that Parker had overlooked the lack of fit between the referendum vote in many regions and their obvious economic interests, and had not explored the likely impact of other factors, including the press, the Church, the union movement, and the 'frontier' mentality of migratory work-forces. The federal campaigns, Blainey concluded, 'were not calm and dispassionate controversies'; Federation 'may possibly have been achieved quite independently of the economic interests of most electors'.[6]

Given the complexity, even impossibility of precisely mapping regional interests and issues with campaigns, personalities and other influences, a definite conclusion on the merits of these arguments cannot be reached. There is certainly evidence to support both sides, both the idea of Federation as a 'business contract' and Federation as a national movement that transcended material concerns. What is important here is to ask why regional interests, which had always existed, were turned in the last decade of the century towards creating a *nation* and why, despite the conclusion reached by Select Committees in several colonies that Federation would be financially injurious to their particular interests, the movement to federate still proceeded. It was in the imagined nation that those with particular economic axes to grind saw their solution, rather than through the much less complex process of driving legislation through the colonial parliaments or negotiating, for example, a customs union between the colonies. The representatives of labour, still struggling to establish themselves in their own parliaments, were not yet in a position to gain a great deal from imagining a nation. But the majority too were ultimately enticed by the vision of 'a self-governing nation in these southern seas', the creation of which 'cannot be long delayed if Australia is to be retained for white men'.[7]

Finally, there is the charge of utilitarianism, best known in the work of Hugh Collins, who has argued that, in contrast to the more visionary, idealistic American model, Australia's Federation was a product of convenience rather than conviction, little more than a 'practical adjustment to circumstance'.[8] The utilitarianism of political theorist Jeremy Bentham is deeply embedded, Collins argues, in the Australian political landscape; it manifests itself in individualism, in 'institutional means of securing that public good which maximises private interest',[9] in lack of imagination or vision, and in the co-ordination of interests rather than social consent or contract.

But, if Australians seemed to be lacking in intellectual passion, interested primarily in material goals and excited by material pleasures (as visitors from overseas frequently remarked), this did not make them any less interested in social and political experiment, nor any less romantic about the country and the culture around them. If they did indeed seek institutional solutions in order to maximise private interest, they did so also to resolve social problems. If they were utilitarian, they drew less upon the ideas of Bentham than upon the later work of John Stuart Mill, for whom utilitarianism was a framework for democracy and human development. If they sought to balance interests, they did so by pursuing a social compact that went far beyond a material solution. If they envisaged institutional forms for this compact, they did so in visionary terms, much as the social blueprint Utopias of the Federation period had done.

This book has attempted to show that Australians were capable of both pragmatism and romanticism, that indeed their combination was characteristic of Australian life and that in the political culture which had developed by the end of the last century, romanticism was allowed to prevail, if only briefly, in the key Utopian moment out of which the practical arrangements of Federation emerged.

Epilogue

Water flows under the bridge. One hundred years have passed since the debates and struggles of the 1890s that gave rise to the Australian Commonwealth. Australians find themselves again in the *fin de siècle*, and even more magically in a *fin de* millennium. It is again a time of deep paradoxes, where predictions of the future and anticipation mingle with economic gloom and political turmoil. But the outlook this time, is much less optimistic. The people of the 1890s felt able to imagine and indeed to make a new nation. Australians in the 1990s are looking back and assessing the fruits of that earlier constructive age. In the eyes of many, the Commonwealth Constitution is now fundamentally flawed.

It is, however, far from the first time the Constitution has been under scrutiny this century. Indeed, scarcely a decade has gone by since Federation without some form of official review, leading to recommendations for its alteration. By 1927, the year the Commonwealth Parliament moved to Canberra, two successful (and thirteen unsuccessful) referendum questions had already been put to the voters, and a major shift in constitutional interpretation had been accomplished by the High Court. That year, a full Royal Commission on the Constitution was appointed by the Nationalist Bruce government with the tasks of inquiring into the powers of the Commonwealth 'and the working of the Constitution since Federation'.[1]

Of its ten specific subjects for inquiry, one, Aviation, had only come into existence after the completion of the Constitution. Some, like the Interstate Commission, would come and go as issues over the years, while New States would take another seventy years to be tested, only to fail in 1998 in the Northern Territory Statehood referendum on the eve of the centenary of Federation. But a good number of the rest—taxation, trade and commerce, company law, and health—remain constant, intractable issues for the constitutional relations between the Commonwealth and the States. Less than thirty years after the Constitution was enacted, these and other matters had been identified (and by a conservative government) as more or less inadequately addressed by its terms.

216

Epilogue 217

The 1927 Royal Commission received submissions from the State Governments and the public, as well as many organisations, including women's organisations and the Australian Natives Association. Those few members of the Conventions of the 1890s who were still alive—Joseph Carruthers, John Cockburn, Patrick Glynn, Andrew Henning, Henry Higgins, Isaac Isaacs, Walter James, Neil Lewis, Alexander Peacock, John Quick, Josiah Symon, and Robert Garran[2]—were invited to contribute submissions. But all the consultation and wisdom in the Commonwealth could not produce a successful review of the Constitution's adequacy in the light of experience and changed conditions.

It is one of the curious features of a Constitution, that no matter how perilous were the processes by which it was established and how slender the majorities that supported it at the time, it becomes almost overnight a sacred document. It must, or the legitimacy and authority of the nation–state which it founds will be in doubt. As a genuine marriage is distinguished from a fake one—not by the legal act alone, but by the belief in what it signifies—so must the constitutional nation be borne along by faith.

All the same, from 1901 on, practical realities and party policies have repeatedly generated proposals for change. These have clashed again and again with the very sense of permanency that the Australian Constitution needed from the start and managed quickly to acquire. Like the recommendations of the Royal Commission of 1927, almost all proposals have come to nothing.

It is a continuing source of mystery and frustration (for those who think of politics as a rational domain) that Australians have been reluctant to change their Constitution. Famously, only eight out of a total of the forty-two referendum questions put between 1906 and 1988 have been passed. One attempt made by governments to get around this impasse has been by calling a 'Convention' rather than simply a Committee or Commission of inquiry. The use of the term self-consciously conveys—as it did last century—something of a higher order than the routine Parliamentary processes: something that might have such authority and weight behind it, that its recommendations would appear as instructions to those with the power to make change. The strategy was successful in the 1890s. Would it work again, this time to alter the work done by the original 'People's' Conventions?

This strategy was tested in 1942 by the Curtin Labor Government and again between 1973 and 1985 when a series of Constitutional Conventions involving all three tiers of government met around the nation, producing recommendations for constitutional alteration. The hoped-for result was not achieved, even if a tenuous link might be found between the successful referendums of 1946 and 1977 and concerns of these

218   *Epilogue*

preceding Conventions. But a bi-partisan Joint Parliamentary Committee, established in 1956 and a Constitutional Commission, in 1985, failed to have even a fortuitous coincidence with a successful referendum, in the latter case, its many recommendations turning into four utterly doomed referendum questions in 1988.

Where then do Australians stand with regard to their Constitution at the end of the twentieth century? They will have a chance, once more, to test themselves. Another Convention has taken place. Its task this time was making recommendations about whether Australia should become a republic and, if so, what sort of Constitutional alterations would achieve this. The result of years of pro-republican lobbying, an Advisory Committee report in 1993 (commissioned by the previous government), and the pressure of public opinion, the Convention was held in Canberra between 2 and 13 February 1998. One hundred and fifty two delegates, half of them appointed, half popularly elected, spent ten days in debate and negotiations, attempting to find common ground despite vast personal differences on the issue.

The Convention was, in some respects, deliberately modelled on the Convention of 1897–98 and was self-consciously styled a 'people's convention'. But it differed in important ways too: it consisted of delegates who were opposed to change as well as those who wanted it, and among those who wanted change, of advocates of numerous different (and often conflicting) models of achieving it. Politicians made up half the appointed delegates, and had not been allowed to stand for election. Women and indigenous Australians had a significant presence. Instead of identical representation for each of the states, numbers of delegates were calculated roughly on a state population basis. Numerous proxies, neither appointed nor elected, took the places of absent delegates throughout the Convention.

At the end, a conclusion favouring a republic was reached. On the final day of the Convention, 13 February 1998, the Prime Minister, John Howard, promised that there would be a referendum on the question the following year. Although a Monarchist, he had accepted the majority's position. He had originally promised to hold a plebiscite on Australia's becoming a republic, if no 'clear view' had emerged from the Convention, and he was relieved of having to adhere to such a difficult undertaking. The model produced by the ten days debate was not too unpalatable for conservatives, and was in fact more likely to alienate those who wanted fundamental constitutional change, in particular direct popular election of the new Head of State.

With the re-assuring title of 'bi-partisan model', the Convention model proposed a joint sitting of the Houses of Parliament to ratify, by a two-thirds majority vote, a choice for the republican Head of State suggested by the Prime Minister, chosen from a list of public nominations. In a conflict between the two offices, dismissal of the Head of State would remain in the hands of the Prime Minister, to be ratified by a simple majority of the House of Representatives. The Head of State's powers would not be codified, and would remain as far as possible those held by the Governor-General.

Australians are again drawn into a process of following an ostensibly American model and at the same time resisting *becoming* American. The simple fact that the 1998 Convention did not commit itself to the name 'President' for a republican Head of State is suggestive of this tension, even though it is probable that President will eventually be settled for. The highly popular alternative of a directly elected Head of State still remains to be accommodated, and fear of following the American model too far may be one of the best hopes for the equally adamant anti-election republicans to defeat direct election.

Those who oppose the referendum in 1999 because they do not like the Convention model will, like the anti-Billites in 1898, have trouble convincing people that they are sincere in their support for the ultimate cause, and only critical of the fine-print. Everyone will have trouble getting past the sense that sacred documents should not be changed, even though direct constitutional relations between Australia and Britain have long been severed, and the material impact of a republican constitution will be very small. But, paradoxically, the older and more 'sacred' an institution, the more it can withstand change. A tradition of defeating referendums may not prove an obstacle, if proponents of the republic can convince the voters that the essential, sacred core of the Constitution will remain untouched. The prospect of a new century will again assist in achieving that other necessary ingredient, the willingness to imagine change.

'All history takes in the appearance of inevitableness after the event' wrote Alfred Deakin at the completion of Federation.[3] When people speak in the 1990s of the 'inevitable republic', this is simply a way of indicating that they are, in fact, prepared to accept it at some point. They mean that the conditions and values of the present are ready to accommodate such constitutional change, where they were not in the past. People spoke of Federation as inevitable long before it was any such thing. That became a type of a self-fulfilling prophesy. But while the cultural landscape had been prepared, the political work had still to be done. If history is any guide, although cultural preparation for the republic has gone a long way, what follows politically from the 1998 Constitutional Convention will be more complex than a single referendum. But history has a habit of being perverse and disproving those who make predictions. Only the historian of the future will know which way the water has flown.

Appendix
Key Sections of the Constitution

PREAMBLE

Whereas the people of New South Wales, Victoria, South Australia, Queensland, and Tasmania, humbly relying on the blessing of Almighty God, have agreed to unite in one indissoluble Federal Commonwealth under the Crown of the United Kingdom of Great Britain and Ireland, and under the Constitution hereby established . . . Be it therefore enacted . . . as follows:—

COVERING CLAUSE 3

It shall be lawful for the Queen, with the advice of the Privy Council, to declare by proclamation that, on and after a day therein appointed, not being later than one year after passing of this Act, the people of New South Wales, Victoria, South Australia, Queensland, and Tasmania, and also, if Her Majesty is satisfied that the people of Western Australia have agreed thereto, of Western Australia, shall be united in a Federal Commonwealth under the name of the Commonwealth of Australia . . .

SECTIONS:

7. The Senate shall be composed of senators for each State, directly chosen by the people of the State, voting, until the Parliament otherwise provides, as one electorate.

But until Parliament of the Commonwealth otherwise provides, the Parliament of the State of Queensland, if that State be an Original State, may make laws dividing the State into divisions and determining the number of senators to be chosen for each division, and in the absence of such provision the State shall be one electorate.

24. The House of Representatives shall be composed of members directly chosen by the people of the Commonwealth, and the number of such members shall be, as nearly as practicable, twice the number of the senators . . .

41. No adult person who has or acquires a right to vote at elections for the more numerous House of the Parliament of a State shall, while the right continues, be prevented by any law of the Commonwealth from voting at elections for either House of the Parliament of the Commonwealth.

44. Any person who—

Key Sections of the Constitution   221

(i)   Is under any acknowledgment of allegiance, obedience, or adherence to a foreign power, or is a subject or a citizen or entitled to the rights or privileges of a subject or a citizen of a foreign power: . . . shall be incapable of being chosen or of sitting as a senator or a member of the House of Representatives.

49.   The powers, privileges, and immunities of the Senate and of the House of Representatives, and of the members and the committees of each House, shall be such as are declared by the Parliament, and until declared shall be those of the Commons House of Parliament of the United Kingdom, and of its members and committees, at the establishment of the Commonwealth.

51.   The Parliament shall, subject to this Constitution, have power to make laws for the peace, order, and good government of the Commonwealth with respect to:—

(v)   Postal, telegraphic, telephonic, and other like services:

(vi)   The naval and military defence of the Commonwealth and of the Several States . . .

(vii)   Lighthouses, lightships, beacons and buoys:

(ix)   Quarantine:

(xi)   Census and statistics:

(xii)   Currency, coinage, and legal tender:

(xvii)   Bankruptcy and insolvency:

(xix)   Naturalization and aliens:

(xxi)   Marriage:

(xxii) Divorce and matrimonial causes; and in relation thereto, parental rights, and the custody and guardianship of infants:

(xxiii)   Invalid and old-age pensions:

(xxiiiA)   The provision of maternity allowances, widows' pensions, child endowment, unemployment, pharmaceutical, sickness and hospital benefits, medical and dental services (but not so as to authorize any form of civil conscription), benefits to students and family allowances:

(xxvi)   The people of any race, other than the aboriginal race in any State, for whom it is deemed necessary to make special laws:

(xxvii)   Immigration and emigration:

(xxix)   External affairs:

(xxxiv)   Railway construction and extension in any State with the consent of that State:

(xxxv)   Conciliation and arbitration for the prevention and settlement of industrial disputes extending beyond the limits of any one State:

(xxxvii)   Matters referred to the Parliament of the Commonwealth by the Parliament or Parliaments of any State or States . . .

53.   Proposed laws appropriating revenue or moneys, or imposing taxation, shall not originate in the Senate . . .

The Senate may not amend proposed laws imposing taxation, or proposed laws appropriating revenue or moneys for the ordinary annual services of the Government . . .

The Senate may at any stage return to the House of Representatives any proposed law which the Senate may not amend, requesting, by message, the omission or amendment of any items or provisions therein. And the House of

222   *Appendix*

Representatives may, if it thinks fit, make any of such omissions or amendments, with or without modifications.

Except as provided in this section, the Senate shall have equal power with the House of Representatives in respect of all proposed laws.

59.   The Queen may disallow any law within one year from the Governor-General's assent, and such disallowance on being made known by the Governor-General by speech or message to each of the Houses of the Parliament, or by Proclamation, shall annul the law from the day when the disallowance is so made known.

74.   No appeal shall be permitted to the Queen in Council from a decision of the High Court upon any question, howsoever arising, as to the limits inter se of the Constitutional powers of the Commonwealth and those of any State or States, or as to the limits inter se of the Constitutional powers of any two or more States, unless the High Court shall certify that the question is one which ought to be determined by Her Majesty in Council . . .

88.   Uniform duties of customs shall be imposed within two years after the establishment of the Commonwealth.

90.   On the imposition of uniform duties of customs the power of the Parliament to impose duties of customs and of excise, and to grant bounties on the production or export of goods, shall become exclusive . . .

92.   On the imposition of uniform duties of customs, trade, commerce, and intercourse among the States, whether by means of internal carriage or ocean navigation, shall be absolutely free.

95.   Notwithstanding anything in this Constitution, the Parliament of the State of Western Australia, if that State be an Original State, may, during the first five years after the imposition of uniform duties of customs, impose duties of customs on goods passing into that State and not originally imported from beyond the limits of the Commonwealth; and such duties shall be collected by the Commonwealth . . .

99.   The Commonwealth shall not, by any law or regulation of trade, commerce, or revenue, give preference to one State or any part thereof over another State or any part thereof.

100.   The Commonwealth shall not by any law or regulation of trade or commerce, abridge the right of a State or of the residents therein to the reasonable use of the waters of rivers for conservation or irrigation.

106.   The Constitution of each State of the Commonwealth shall, subject to this Constitution, continue as at the establishment of the Commonwealth, or as at the admission or establishment of the State, as the case may be, until altered in accordance with the Constitution of the State.

109.   When a law of a State is inconsistent with a law of the Commonwealth, the latter shall prevail, and the former shall, to the extent of the inconsistency, be invalid.

111.   The Parliament of a State may surrender any part of the State to the Commonwealth, and upon such surrender, and the acceptance thereof by the Commonwealth, such part of the State shall become subject to the exclusive jurisdiction of the Commonwealth.

113. All fermented, distilled, or other intoxicating liquids passing into any State or remaining therein for use, consumption, sale, or storage, shall be subject to the laws of the State as if such liquids had been produced in the State.

114. A State shall not, without the consent of the Parliament of the Commonwealth, raise or maintain any naval or military force . . .

116. The Commonwealth shall not make any law for establishing any religion, or for imposing any religious observance, or for prohibiting the free exercise of any religion, and no religious test shall be required as a qualification for any office or public trust under the Commonwealth.

117. A subject of the Queen, resident in any State, shall not be subject in any other State to any disability or discrimination which would not be equally applicable to him if he were a subject of the Queen resident in such other State.

119. The Commonwealth shall protect every State against invasion and, on the application of the Executive Government of the State, against domestic violence.

125. The seat of the Government of the Commonwealth shall be determined by the Parliament, and shall be within territory which shall have been granted to or acquired by the Commonwealth, and shall be vested in and belong to the Commonwealth, and shall be in the State of New South Wales, and be distant not less than one hundred miles from Sydney.

Such territory shall contain an area of not less than one hundred square miles . . .

The Parliament shall sit at Melbourne until it meet at the seat of Government.

127. In reckoning the numbers of the people of the Commonwealth, or of a State or other part of the Commonwealth, aboriginal natives shall not be counted.

128. This Constitution shall not be altered except in the following manner:—The proposed law for the alteration thereof must be passed by an absolute majority of each House of the Parliament, and not less than two nor more than six months after its passage through both Houses the proposed law shall be submitted in each State to the electors qualified to vote for the election of members of the House of Representatives.

. . . When a proposed law is submitted to the electors the vote shall be taken in such manner as the Parliament prescribes. But until the qualification of electors of members of the House of Representatives becomes uniform throughout the Commonwealth, only one-half the electors voting for and against the proposed law shall be counted in any State in which adult suffrage prevails.

And if in a majority of the States a majority of the electors voting approve the proposed law, and if a majority of all the electors voting also approve the proposed law, it shall be presented to the Governor-General for the Queen's assent. . . .

Notes

ABBREVIATIONS

ANA	Australian Natives' Association
AFL	Australasian Federation League
Conference Debates 1890	*Official Record of the Proceedings and Debates of the Australasian Federation Conference*, Melbourne: Government Printer, 1890
Convention Debates 1891, 1897, 1898	*Official Record of the Debates of the Australasian Federal Convention*, vols. I–V, Sydney, 1891, Adelaide, Sydney, Melbourne, 1897–1898, Sydney: Legal Books, 1986
Council Debates	*Official Record of the Debates of the Federal Council of Australasia*, sixth session, Hobart: 1895
ML	Mitchell Library, Sydney
NLA	National Library of Australia
Quick and Garran	John Quick and Robert Garran, *The Annotated Constitution of the Australian Commonwealth*, Sydney: Angus & Robertson, 1901
SMH	*Sydney Morning Herald*
WCTU	Woman's Christian Temperance Union
WFL	Women's Federal League
WSL	Womanhood Suffrage League of New South Wales

INTRODUCTION

1 The classic is J. A. La Nauze's *The Making of the Australian Constitution* (Melbourne University Press, 1972). Scott Bennett's invaluable edited two-volume collection of documents, *The Making of the Commonwealth* and *Federation* (Melbourne: Cassell Australia, 1971 and 1975), complement this work. With the exception of Bennett's *Federation*, no single work devoted to Federation alone has appeared since the first decade of the century. Most

Notes (pages 1–9)   225

recently, W. G. McMinn's *Nationalism and Federalism in Australia* (Melbourne: Oxford University Press, 1994) and Robert Birrell's *A Nation of Our Own: Citizenship and Nation-building in Federation Australia* (Melbourne: Longman, 1995) come closest to a full account of Federation history. The detailed bibliography in L. F. Crisp's *Federation Fathers* (Melbourne University Press, 1990) lists a number of theses and articles on Federation in individual states, as well as studies of particular political movements. The bibliography ends at 1980, but there have been no published studies of this kind since.

2 R. A. Gollan, 'Nationalism, the Labour Movement and the Commonwealth, 1880–1900', in Gordon Greenwood (ed.), *Australia: A Social and Political History* (Sydney: Angus & Robertson, 1977); Susan Magarey, et al. (eds), *Debutante Nation: Feminism Contests the 1890s* (Sydney: Allen & Unwin, 1993); John Docker, *The Nervous Nineties: Australian Cultural Life in the 1890s* (Melbourne: Oxford University Press, 1991).

3 For example, Ernest Scott, *A Short History of Australia* (Melbourne: Oxford University Press, 1916); A. G. L. Shaw, *The Story of Australia* (London: Faber & Faber, 1954).

4 Robert Garran, 'The Federation Movement and the Founding of the Commonwealth', in Ernest Scott (ed.), *Australia*, vol. VII, part I, of the *Cambridge History of the British Empire* (Cambridge University Press, reprint 1988), p. 425.

5 'Federal Council of Australasia Act, 14 August 1885', in C. M. H. Clark (ed.), *Select Documents in Australian History*, vol. II, 1851–1900 (Sydney: Angus & Robertson, 1977), p. 457.

6 La Nauze, *The Making of the Australian Constitution*, p. 86.

7 J. A. La Nauze, *The Hopetoun Blunder* (Melbourne University Press, 1957).

1 COLONIAL NUPTIALS

1 Gavin Souter, *Lion and Kangaroo: The Initiation of Australia* (Sydney: Sun Australia, 1992), p. 31.

2 *Council Debates*, 1895, p. 75.

3 Report of meeting, 30 May 1898, unidentified newspaper cutting, Rose Scott papers, ML.

4 *Argus*, 24 January 1895.

5 Most recently W. G. McMinn, *Nationalism and Federalism in Australia* (Melbourne: Oxford University Press, 1994).

6 Stephen Alomes, 'Ceremonial Visions of Australia', *Journal of Australian Studies*, no. 20, May 1987.

7 *SMH*, 21 June 1897.

8 *Bulletin*, 19 June 1897.

9 Souvenir booklet, 'with compliments of W. D. and H. O. Wills Ltd' (London: 1897).

10 E. K. Knight, *With The Royal Tour* (London: Longmans, Green & Co., 1902), p. 111.

11 Robert Freestone and Sharon Veale, 'The Street Beautiful: Triumphal Arches and Urban Improvement in Sydney, 1888–1925', *Public History Review*, vol. 4, 1996.

226 *Notes (pages 9–21)*

12 *Argus*, 2 January 1901.
13 *Courrier Australien*, 22 December 1900. They conceded, a fortnight later, that much less disorder had been experienced than they had expected (5 January 1901).
14 *Argus*, 2 January 1901.
15 Sidney Flavell, *A Voyage to Australia, Together with a Descriptive Account of the Inauguration of the Commonwealth* (Leamington Spa: Leamington Publishing Co., 1902).
16 *Age*, 7 May 1901.
17 *Sydney Mail*, 5 January 1901.
18 *Courrier Australien*, 5 January 1901.
19 Knight, *With The Royal Tour*, p. 107.
20 *Review of Reviews*, 15 December 1900.
21 *SMH*, 2 January 1901.
22 *Nordern*, 26 January 1901.
23 *Nordern*, 18 May 1901; 26 January 1901 (trans.).
24 *Australische Zeitung*, 12 December, 19 December 1900 (trans.).
25 *Chinese Australian Herald*, 15 December 1900 (trans.).
26 *Age*, 8 May 1901.
27 *Daily Record* (Rockhampton), 2 January 1901. The paper commented: 'Of course, nothing of the kind was contemplated', and the organiser had expressed his regret at the misunderstanding.
28 *Age*, 8 May 1901.
29 *SMH*, 14 January 1901.
30 *Geraldton World*, 4 January 1901.
31 One Walgett woman, a nine-year-old in 1901, when interviewed in her very old age by D. I. McDonald, 'scarcely remembered the Federation celebrations'. From McDonald's 'The Great and Long-looked for Day', *Canberra Historical Journal*, no. 24, September 1989.
32 10 September, 9 October 1900, Record of Proceedings of the Municipal Council of the City of Sydney, City of Sydney Archives.
33 *Review of Reviews*, 15 December 1900.
34 J. J. Keenan, *The Inaugural Celebrations of the Commonwealth of Australia* (Sydney: Government Printer, 1904), p. 5.
35 Record of Proceedings of the Municipal Council of the City of Sydney, 1900, City of Sydney Archives.
36 *Argus*, 2 January 1901.
37 Public notices of caution and detailed instructions to police were issued. Memo, Police Department, Inspector General's Office, 14 December 1900, NSW State Archives.
38 *Bulletin*, 29 December 1900.
39 *SMH*, 10 January 1901.
40 *Review of Reviews*, 15 December 1900.
41 *Town and Country Journal*, 12 January 1901.
42 'State Government Manifesto', *Daily Telegraph*, 27 April 1901.
43 *Daily Telegraph*, 10 January 1901.
44 *SMH*, 10 January 1901.
45 *SMH*, 14 January 1901.

Notes (pages 21–32) 227

46 *Hebrew Standard*, 18 January 1901.
47 *SMH*, 2 January 1901.
48 Edward Porter ('Lyon Harvey'), *Commonwealth Day, or Sydney En Fête* (Sydney: 1901), p. 11.
49 *Evening Journal* (Adelaide), 2 January 1901.
50 Alfred Deakin, *The Federal Story* (Melbourne: Robertson & Mullens, 1944), p. 112.
51 *SMH*, 2 January 1901.
52 Deakin, *The Federal Story*, p. 166.

2 THE IMAGINARY NATION

1 Henry Parkes, *Conference Debates* 1890, p. 48.
2 Benedict Anderson has described this process in his work on the genesis of modern nations: *Imagined Communities* (London: Verso, 1983).
3 *Commonwealth*, 1 October 1894.
4 K. H. Bailey, 'Self-Government in Australia', in Ernest Scott (ed.), *Australia*, vol. VII, part I, of the *Cambridge History of the British Empire* (Cambridge University Press, reprint 1988), p. 416.
5 Quoted in Gavin Souter, *Acts of Parliament* (Melbourne University Press, 1988), p. 74.
6 J. A. La Nauze, *The Making of the Australian Constitution* (Melbourne University Press, 1972), p. 270.
7 *Conference Debates* 1890, p. 225.
8 *Ibid.*, pp. 76–7.
9 Notes for speech, 1899, Rose Scott papers, ML.
10 Anderson, *Imagined Communities*, p. 19.
11 *Age*, 24 January 1895.
12 Griffith, in W. Gay and M. E. Sampson (eds), *The Commonwealth and the Empire* (Sydney: George Robertson and Co., 1895), pp. 6–7.
13 *Conference Debates* 1890, p. 113.
14 Luke Trainor, *British Imperialism and Australian Nationalism* (Cambridge University Press, 1994).
15 C. Blackton, 'Australian Nationality and Nationalism: The Imperial Federationist Interlude', *Historical Studies*, vol. 7, no. 25, 1955.
16 *Bulletin*, 22 December 1900.
17 Meeting, Town Hall, Perth, 25 July 1900, *West Australian*, 26 July 1900.
18 Alfred Deakin, *The Federal Story* (Melbourne: Robertson & Mullens, 1944), p. 111.
19 Scott Bennett (ed.), *The Making of the Commonwealth* (Melbourne: Cassell Australia, 1971), p. 77.
20 Graeme Davison, *The Unforgiving Minute: How Australians Learned to Tell the Time* (Melbourne: Oxford University Press, 1993), p. 74.
21 *Woman's Voice*, 23 February 1895.
22 The only source for this seems to be Robert Garran, who says, in his later autobiography, that Barton's epigram would have gone unrecorded, had he himself not noted it down. *Prosper the Commonwealth* (Sydney: Angus & Robertson, 1958), p. 101. Garran then employed the phrase on the title page

228   *Notes (pages 32–44)*

of his *The Coming Commonwealth* (Sydney: Angus & Robertson, 1897), and it appeared again among the mottoes on the Citizens' Commonwealth Arch in Sydney, at the inauguration of the Commonwealth.

23 Quoted in Bennett, *The Making of the Commonwealth*, p. 108.
24 Russel Ward, *The Australian Legend*, 2nd edn (Melbourne: Oxford University Press, 1966).
25 Vance Palmer, *The Legend of the Nineties* (Melbourne University Press, 1963), p. 154.
26 Ward, *The Australian Legend*, p. 228.
27 Chris Wallace-Crabbe (ed.), *The Australian Nationalists* (Melbourne: Oxford University Press, 1971), Introduction, p. x.
28 Completed after Quick's death in 1932, by E. Morris Miller (Melbourne University Press, 1940).
29 'Australian Art', *Commonwealth*, November 1894.
30 *Evening News*, 8 February 1897.
31 *Bulletin*, 4 June 1898.
32 W. G. McMinn, *Nationalism and Federalism in Australia* (Melbourne: Oxford University Press, 1994).
33 Alfred Deakin, 'The Federal Council of Australasia', *Review of Reviews*, 20 February 1895.
34 Gabriel de Foigny, 'A New Discovery of Terra Incognita Australis' (1676), in Marie Louise Berneri (ed.), *Journey Through Utopia* (New York: Schocken Books, 1971), p. 197.
35 J. A. Williamson, 'The Exploration of the Pacific', in Scott, *Australia*.
36 See Krishan Kumar, *Utopia and Anti-Utopia in Modern Times* (Oxford: Basil Blackwell, 1987).
37 Williamson, 'The Exploration of the Pacific', in Scott, *Australia*.
38 Paul Carter, *The Road to Botany Bay* (London: Faber & Faber, 1987), p. 314.
39 Catherine Helen Spence, *A Week in the Future* (1888) (Sydney: Hale & Iremonger, 1988).
40 Kumar, *Utopia and Anti-Utopia*.
41 James Anthony Froude, *Oceana, or England and Her Colonies* (London: Longmans, Green and Co., 1886), p. 2.
42 Parkes to Froude. Quoted in Luke Trainor, *British Imperialism and Australian Nationalism*, pp. 98–9.
43 A. Nugent Robertson, *Federation and Afterwards: A Fragment of History (AD 1898–1912)* (Sydney: Angus & Robertson, 1897), p. 17, p. 21, p. 19.
44 William Lane ('Sketcher'), 'Yellow or White?', *Boomerang*, 25 February 1888.
45 L. J. Blake, 'Village Settlements', *Victorian Historical Magazine*, vol. 37, no. 4, 1966.
46 Gavin Souter, *A Peculiar People* (Sydney: Angus & Robertson, 1968).
47 Notes for speech, 1899, Rose Scott papers, ML.
48 See W. Pember Reeves, *State Experiments in Australia and New Zealand* (London: Grant Richards, 1902).
49 B. R. Wise, 'The Struggle for Union', *Lone Hand*, 2 September 1912.
50 T. Holme, 'Federation', Sydney, 1898, in Scott Bennett (ed.), *Federation* (Melbourne: Cassell Australia, 1971), p. 51.
51 'Freedom's Greatest Victory', *Brisbane Courier*, 1 January 1901.

Notes (pages 44–59)   229

52 'The Centenary of Federation: An Anticipation', *SMH*, 24 May 1898.
53 'Forecast. News from Australia 2000 AD. Extract from the London Times, August 23, 2000 AD', *Cosmos*, 31 March 1899.
54 *Daily Telegraph*, 1 January 1901.
55 *SMH*, 2 January 1901.

3 IMAGINED CONSTITUTIONS

1 Geoffrey Sawer, *Australian Federalism in the Courts* (Melbourne University Press, 1967), p. 208.
2 *Convention Debates* 1898, pp. 215–25.
3 W. J. Hudson and M. P. Sharp, *Australian Independence: Colony to Reluctant Kingdom* (Melbourne University Press, 1988).
4 Brian de Garis, 'The Colonial Office and the Commonwealth Constitution Bill', in A. W. Martin (ed.), *Essays in Australian Federation* (Melbourne University Press, 1969).
5 James Anthony Froude, *Oceana, or England and Her Colonies* (London: Longmans, Green & Co., 1886), p. 91.
6 R. W. Dale, *Impressions of Australia* (London: Hodder & Stoughton, 1889).
7 Reproduced in C. M. H. Clark (ed.), *Select Documents in Australian History*, vol. II, 1851–1900 (Sydney: Angus & Robertson, 1977), p. 469.
8 David Christie Murray, *The Cockney Columbus* (London: Downey & Co., 1898), p. 189.
9 *Republican*, vol. 2, no. 1, February 1888.
10 Marian Aveling, 'A History of the Australian Natives' Association, 1871–1900', PhD thesis, Monash University, 1970.
11 Murray, *The Cockney Columbus*, p. 190.
12 David B. Swinfen, *Imperial Appeal: The Debate on the Appeal to the Privy Council, 1833–1986* (Manchester University Press, 1987).
13 Quoted in J. A. La Nauze, *The Making of the Australian Constitution* (Melbourne University Press, 1972), p. 24.
14 Quoted in L. F. Crisp, *Federation Fathers* (Melbourne University Press, 1990), p. 78.
15 *Brisbane Courier*, 16 June 1894; *Bulletin*, 30 June 1894, quoted in Crisp, *Federation Fathers*, p. 80, p. 82.
16 Crisp, *Federation Fathers*, pp. 90–1.
17 Quoted, in *ibid.*, p. 102.
18 Quoted in L. F. Crisp, *Australian National Government*, 4th edn (Melbourne: Longman Cheshire, 1978), p. 28.
19 Hugh Anderson (ed.), *Tocsin: Radical Arguments Against Federation, 1897–1900* (Melbourne: Drummond, 1977), p. 106.
20 Petitions and correspondence received by the Federal Convention are held in the Australian Archives in Canberra (series R216).
21 NLA MS429.
22 Murray, *The Cockney Columbus*, p. 279.
23 By Mr P. J. Holdsworth, read to the Bathurst People's Federal Convention, 1896. *Proceedings of the Bathurst People's Federal Convention* (Sydney, 1897), p. 188.
24 Major-General French, letter to editor, *SMH*, 13 June 1899.

230 *Notes (pages 59–70)*

25 Thomas Smeaton, 'The Federal City', *United Australia*, 20 September 1901.
26 *Convention Debates* 1898, pp. 702–3.
27 *Ibid.*, p. 1813.
28 *Clipper*, 16 April 1898, in Scott Bennett (ed.), *Federation* (Melbourne: Cassell Australia, 1975), p. 43.
29 W. Pember Reeves, *State Experiments in Australia and New Zealand* (London: Grant Richards, 1902).
30 *Worker*, 11 February 1899.
31 *Courrier Australien*, 8 April 1899.
32 *SMH*, 23 May 1898.
33 *Age,* 25 May 1898.
34 Alfred Deakin, *The Federal Story* (Melbourne: Robertson & Mullens, 1944), p. 166.

4 MODELS FOR A NATION

1 *Conference Debates* 1890, pp. 10–11.
2 *Ibid.*, pp. 45–6.
3 *Ibid.*, p. 71.
4 *Ibid.*, pp. 133–4.
5 *Ibid.*, pp. 212–13.
6 *Convention Debates*, 1891, p. 110.
7 *Convention Debates*, Adelaide, 1897, p. 222.
8 *West Australian*, 20 June 1899.
9 *Worker*, 6 May 1899.
10 *SMH*, 3 May 1898.
11 *Age*, 1 August 1893.
12 *Proceedings of the Bathurst People's Federal Convention* (Sydney, 1897), p. 98.
13 *Conference Debates* 1890, p. 124.
14 Keith Sinclair, 'Why New Zealanders are not Australians: New Zealand and the Australian Federation Movement, 1881–1901', in Keith Sinclair (ed.), *Tasman Relations: New Zealand and Australia, 1788–1988* (Auckland University Press, 1988), p. 102.
15 *West Australian*, 2 January 1901.
16 *Progress*, 19 August 1899.
17 *Convention Debates* 1898, p. 755.
18 *Clipper*, 17 June 1899.
19 Reported in the *Riverine Grazier*, 16 June 1899.
20 *Convention Debates*, Adelaide, 1897, pp. 213–14.
21 Richard White, *Inventing Australia* (Sydney: Allen & Unwin, 1981), p. 51.
22 Russel Ward, *The Australian Legend*, 2nd edn (Melbourne: Oxford University Press, 1966), p. 132.
23 For example, the Bishop of Riverina, *Riverine Grazier*, 4 July 1899.
24 *Worker*, 11 February 1899.
25 *Convention Debates*, Adelaide, 1897, pp. 1184–5.
26 *SMH*, 28 March 1898.

27 *SMH*, 23 April 1898.
28 *Ibid.*
29 *SMH*, 26 April 1898. A further article by Piddington, 'Equal Representation in the Senate: The Civil War in America', followed in the *Daily Telegraph*, 14 May 1898.
30 *Conference Debates* 1890, p. 106.
31 *Ibid.*, pp. 105–7.
32 John Reynolds, 'A. I. Clark's American Sympathies and His Influence on Australian Federation', *Australian Law Journal*, vol. 32, July 1958.
33 Including, it is thought, Robert Garran's *The Coming Commonwealth* (Sydney: Angus & Robertson, 1897).
34 Will M. Whitely, 'Some Australian Characteristics', *Cosmos*, January 1899.
35 Sir Robert Stout, 'Two Types of Democracy', *Review of Reviews*, December 1900.
36 *Conference Debates* 1890, pp. 134–5.
37 *Ibid.*, p. 250, p. 253.
38 *Ibid.*, p. 226.
39 J. A. La Nauze, 'The Name of the Commonwealth of Australia', *Historical Studies*, vol. 15, no. 57, 1971.
40 *SMH*, 24 August 1897.
41 *SMH*, 20 August 1897.
42 *Age*, 24 May 1898.
43 *Age*, 24 January 1895.
44 *Convention Debates* 1891, pp. 550–7.
45 G. B. Barton, *The Draft Bill to Constitute the Commonwealth of Australia* (Sydney: 1891).
46 *Convention Debates* 1891, pp. 550–7.
47 La Nauze, 'Name of the Commonwealth', p. 62.
48 In C. M. H. Clark (ed.), *Select Documents in Australian History*, vol. II, 1851–1900 (Sydney: Angus & Robertson, 1977), p. 496.

5 THINGS PROPERLY FEDERAL

1 'Report of Major-General Edwards . . . with a Memorandum containing Proposals for the Reorganisation of the Australian Forces', Victoria, 1889, in C. M. H. Clark (ed.), *Select Documents in Australian History*, vol. II, 1851–1900 (Sydney: Angus & Robertson, 1977), p. 467.
2 Kevin Livingston, 'Anticipating Federation: The Federalising of Telecommunications in Australia', *Australian Historical Studies*, vol. 26, April 1994.
3 *Council Debates* 1895, p. 24.
4 *Conference Debates* 1890, pp. 126–7.
5 John Mordike, *An Army for a Nation* (Sydney: Allen & Unwin, 1992).
6 *SMH*, 16 June 1899.
7 Mordike, *An Army for a Nation*.
8 *West Australian*, 20 June 1899.
9 *Conference Debates* 1890, p. 133.
10 *Ibid.*, p. 52.

232 *Notes (pages 84–96)*

11 *Ibid.*, p. 56, pp. 58–9.
12 From 'Extract of Proceedings of the Intercolonial Conference, 1883', in Clark, *Select Documents*, p. 453.
13 'Henry Parkes's speech, Intercolonial Conference, Sydney, 1881', in Clark, *Select Documents*, p. 452.
14 W. G. McMinn, *Nationalism and Federalism in Australia* (Melbourne: Oxford University Press, 1994).
15 Alfred Deakin, *The Federal Story* (Melbourne: Robertson & Mullens, 1944), p. 14.
16 *Conference Debates* 1890, pp. 66–7.
17 Section 51 (xxxvii). See Quick and Garran, pp. 648–9.
18 *Conference Debates* 1890, p. 173.
19 *Ibid.*, p. 207.
20 *Convention Debates* 1891, p. 301.
21 *Proceedings of the Bathurst People's Federal Convention* (Sydney: 1897), p. 94.
22 'The Democratic Influence', *Brisbane Courier*, 1 January 1901.
23 James Backhouse Walker, *Prelude to Federation*, ed. Peter Benson Walker (Hobart: O.B.M. Publishing Co., 1976), pp. 126–7.
24 *Council Debates* 1895, p. 23.
25 *Ibid.*, pp. 7–8.
26 *Brisbane Courier*, 1 February 1895.
27 *Council Debates* 1895, pp. 17–18.
28 *Ibid.*, p. 14.
29 *Convention Debates* 1898, p. 216.
30 *Hobart Mercury*, 29 January 1895.
31 Hilary Golder, *Divorce in 19th Century New South Wales* (Kensington: University of New South Wales Press, 1988).
32 *West Australian*, 23 July 1900.
33 *Convention Debates*, Sydney, 1897, p. 1078.
34 Quick and Garran, p. 610.
35 *Convention Debates*, Sydney, 1897, p. 1081.
36 *Ibid.*, p. 1082.
37 Judith Godden, 'British Models and Colonial Experience: Women's Philanthropy in Late 19th Century Sydney', *Journal of Australian Studies*, no. 19, November 1986.
38 *West Australian*, 15 June 1899.
39 William Cullen to Rose Scott, quoted in Judith Allen, *Rose Scott* (Melbourne: Oxford University Press, 1994), p. 146.
40 Frank J. Donohue, 'Our Social Conditions', in Frank Hutchinson (ed.), *New South Wales* (Sydney: Government Printer, 1896), p. 301.
41 *Convention Debates*, Sydney, 1897, pp. 1076–7.
42 R. Norris, *The Emergent Commonwealth* (Melbourne University Press, 1975), p. 169.
43 *Convention Debates* 1898, pp. 1992–3.
44 *Convention Debates*, Sydney, 1897, p. 1086.
45 *Convention Debates* 1898, pp. 1994–5.

Notes (pages 96–107)   233

46 *Ibid.*, p. 191.
47 *Ibid.*, pp. 183–4, p. 187.
48 Quick and Garran, p. 631.
49 In cases such as *Australian Capital TV* v. *Commonwealth* (1992); *Nationwide News Pty Ltd* v. *Wills* (1992); *Theophanous* v. *Herald & Weekly Times Ltd* (1994).
50 *Convention Debates*, Adelaide, 1897, p. 1032.
51 Section 100 of the Australian Constitution.
52 John Gunn, *Along Parallel Lines: A History of the Railways of New South Wales* (Melbourne University Press, 1989), p. 210.
53 *Ibid.*, p. 240.
54 *Convention Debates* 1898, p. 161.
55 Section 51 (v) of the Australian Constitution. Emphasis added.

6 WHITE AUSTRALIANS

1 R. Norris, *The Emergent Commonwealth* (Melbourne University Press, 1975), p. 59.
2 *Convention Debates* 1898, p. 666.
3 'Coloured Immigration Restriction Bill, November 1896', South Australia, House of Assembly, 1896, *Debates*.
4 'Minutes of Conference', New South Wales, Legislative Council 1888, *Proceedings and Papers*.
5 *Ibid.*
6 'Papers on Chinese Immigration', Victoria, Legislative Assembly 1888, *Votes and Proceedings*.
7 *SMH*, 25 November 1887.
8 Unidentified press cutting, 23 November 1887, Quong Tart papers, ML.
9 *Conference Debates* 1890, p. 222.
10 Vicki Pearce, ' "A Few Viragos on a Stump": The Womanhood Suffrage Campaign in Tasmania, 1880–1920', *Tasmanian Historical Research Association*, vol. 32, no. 4, December 1985.
11 John Foster Fraser, *Australia: The Making of a Nation* (London: Cassell & Co., 1910), p. 214, pp. 221–2.
12 E. K. Knight, *With The Royal Tour* (London: Longmans, Green & Co., 1902), p. 170.
13 E. W. Cole, *Better Side of the Chinese Character: Its Relation to a White Australia and the Development of our Tropical Territory* (Melbourne: Coles Book Arcade, *c.* 1905), p. 22 (original emphasis).
14 Petition to Executive Council of NSW, 1883, ML.
15 Address to Sir Robert Duff, n.d., ML.
16 *Daily Telegraph*, 27 July 1903.
17 Margaret Tart, *The Life of Quong Tart: Or, How a Foreigner Succeeded in a British Community* (Sydney: 1911), p. 9.
18 *Ibid.*, p. 99.
19 See Andrew Markus, *Fear and Hatred* (Sydney: Hale & Iremonger, 1979), p. 223.
20 'Papers on Chinese Immigration', Victoria, Legislative Assembly, 1888, *Votes and Proceedings*.

234 *Notes (pages 109–120)*

21 Marilyn Lake, 'The Politics of Respectability: Identifying the Masculinist Context', in Susan Magarey, et al. (eds), *Debutante Nation: Feminism Contests the 1890s* (Sydney: Allen & Unwin, 1993).
22 Luke Trainor, *British Imperialism and Australian Nationalism* (Cambridge University Press, 1994).
23 *SMH*, 25 August 1896.
24 *Ibid.*
25 *Evening News*, 24 August 1896.
26 Edward Said, *Orientalism* (London: Routledge & Kegan Paul, 1978).
27 *SMH*, 19 May 1898.
28 *Australian Woman*, 16 June 1894.
29 *Conference Debates* 1890, pp. 125–6.
30 Quick and Garran, p. 984.
31 Geoffrey Sawer, 'The Australian Constitution and the Australian Aborigine', *Federal Law Review*, vol. 2, no. 17, 1966.
32 *Convention Debates*, Adelaide, 1897, p. 1020.
33 In Scott Bennett (ed.), *Federation* (Melbourne: Cassell Australia, 1975), p. 139.
34 Tom Clarke and Brian Galligan, ' "Aboriginal Native" and the Institutional Construction of the Australian Citizen 1901–48', *Australian Historical Studies*, no. 105, October 1995.
35 Markus, *Fear and Hatred*, p. 240.
36 *SMH*, 21 April 1898.
37 *Australasian Federation League Seventh Annual Report* (Sydney: Government Printer, 1901), p. 12.
38 Maurice Ollivier (ed.), *The Colonial and Imperial Conferences from 1887–1937* (Ottawa: 1954), vol. I, p. 139.
39 Sawer, 'The Australian Constitution'.
40 *Convention Debates* 1898, p. 232.
41 Bennett, *Federation*, p. 61.
42 *Daily Telegraph*, 9 June 1899.
43 Mary Douglas, *Purity and Danger* (London: Ark Paperbacks, 1984), pp. 1–2.

7 AUSTRALIAN NATIVES

1 Bernard Wise, *Convention Debates* 1898, p. 2188.
2 Marilyn Lake, 'Between Old Worlds and New', in Caroline Daley and Melanie Nolan (eds), *Suffrage and Beyond* (Auckland University Press/Pluto Press, 1994), p. 277.
3 R. W. Dale, *Impressions of Australia* (London: Hodder & Stoughton, 1889), p. 10.
4 James Anthony Froude, *Oceana, or England and Her Colonies* (London: Longmans, Green & Co., 1886), p. 138.
5 Extract in C. M. H. Clark (ed.), *Select Documents in Australian History*, vol. II, 1851–1900 (Sydney: Angus & Robertson, 1977), p. 814.
6 Samuel Clemens, *Following the Equator* (New York: Hartford, 1897), p. 130, p. 138, p. 213.

Notes (pages 121–129)   235

7 John Clifford, *God's Greater Britain* (London: James Clarke & Co., 1899), p. 6.
8 *Ibid.*, p. 9, p. 110.
9 John Foster Fraser, *Australia: The Making of a Nation* (London: Cassell & Co., 1910), p. 250, p. 8.
10 Beatrice Webb and Sidney Webb, *The Webbs' Australian Diary*, ed. A. G. Austin (Melbourne: Pitman & Sons, 1965).
11 *Ibid.*, p. 46.
12 John Docker, *The Nervous Nineties: Australian Cultural Life in the 1890s* (Melbourne: Oxford University Press, 1991), p. 56.
13 Albert Métin, *Le Socialisme Sans Doctrines* (1902), trans. Russel Ward as *Socialism Without Doctrine* (Sydney: Alternative Publishing Co., 1977).
14 James Bryce, *Modern Democracies* (London: 1921).
15 Webb and Webb, *The Webbs' Australian Diary*, pp. 107–8.
16 *Echo*, 30 December 1898 (appendix to *ibid.*).
17 Philip E. Muskett, *The Art of Living in Australia* (London: Eyre & Spottiswood, 1893), pp. v–vi.
18 *Ibid.*, p. xix.
19 Ernest Moon, 'Some Aspects of Australian Life', *Blackwoods Magazine*, March 1888.
20 Marian Quartly, 'Mothers and Fathers and Brothers and Sisters: The AWA and the ANA and Gendered Citizenship', in Renate Howe (ed.), *Women and the State: Australian Perspectives* (Melbourne: La Trobe University Press, 1993).
21 Janet Pettman, 'The Australian Natives' Association and Federation in South Australia', in A. W. Martin (ed.), *Essays in Australian Federation* (Melbourne University Press, 1969).
22 Reported by C. Gavan Duffy in *My Life in Two Hemispheres* (1898), extract in Clark, *Select Documents*, p. 810.
23 *Hobart Mercury*, 29 January 1898.
24 *SMH*, 19 April 1898.
25 *SMH*, 25 April 1898.
26 *Proceedings of the Bathurst People's Federal Convention* (Sydney: 1897), p. 189.
27 *Hobart Mercury*, 29 January 1895.
28 William Thorpe, 'Archibald Meston and Aboriginal Legislation in Colonial Queensland', *Historical Studies*, vol. 21, no. 82, 1984.
29 Henry Reynolds, *Dispossession* (Sydney: Allen & Unwin, 1989).
30 *Ibid.*, p. 199.
31 Regina Ganter and Ros Kidd, 'The Powers of Protectors: Conflicts Surrounding Queensland's 1897 Aboriginal Legislation', *Australian Historical Studies*, no. 101, October 1993.
32 *Ibid.*, p. 554.
33 See sections 34 (i) and (ii), and 44 (i)–(v) of the Constitution.
34 *Dawn*, September 1900.
35 *Sands Directory*, 1876, ML.
36 Geoffrey Bolton, *Spoils and Spoilers*, 2nd edn (Sydney: Allen & Unwin, 1992).
37 *SMH*, 28 February 1895.

236   *Notes (pages 129–140)*

38 *SMH*, 5 March 1895.
39 *SMH*, 2 October 1895.
40 'Native Flora Protection Bill, second reading, 23 November', New South Wales, Legislative Assembly 1897, *Parliamentary Debates*.
41 *SMH*, 14 August 1897.
42 *SMH*, 16 August 1897.
43 *Australian Federalist*, no. 4, 14 May 1898.
44 Richard White, *Inventing Australia* (Sydney: Allen & Unwin, 1981).
45 Clark, *Select Documents*, pp. 800–1.
46 Alfred Deakin, 'The Federal Council of Australasia', *Review of Reviews*, 20 February 1895.
47 In W. Gay and M. E. Sampson (eds), *The Commonwealth and the Empire* (Sydney: George Robertson and Co., 1895).

8 THE PEOPLE

1 'Federal Hymn' (last verse) by the Rev. Professor Gosman, read at the Bathurst People's Federal Convention, November 1896, *Proceedings of the Bathurst People's Federal Convention* (Sydney: 1897).
2 Robert Garran, *Prosper the Commonwealth* (Sydney: Angus & Robertson, 1958), p. 105.
3 John Quick and Robert Garran, *The Annotated Constitution of the Australian Commonwealth* (Sydney: 1901), known simply as Quick and Garran.
4 Garran, *Prosper the Commonwealth*, p. 137.
5 Quick and Garran, p. 154.
6 Garran, *Prosper the Commonwealth*, p. 103.
7 John Quick, *Sir John Quick's Notebook*, ed. L. E. Fredman (Newcastle: 1965).
8 Alfred Deakin, *The Federal Story* (Melbourne: Robertson & Mullens, 1944), p. 56.
9 *Corowa Free Press*, 15 February 1895.
10 Quick and Garran, p. 154.
11 Deakin, *The Federal Story*, p. 55.
12 Stuart Macintyre, 'Corowa and the Voice of the People', *Canberra Historical Journal*, no. 33, March 1994.
13 Quick, *Sir John Quick's Notebook*.
14 Deakin, *The Federal Story*, p. 56.
15 *Argus*, 24 January 1895.
16 *Age,* 30 January 1895.
17 *Council Debates* 1895, p. 70.
18 *Ibid.*, p. 74.
19 *Ibid.*, p. 84.
20 *Ibid.*, p. 91.
21 *Daily Telegraph*, 4 February 1895.
22 *Council Debates* 1895, p. 86. Also B. R. Wise, *The Making of the Australian Commonwealth* (London: Longmans Green, 1913), p. 195.
23 Parkes to Lord Carrington, 1 November 1891, ML, Parkes Correspondence, vol. 46, A916/179.

Notes (pages 141–153) 237

24 *Brisbane Courier*, 29 January, 2 February 1895.
25 G. B. Barton, *The Troubles of Australian Federation* (pamphlet) (Sydney: 1901).
26 *SMH*, 3 May 1898.
27 L. F. Crisp, *Australian National Government*, 4th edn (Melbourne: Longman Cheshire, 1978); R. W. Connell and T. Irving, *Class Structure in Australian History* (Melbourne: Longman Cheshire, 1980).
28 *Cosmos*, November 1894.
29 W. Gay and M. E. Sampson (eds), *The Commonwealth and the Empire* (Sydney: George Robertson and Co., 1895), p. 19.
30 *Proceedings, Bathurst Convention*, p. 14.
31 *Bathurst Daily Times*, 13 November 1896.
32 Quick and Garran, p. 163.
33 Garran, *Prosper the Commonwealth*, p. 108.
34 *Proceedings, Bathurst Convention*, p. 90.
35 *Ibid.*, pp. 93–4.
36 *Ibid.*, pp. 101–2.
37 *Bulletin*, 28 November 1896.
38 New South Wales, Legislative Assembly 1895, *Parliamentary Debates*, pp. 1938–9.
39 *Daily Telegraph*, 13 April 1898.
40 Lilian Tomm, 'The Referendum in Australia and New Zealand', *Contemporary Review*, August 1897.
41 *Convention Debates* 1891, p. 892.
42 The Constitution includes the term 'the people' in sections 7 and 24, to refer to the electors. High Court interpretation of these sections has not yet produced a clear indication of what else 'the people' may here mean.
43 *Convention Debates*, Adelaide, 1897, p. 1025.
44 *Ibid.*, p. 1205.
45 An error in the recording of the speech made by Frederick Holder ironically captures an alternative way of seeing the problem: halving the vote, Holder is recorded as saying, 'would overcome the men difficulty connected with the matter'. *Ibid.*, p. 1207.
46 *Ibid.*, p. 1205.
47 *Ibid.*, p. 1208.
48 *Convention Debates* 1898, p. 764.
49 *Ibid.*, p. 2188.
50 *Ibid.*, p. 2217.
51 *Ibid.*, p. 717.
52 *Ibid.*, p. 719.
53 *Ibid.*, p. 722.
54 *Ibid.*, p. 725.
55 *Ibid.*, p. 738.
56 *Ibid.*, p. 759.
57 *Ibid.*, p. 742.
58 *Ibid.*, p. 763.
59 *Review of Reviews*, 15 June 1898.

238   *Notes (pages 153–168)*

60   R. S. Parker, 'Australian Federation: The Influence of Economic Interests and Political Pressures', *Historical Studies*, vol. 4, no. 13, 1949.
61   Crisp, *Australian National Government*, p. 12.
62   W. G. McMinn, *Nationalism and Federalism in Australia* (Melbourne: Oxford University Press, 1994), p. 180, p. 190.
63   Scott Bennett (ed.), *Federation* (Melbourne: Cassell Australia, 1975), pp. 17–21. Also R. Norris, *The Emergent Commonwealth* (Melbourne University Press, 1975), chapter 1.
64   *Dawn*, 1 April 1899.
65   *Convention Debates* 1898, p. 747.
66   *Ibid.*, p. 725.

9 CITIZENS

1   *Australian Digest* (Sydney: Law Book Co., 1989), vol. 6.
2   South Australia, House of Assembly 1896, *Debates*.
3   Quick and Garran, p. 600.
4   'Petition from the Womanhood Suffrage League of New South Wales', *Convention Debates*, Adelaide, 1897, p. 32.
5   *Convention Debates* 1898, p. 665.
6   *Ibid.*, pp. 672–3.
7   *Ibid.*, p. 674.
8   *Ibid.*, p. 677.
9   *Ibid.*, p. 1750.
10   *Ibid.*, pp. 1793–4.
11   *Sykes* v. *Cleary and Others* (1992).
12   *Convention Debates*, Adelaide, 1897, p. 736.
13   F. Stroud, *The Judicial Dictionary of Words and Phrases Judicially Interpreted* (London: Sweet and Maxwell, 1890).
14   *Convention Debates* 1898, p. 1787.
15   J. A. La Nauze, *The Making of the Australian Constitution* (Melbourne University Press, 1972), p. 321.
16   *Convention Debates* 1898, p. 687.
17   *Ibid.*, p. 689.
18   *Age*, 1 January 1901.
19   Most notably, *Australian Capital TV* v. *Commonwealth* (1992), and *Nationwide News Pty Ltd* v. *Wills* (1992).
20   *Brisbane Courier*, 1 January 1901.
21   *SMH*, 2 January 1901.
22   *Champion*, 22 June 1895.
23   *Age*, 1 August 1893.
24   *South Australian Register*, 19 April 1898.
25   *Kalgoorlie Miner*, 11 July 1900.
26   *Bathurst Times*, 12 June 1899.
27   *Worker*, 6 May 1899.
28   *Convention Debates* 1898, p. 654.
29   Richard Ely, *Unto God and Caesar* (Melbourne University Press, 1971).

Notes (pages 168–178) 239

30 *Convention Debates* 1898, p. 656.
31 *Ibid.*, p. 657.
32 Stuart Macintyre, *Colonial Liberalism: The Lost World of Three Victorian Visionaries* (Melbourne: Oxford University Press, 1991).
33 *Convention Debates* 1898, p. 2509.
34 *Brisbane Courier*, 1 January 1901.

10 HALF THE NATION

1 National President's (Mrs Nicholls) Address, WCTU Third Triennial Convention, Brisbane, 1897, Minutes, ML, MSS 3641/MKL 2008.
2 Letter, n.d., in Mrs E. J. Ward, *Out of Weakness Made Strong: The Life of Mrs E. J. Ward* (Sydney, 1903), p. 94.
3 Press cutting, n.d., Rose Scott papers, ML, MSS 38/35.
4 National President's Address, WCTU Third Triennial Convention, Brisbane, 1897, ML, MSS 3641/MKL 2008.
5 Judith Godden, 'British Models and Colonial Experience: Women's Philanthropy in Late 19th Century Sydney', *Journal of Australian Studies*, no. 19, November 1986.
6 *Australian Woman*, 25 April 1894.
7 *Champion*, edited by Henry Champion, appeared from 1895–1897. On the *Bulletin* and women, see John Docker, *The Nervous Nineties: Australian Cultural Life in the 1890s* (Melbourne: Oxford University Press, 1991).
8 Alison Mackinnon, 'The State as an Agent of Demographic Change? The Higher Education of Women and Fertility Decline 1880–1930', in Renate Howe (ed.), *Women and the State: Australian Perspectives* (Melbourne: La Trobe University Press, 1993).
9 J. L. Parsons, *Women as Citizens* (pamphlet) (Adelaide: 1895), p. 13.
10 Maybanke Anderson (Wolstenholme), Obituary for Rose Scott, *SMH*, 2 May 1925.
11 *Ibid.*
12 Quoted in Ward, *Out of Weakness Made Strong*, p. 63.
13 Beatrice Webb and Sidney Webb, *The Webbs' Australian Diary*, ed. A. G. Austin (Melbourne: Pitman & Sons, 1965), p. 23.
14 Parsons, *Women as Citizens*.
15 Emily Soldene, 'Sydney Week by Week', Rose Scott papers, ML, MSS 35/63.
16 National President's Address, WCTU Third Triennial Convention, Brisbane, 1897, Minutes, ML, MSS 3641/MKL 2008.
17 *Cosmos*, October 1894.
18 *United Australia*, July 1900.
19 'The Woman's Column', *Worker*, 11 April 1896.
20 Quick and Garran, p. 475.
21 C. H. Spence, *Autobiography* (Adelaide: 1910).
22 Minutes, WCTU Convention, Brisbane, 1897.
23 *Convention Debates*, Adelaide, 1897, p. 720.
24 Spence, *Autobiography*.
25 *South Australian Register*, 8 March 1897.

240   *Notes (pages 178–190)*

26 Spence to Josiah Symon, 17 August [1897], Symon papers, NLA, MS 1736/6/18.
27 *Convention Debates*, Adelaide, 1897, p. 725.
28 *Champion*, 27 February 1897.
29 Letter to Adelaide Convention, 9 April 1897. Australian Archives (series R216).
30 *Convention Debates*, Adelaide, 1897, pp. 32–3.
31 *Ibid.*, p. 637.
32 Audrey Oldfield, *Woman Suffrage in Australia* (Cambridge University Press, 1992).
33 *Australian Star*, 17 February 1897.
34 *Convention Debates*, Adelaide, 1897, p. 717.
35 *Ibid.*, p. 722.
36 *Ibid.*, p. 717.
37 *Ibid.*, p. 721.
38 *Ibid.*, p. 723.
39 WSL Annual Meeting, *c.* 10 June 1897, Rose Scott papers, ML, MSS 38/35.
40 Notes for speech, in *ibid.*
41 Report of meeting, 27 March 1899, in *ibid.*
42 Handwritten speech, in *ibid.*, ML, MSS 38/27.
43 *Ibid.*
44 'A Woman's World', *The People and the Collectivist*, 17 June 1899.
45 *Daily Telegraph*, May 1898.
46 *West Australian*, 30 July 1900.
47 Handwritten speech, Rose Scott papers, ML, MSS 38/27.
48 Cutting, *Australian Star*, in *ibid.*
49 *SMH*, 21 April 1898.
50 *Evening News*, 8 February 1897.
51 *Bathurst Daily Times*, 17 November 1896.
52 WFL pamphlet, Rose Scott papers, ML, MSS 38/27.
53 WFL open letter, 25 April 1898, in *ibid.*, ML, MSS 38/63.
54 *Ibid.*
55 Jan Roberts, *Maybanke Anderson: Sex, Suffrage and Social Reform* (Sydney: Hale & Iremonger, 1993).
56 *Federalist*, no. 10, 25 June 1898.
57 *Woman's Voice*, 1894.
58 *Woman's Voice*, 1895.
59 Handwritten speech, Rose Scott papers, ML, MSS 38/27.
60 *Daily Telegraph*, 14 June 1899.
61 Rose Scott papers, ML, MSS 38/27.
62 *Riverine Grazier*, 12 May 1899.
63 *Ibid.*
64 *Hay Standard*, 20 May 1899.
65 *Riverine Grazier*, 19 May 1899.
66 *Hay Standard*, 10 June 1899.
67 *Hay Standard*, 24 May 1899.
68 *Hay Standard*, 14 June 1899.
69 *Riverine Grazier*, 9 June 1899.
70 *Riverine Grazier*, 14 July 1899.

Notes (pages 191–201) 241

71 See Oldfield, *Woman Suffrage*, p. 55, for discussion of the theory that Sir John Forrest granted women the vote to control the radical goldfields.
72 WCTU to Charles Kingston, 18 September 1900, Premier's Department records, WA State Archives.
73 *Kalgoorlie Miner*, 12 July, 31 July 1900. Other reports of women's meetings are to be found in the *Kalgoorlie Miner* on 6, 11, 17, 18, 19, 20, 23, 25, 27, 31 July, and on 1 August 1900.
74 F. Alexander, *Moving Frontiers* (Melbourne: 1947), discussed in Geoffrey Blainey, 'The Role of Economic Interests in Australian Federation', *Historical Studies*, vol. 4, no. 15, 1950.
75 Rose Scott papers, n.d., ML, MSS 38/35.
76 *United Australia*, April 1900.
77 *United Australia*, July 1900.
78 *United Australia*, October 1900.
79 *Hay Standard*, 19 July 1899.
80 *SMH*, 9 January 1901.
81 Madeleine Onslow, 'Woman's Position in the Commonwealth', *United Australia*, January 1901.

11 THE FEDERAL COMPACT

1 Rosemary Pringle, 'Public Opinion in the Federal Referendum Campaigns in New South Wales 1898–1899', *Journal of the Royal Australian Historical Society*, vol. 65, pt 4, 1979.
2 *Adelaide Advertiser*, 4 June 1898.
3 'Petition to Her Majesty the Queen from Persons Residing on the Eastern Goldfields, 1900', in Scott Bennett (ed.), *Federation* (Melbourne: Cassell Australia, 1975), p. 239.
4 *Adelaide Advertiser*, 4 June 1898.
5 *Daily Telegraph*, 30 May 1898.
6 *West Australian*, 14 June 1899.
7 *SMH*, 6 June 1899.
8 *Proceedings of the Bathurst People's Federal Convention* (Sydney: 1897), p. 99.
9 J. W. Gough, *The Social Contract: A Critical Study of its Development* (Oxford: Clarendon Press, 1936).
10 This is the approach associated with the early liberal social contract theorist, John Locke: *Two Treatises of Government* (1690). The idea of compact is closer to Rousseau's idea of social contract, one shaped by the 'common will' rather than individual consent: *The Social Contract* (1762).
11 *Convention Debates* 1891, p. 884.
12 *Ibid.*, p. 888.
13 *Ibid.*, p. 890.
14 *Ibid.*, p. 893.
15 Quick and Garran, pp. 988–9.
16 Rose Scott papers, n.d., ML.
17 *Ibid.*

242 *Notes (pages 202–214)*

18 James Backhouse Walker, *Prelude to Federation*, ed. Peter Benson Walker (Hobart: O.B.M. Publishing Co., 1976), p. 152.
19 John Latham, 'The Interpretation of the Constitution', in R. Else-Mitchell (ed.), *Essays on the Australian Constitution* (Sydney: Law Book Co., 1952), p. 5.
20 Brian Galligan, *A Federal Republic* (Cambridge University Press, 1995), p. 29.
21 John Mordike, *An Army for a Nation* (Sydney: Allen & Unwin, 1992).
22 *Commonwealth Parliamentary Debates*, vol. 1, May–June, 1901, p. 18.
23 Brian de Garis, 'The Colonial Office and the Commonwealth Constitution Bill', in A. W. Martin (ed.), *Essays in Australian Federation* (Melbourne University Press, 1969).
24 Colonial Office, correspondence, 29 March 1900, NLA, Barton papers, MS 51/6/1014.
25 Alfred Deakin, *The Federal Story* (Melbourne: Robertson & Mullens, 1944), pp. 143-5.
26 Justice Lionel Murphy, 'The China Ocean Case', in A. L. Blackshield, et al. (eds), *The Judgments of Justice Lionel Murphy* (Sydney: Primavera Press, 1986).
27 *West Australian*, 15 June 1899.
28 *West Australian*, 16 June 1899.
29 Mark McKenna, 'Tracking the Republic', in David Headon, et al. (eds), *Crown or Country: The Traditions of Australian Republicanism* (Sydney: Allen & Unwin, 1994).
30 *SMH*, 21 June 1897.
31 *Bulletin*, 19 June 1897.
32 *Argus*, 12 June, 22 June 1897.
33 John Quick, 'Is Secession Possible?', *Life*, vol. III, no. 10, 1906.
34 Christopher Besant, 'Two Nations, Two Destinies: A Reflection on the Significance of the Western Australian Secession Movement to Australia, Canada and the British Empire', *University of Western Australia Law Review*, vol. 20, no. 2, 1990.
35 *Ibid.*, p. 249.
36 Quick and Garran, p. 294.
37 Section 59 of the Constitution.

CONCLUSION

1 H. V. Evatt, *Australian Labour Leader* (Sydney: Angus & Robertson, 1940). L. F. Crisp, *Australian National Government*, 4th edn (Melbourne: Longman Cheshire, 1978).
2 Brian Fitzpatrick, *The Australian People* (Melbourne University Press, 1946), p. 232.
3 R. S. Parker, 'Australian Federation: The Influence of Economic Interests and Political Pressures', *Historical Studies*, vol. 4, no. 13, 1949; R. Norris, *The Emergent Commonwealth* (Melbourne University Press, 1975), chapter 6.
4 Parker, *ibid.*
5 John Bastin, 'Federation and Western Australia', *Historical Studies*, vol. 5, no. 17, 1951. Patricia Hewett, 'Aspects of Campaigns in South-Eastern New

South Wales at the Federation Referenda of 1898 and 1899', in A. W. Martin (ed.), *Essays in Australian Federation* (Melbourne University Press, 1969).

6 Geoffrey Blainey, 'The Role of Economic Interests in Australian Federation', *Historical Studies*, vol 4, no. 15, 1950, pp. 235–6.

7 *Worker*, 21 August 1895.

8 Hugh Collins, 'Political Ideology in Australia: The Distinctiveness of a Benthamite Society', in Stephen Graubard (ed.), *The Daedalus Symposium* (Sydney: Angus & Robertson, 1985).

9 *Ibid.*, p. 148.

EPILOGUE

1 *Report of the Royal Commission on the Constitution*, Canberra, Government Printer, 1929.

2 Andrew Thynne, a Queensland delegate at the Federation Convention in 1891, died in 1927.

3 Deakin, *The Federal Story*, Melbourne, Robertson & Mullens, 1944, p. 166.

Select Bibliography

COLLECTIONS OF DOCUMENTS

Alomes, Stephen, and Jones, Catherine (eds), *Australian Nationalism*, Sydney: Angus & Robertson, 1991.

Anderson, Hugh (ed.), *Tocsin: Radical Arguments Against Federation, 1897–1900*, Melbourne: Drummond, 1977.

Bennett, Scott (ed.), *The Making of the Commonwealth*, Melbourne: Cassell Australia, 1971.

Bennett, Scott (ed.), *Federation*, Melbourne: Cassell Australia, 1975.

Clark, C. M. H. (ed.), *Select Documents in Australian History*, vol. II, 1851–1900, Sydney: Angus & Robertson, 1977.

CONTEMPORARY WORKS

Ackerman, Jessie, *Australia from a Woman's Point of View*, London: Cassell & Co., 1913.

Andrade, David, *The Melbourne Riots and How Harry Holdfast and His Friends Emancipated the Workers*, Melbourne: 1892.

Astley, William ('Price Warung'), *Bathurst: The Ideal Federal Capital*, Bathurst: 1901.

Baker, Richard Chaffey, *A Manual of Reference for the Use of the Members of the National Australasian Convention*, Adelaide: W. K. Thomas & Co., 1891.

Baker, Richard Chaffey, *Federation*, Adelaide: 1897.

Barton, G. B., *The Draft Bill to Constitute the Commonwealth of Australia*, Sydney: 1891.

Barton, G. B., *The Troubles of Australian Federation* (pamphlet), Sydney: 1901.

Bryce, James, *The American Commonwealth*, London: 1888.

Bryce, James, *Modern Democracies*, London: 1921.

Clemens, Samuel, *Following the Equator*, New York: Hartford, 1897.

Clifford, John, *God's Greater Britain*, London: James Clarke & Co., 1899.

Cole, E. W., *Better Side of the Chinese Character: Its Relation to a White Australia and the Development of our Tropical Territory*, Melbourne: Coles Book Arcade, c. 1905.

Dale, R. W., *Impressions of Australia*, London: Hodder & Stoughton, 1889.

Deakin, Alfred, 'The Federal Council of Australasia', *Review of Reviews*, 20 February 1895.

Select Bibliography 245

Deakin, Alfred, *The Federal Story*, Melbourne: Robertson & Mullens, 1944.
de Foigny, Gabriel, 'A New Discovery of Terra Incognita Australis' (1676), in Marie Louise Berneri (ed.), *Journey Through Utopia*, New York: Schocken Books, 1971.
Dilke, Charles, 'The Commonwealth of Australia', *The Forum*, vol. 11, June 1891.
Flavell, Sidney, *A Voyage to Australia, Together with a Descriptive Account of the Inauguration of the Commonwealth*, Leamington Spa: Leamington Publishing Co., 1902.
Fraser, John Foster, *Australia: The Making of a Nation*, London: Cassell & Co., 1910.
Froude, James Anthony, *Oceana, or England and Her Colonies*, London: Longmans, Green and Co., 1886.
Garran, Robert, *The Coming Commonwealth*, Sydney: Angus & Robertson, 1897.
Garran, Robert, 'The Federation Movement and the Founding of the Commonwealth', in Ernest Scott (ed.), *Australia*, vol VII, part I, of the Cambridge History of the British Empire, Cambridge University Press, (1933) reprint 1988.
Garran, Robert, *Prosper the Commonwealth*, Sydney: Angus & Robertson, 1958.
Gay, W., and Sampson, M. E. (eds), *The Commonwealth and the Empire*, Sydney: George Robertson and Co., 1895.
Hamilton, Alexander, Madison, James, and Jay, John, *The Federalist* (1787–1788), London: J. M. Dent, 1992.
Hutchinson, Frank (ed.), *New South Wales*, Sydney: Government Printer, 1896.
James, Walter, 'The James Papers: Letters on Federalism', *Australian Quarterly*, vol. 21, no. 4, 1949.
Kingston, C. K., *The Democratic Element in Australian Federation*, Adelaide: 1897.
Knight, E. K., *With The Royal Tour*, London: Longmans, Green & Co., 1902.
Lane, William ('Sketcher'), 'Yellow or White?', *Boomerang*, 25 February 1888.
Mackay, Kenneth, *The Yellow Wave*, London: Richard Bentley and Son, 1895.
Métin, Albert, *Le Socialisme Sans Doctrines* (1902), trans. Russel Ward as *Socialism Without Doctrine*, Sydney: Alternative Publishing Co., 1977.
Moon, Ernest, 'Some Aspects of Australian Life', *Blackwoods Magazine*, March 1888.
Murray, David Christie, *The Cockney Columbus*, London: Downey & Co., 1898.
Muskett, Philip E., *The Art of Living in Australia*, London: Eyre & Spottiswood, 1893.
Official Record of the Debates of the Australasian Federal Convention, vols I–V (Sydney, 1891, Adelaide, Sydney, Melbourne, 1897–1898), Sydney: Legal Books, 1986.
Official Record of the Debates of the Federal Council of Australasia, sixth session, Hobart: 1895.
Official Record of the Proceedings and Debates of the Australasian Federation Conference, Melbourne: Government Printer, 1890.
Ollivier, Maurice (ed.), *The Colonial and Imperial Conferences from 1887–1937*, vol. I, Ottawa: 1954.

246   *Select Bibliography*

Onslow, Madeleine, 'Woman's Position in the Commonwealth', *United Australia*, January 1901.

Parkes, Henry, *The Chinese in Australia*, Second Reading Speech, Legislative Assembly, Sydney: Government Printer, 1888.

Parkes, Henry, *Fifty Years in the Making of Australian History*, London: 1892.

Parsons, J. L., *Women as Citizens* (pamphlet), Adelaide: 1895.

Porter, Edward ('Lyon Harvey'), *Commonwealth Day, or Sydney En Fête*, Sydney: 1901.

'A Post-Card Plebiscite on the Federal Bill', *Review of Reviews*, 15 May 1898.

Proceedings of the Bathurst People's Federal Convention, Sydney: 1897.

Quick, John, 'Is Secession Possible?', *Life*, vol. III, no. 10, 1906.

Quick, John, *Australian Literature*, completed by E. Morris Miller, Melbourne University Press, 1940.

Quick, John, *Sir John Quick's Notebook*, ed. L. E. Fredman, Newcastle: 1965.

Quick, John, and Garran, Robert, *The Annotated Constitution of the Australian Commonwealth*, Sydney: Angus & Robertson, 1901.

Reeves, W. P., 'Attitude of New Zealand', *Empire Review*, vol. I, no. 1, 1901.

Reeves, W. Pember, *State Experiments in Australia and New Zealand*, London: Grant Richards, 1902.

Reid, George, 'The Conference of the Premiers at Hobart', *Review of Reviews*, February 1895.

Reid, George, 'The Outlook of Federation', *Review of Reviews*, January 1897.

Reid, George, 'The Australian Premiers in England', *Review of Reviews*, September 1897.

Reid, George, *My Reminiscences*, London: 1917.

Robertson, A. Nugent, *Federation and Afterwards: A Fragment of History (AD 1898–1912)*, Sydney: Angus & Robertson, 1897.

Spence, C. H., *A Week in the Future* (1888), Sydney: Hale & Ironmonger, 1988.

Spence, C. H., 'An Australian's Impressions of America', *Harper's New Monthly Magazine*, July 1894.

Spence, C. H., 'Woman's Place in the Commonwealth', *United Australia*, April 1900.

Spence, C. H., *Autobiography*, Adelaide: 1910.

Stout, Sir Robert, 'Two Types of Democracy', *Review of Reviews*, December 1900.

Stroud, F., *The Judicial Dictionary of Words and Phrases Judicially Interpreted*, London: Sweet and Maxwell, 1890.

Tart, Margaret, *The Life of Quong Tart: Or, How a Foreigner Succeeded in a British Community*, Sydney: 1911.

Tomm, Lilian, 'The Referendum in Australia and New Zealand', *Contemporary Review*, August 1897.

Tucker, Horace, *The New Arcadia: An Australian Story*, London: George Robertson and Co., 1896.

Walker, James Backhouse, *Prelude to Federation*, ed. Peter Benson Walker, Hobart: O.B.M. Publishing Co., 1976.

Ward, Mrs E. J., *Out of Weakness Made Strong: The Life of Mrs E. J. Ward*, Sydney: 1903.

Webb, Beatrice, and Webb, Sidney, *The Webbs' Australian Diary*, ed. A. G. Austin, Melbourne: Pitman & Sons, 1965.

Select Bibliography 247

Whitely, Will M., 'Some Australian Characteristics', *Cosmos*, January 1899.

Wise, B. R., 'The Struggle for Union', *Lone Hand*, 2 September 1912.

Wise, B. R., *The Making of the Australian Commonwealth*, London: Longmans & Green, 1913.

LATER WORKS

Albinski, Nan Bowman, 'Visions of the Nineties', *Journal of Australian Studies*, no. 20, May 1987.

Allen, Judith, *Rose Scott*, Melbourne: Oxford University Press, 1994.

Alomes, Stephen, 'Ceremonial Visions of Australia', *Journal of Australian Studies*, no. 20, May 1987.

Alomes, Stephen, *A Nation at Last*, Sydney: Angus & Robertson, 1988.

Anderson, Benedict, *Imagined Communities*, London: Verso, 1983.

Archer, Jeff, ' "But is it Australian Nationalism?" ', *Australian Journal of Politics and History*, vol. 36, no. 1, 1990.

Ashton, Paul, *Waving the Waratah*, Sydney: Bicentennial Council, 1989.

Aveling, Marian, 'A History of the Australian Natives' Association, 1871–1900', PhD thesis, Monash University, 1970.

Bastin, John, 'Federation and Western Australia', *Historical Studies*, vol. 5, no. 17, 1951.

Besant, Christopher W., 'Two Nations, Two Destinies: A Reflection on the Significance of the Western Australian Secession Movement to Australia, Canada and the British Empire', *University of Western Australia Law Review*, vol. 20, no. 2, 1990.

Birrell, Robert, *A Nation of Our Own: Citizenship and Nation-building in Federation Australia*, Melbourne: Longman, 1995.

Blackshield, A. L., et al. (eds), *The Judgments of Justice Lionel Murphy*, Sydney: Primavera Press, 1986.

Blackton, C., 'Australian Nationality and Nationalism: The Imperial Federationist Interlude', *Historical Studies*, vol. 7, no. 25, 1955.

Blainey, Geoffrey, 'The Role of Economic Interests in Australian Federation', *Historical Studies*, vol. 4, no. 15, 1950.

Blake, L. J., 'Village Settlements', *Victorian Historical Magazine*, vol. 37, no. 4, 1966.

Bolton, Geoffrey, *Spoils and Spoilers*, 2nd edn, Sydney: Allen & Unwin, 1992.

Bomford, Janette M., *That Dangerous and Persuasive Woman: Vida Goldstein*, Melbourne University Press, 1993.

Burgmann, Verity, *In Our Time: Socialism and the Rise of Labor, 1885–1905*, Sydney: George Allen & Unwin, 1985.

Cannadine, David, and Price, Simon (eds), *Rituals of Royalty: Power and Ceremonial in Traditional Societies*, Cambridge University Press, 1987.

Carter, Paul, *The Road to Botany Bay*, London: Faber & Faber, 1987.

Clarke, Tom, and Galligan, Brian, ' "Aboriginal Native" and the Institutional Construction of the Australian Citizen 1901–48', *Australian Historical Studies*, no. 105, October 1995.

Cole, D., ' "The Crimson Thread of Kinship": Ethnic Ideas in Australia, 1870–1914', *Historical Studies*, vol. 14, no. 56, 1971.

248   *Select Bibliography*

Collins, Hugh, 'Political Ideology in Australia: The Distinctiveness of a Benthamite Society', in Stephen Graubard (ed.), *The Daedalus Symposium*, Sydney: Angus & Robertson, 1985.

Connell, R. W., and Irving, T., *Class Structure in Australian History*, Melbourne: Longman Cheshire, 1980.

Crawford, R. M., *Australia*, London: Hutchinson, 1952.

Crisp, L. F., *Australian National Government*, 4th edn, Melbourne: Longman Cheshire, 1978.

Crisp, L. F., *Federation Fathers*, Melbourne University Press, 1990.

Crowley, F. K. (ed.), *A New History of Australia*, Melbourne: Heinemann, 1974.

Cunneen, Christopher, *King's Men: Australia's Governors-General from Hopetoun to Isaacs*, Sydney: George Allen & Unwin, 1983.

Curthoys, Ann, 'Racism and Class in the Nineteenth Century Immigration Debate', in A. Markus and M. C. Ricklefs (eds), *Surrender Australia?: Essays in the Study and Uses of History*, Sydney: Allen & Unwin, 1985.

Davidson, Alastair, *The Invisible State*, Melbourne: Cambridge University Press, 1991.

Davison, Graeme, *The Unforgiving Minute: How Australians Learned to Tell the Time*, Melbourne: Oxford University Press, 1993.

de Garis, Brian, 'The Colonial Office and the Commonwealth Constitution Bill', in A. W. Martin (ed.), *Essays in Australian Federation*, Melbourne University Press, 1969.

de Garis, Brian, 'Some Reflections on the Problems Involved in Writing a History of the Australian Federal Movement', *Early Days: Journal of the West Australian Historical Society*, vol. VII, 1972.

Docker, John, *The Nervous Nineties: Australian Cultural Life in the 1890s*, Melbourne: Oxford University Press, 1991.

Douglas, Mary, *Purity and Danger*, London: Ark Paperbacks, 1984.

Eddy, John, and Schreuder, Deryck (eds), *The Rise of Colonial Nationalism*, Sydney: Allen & Unwin, 1988.

Ely, Richard, *Unto God and Caesar*, Melbourne University Press, 1971.

Evatt, H. V., *Australian Labour Leader*, Sydney: Angus & Robertson, 1940.

Fitzpatrick, Brian, *The Australian People*, Melbourne University Press, 1946.

Fredman, L. E., 'A Note on the Corowa Conference of 1893', *Journal of the Royal Australian Historical Society*, vol. 4, pt 4, 1963.

Fredman, L. E., ' "Yes–No Reid": A Case For the Prosecution ', *Journal of the Royal Australian Historical Society*, vol. 50, pt 2, 1964.

Freestone, Robert, and Veale, Sharon, 'The Street Beautiful: Triumphal Arches and Urban Improvement in Sydney, 1888–1925', *Public History Review*, vol. 4, 1996.

Galligan, Brian, *A Federal Republic*, Cambridge University Press, 1995.

Ganter, Regina, and Kidd, Ros, 'The Powers of Protectors: Conflicts Surrounding Queensland's 1897 Aboriginal Legislation', *Australian Historical Studies*, no. 101, October 1993.

Godden, Judith, 'British Models and Colonial Experience: Women's Philanthropy in Late 19th Century Sydney', *Journal of Australian Studies*, no. 19, November 1986.

Select Bibliography 249

Golder, Hilary, *Divorce in 19th Century New South Wales*, Kensington: University of New South Wales Press, 1988.

Gollan, R. A., 'The Australian Impact', in Sylvia Bowman (ed.), *Edward Bellamy Abroad*, New York: Twayne, 1962.

Gollan, R. A., 'Nationalism, the Labour Movement and the Commonwealth, 1880–1900', in Gordon Greenwood (ed.), *Australia: A Social and Political History*, Sydney: Angus & Robertson, 1977.

Gollan, Robin, *Radical and Working Class Politics: A Study of Eastern Australia, 1850–1910*, Melbourne University Press, 1967.

Gough, J. W., *The Social Contract: A Critical Study of its Development*, Oxford: Clarendon Press, 1936.

Graubard, Stephen (ed.), *Australia: The Daedalus Symposium*, Sydney: Angus & Robertson, 1985.

Grimshaw, Patricia, Lake, Marilyn, McGrath, Ann, and Quartly, Marian, *Creating a Nation*, Melbourne: McPhee Gribble, 1994.

Gunn, John, *Along Parallel Lines: A History of the Railways of New South Wales*, Melbourne University Press, 1989.

Hammer, W. C. K., 'The Australian Natives' Association's Part in Australian Nationalism, 1871–1901', *ANU Historical Journal*, no. 4, October 1967.

Hancock, W. K., *Australia*, London: Ernest Benn, 1930.

Haward, Marcus, and Warden, James (eds), *An Australian Democrat: The Life, Work and Consequences of Andrew Inglis Clark*, Hobart: University of Tasmania, 1995.

Headon, David, et al. (eds), *Crown or Country: The Traditions of Australian Republicanism*, Sydney: Allen & Unwin, 1994.

Hewett, Patricia, 'Aspects of Campaigns in South-Eastern New South Wales at the Federation Referenda of 1898 and 1899', in A. W. Martin (ed.), *Essays in Australian Federation*, Melbourne University Press, 1969.

Hillman, Wendy, 'The 1900 Federal Referendum in Western Australia', *Studies in West Australian History*, vol. II, March 1978.

Hirst, John, 'Keeping Colonial History Colonial: The Hartz Thesis Revisited', *Historical Studies*, vol. 21, no. 82, 1984.

Hirst, John, 'Egalitarianism', *Australian Cultural Studies*, no. 5, 1986.

Howe, Renate (ed.), *Women and the State: Australian Perspectives*, Melbourne: La Trobe University Press, 1993.

Hudson, W. J., and Sharp, M. P., *Australian Independence: Colony to Reluctant Kingdom*, Melbourne University Press, 1988.

Hurley, Paula, 'Citizen Jane: Federation and First-Wave Feminism in Australia', MA thesis, University of Melbourne, 1994.

Hutchison, John, 'State Festivals, Foundation Myths and Cultural Politics and Immigrant Nations', in Tony Bennett, Pat Buckridge, David Carter and Colin Mercer (eds), *Celebrating the Nation*, Sydney: Allen & Unwin, 1992.

Irving, Helen (ed.), *A Woman's Constitution?: Gender and History in the Australian Commonwealth*, Sydney: Hale & Iremonger, 1996.

Kammen, Michael, *A Machine that Would Go of Itself: The Constitution in American Culture*, New York: Vintage Books, 1987.

Kingston, Beverley, *The Oxford History of Australia*, vol. 3, 1860–1900, 'Glad, Confident Morning', Melbourne: Oxford University Press, 1989.

250 *Select Bibliography*

Kumar, Krishan, *Utopia and Anti-Utopia in Modern Times*, Oxford: Basil Blackwell, 1987.

Lake, Marilyn, 'Between Old Worlds and New', in Caroline Daley and Melanie Nolan (eds), *Suffrage and Beyond*, Auckland University Press/Pluto Press, 1994.

La Nauze, J. A., *The Hopetoun Blunder*, Melbourne University Press, 1957.

La Nauze, J. A., 'A Day to Remember: A Fragment of Narrative History', *Meanjin*, vol. XX, no. 4, 1961.

La Nauze, J. A., *Alfred Deakin: A Biography*, Melbourne University Press, 1965.

La Nauze, J. A., 'Who Are the Fathers?', *Historical Studies*, vol. 13, no. 51, 1968.

La Nauze, J. A., 'A Little Bit of Lawyers' Language: The History of "Absolutely Free", 1890–1900', in A. W. Martin (ed.), *Essays in Australian Federation*, Melbourne University Press, 1969.

La Nauze, J. A. 'The Name of the Commonwealth of Australia', *Historical Studies*, vol. 15, no. 57, 1971.

La Nauze, J. A., *The Making of the Australian Constitution*, Melbourne University Press, 1972.

Latham, John, 'The Interpretation of the Constitution', in R. Else-Mitchell (ed.), *Essays on the Australian Constitution*, Sydney: Law Book Co., 1952.

Lesnoff, Michael, *Social Contract*, London: Macmillan, 1986.

Livingston, Kevin, 'Anticipating Federation: The Federalising of Telecommunications in Australia', *Australian Historical Studies*, vol. 26, April 1994.

Lovejoy, P. 'The Federal Convention: An Analysis of Voting', *Australian Journal of Politics and History*, vol. 18, no. 2, 1972.

McCorkingdale, Isabel (ed.), *Pioneer Pathways: Sixty Years of Citizenship*, Melbourne: WCTU, 1948.

McDonald, D. I., 'The Great and Long-looked for Day', *Canberra Historical Journal*, no. 24, September 1989.

Macintyre, Stuart, *Colonial Liberalism: The Lost World of Three Victorian Visionaries*, Melbourne: Oxford University Press, 1991.

Macintyre, Stuart, 'Corowa and the Voice of the People', *Canberra Historical Journal*, no. 33, March 1994.

McKenna, Mark, 'Tracking the Republic', in David Headon, et al. (eds), *Crown or Country: The Traditions of Australian Republicanism*, Sydney: Allen & Unwin, 1994.

Mackinnon, Alison, 'The State as an Agent of Demographic Change? The Higher Education of Women and Fertility Decline 1880–1930', in Renate Howe (ed.), *Women and the State: Australian Perspectives*, Melbourne: La Trobe University Press, 1993.

McLachlan, Noel, *Waiting for the Revolution*, Melbourne: Penguin, 1989.

McMinn, W. G., 'George Reid and Federation: The Origin of the "Yes-No" Policy', *Historical Studies*, vol. 10, no. 8, 1962.

McMinn, W. G., *George Reid*, Melbourne University Press, 1989.

McMinn, W. G., *Nationalism and Federalism in Australia*, Melbourne: Oxford University Press, 1994.

Madden, A. F., and Morris-Jones, W. H., *Australia and Britain: Studies in a Changing Relationship*, Sydney University Press, 1980.

Magarey, Susan, *Unbridling the Tongues of Women: A Biography of Catherine Helen Spence*, Sydney: Hale & Iremonger, 1985.

Magarey, Susan, Rowley, Sue, and Sheridan, Susan (eds), *Debutante Nation: Feminism Contests the 1890s*, Sydney: Allen & Unwin, 1993.

Markus, Andrew, *Fear and Hatred*, Sydney: Hale & Iremonger, 1979.

Martin, A. W. (ed.), *Essays in Australian Federation*, Melbourne University Press, 1969.

Martin, A. W., *Henry Parkes*, Melbourne University Press, 1980.

Meaney, N. (ed.), *Under New Heavens: Cultural Transmission and the Making of Australia*, Port Melbourne: Heinemann Educational, 1989.

Mordike, John, *An Army for a Nation*, Sydney: Allen & Unwin, 1992.

Murphy, D. J. (ed.), *Labor in Politics: The State Labor Parties in Australia, 1880–1920*, St Lucia: University of Queensland Press, 1975.

Norris, R., 'Economic Influences on the 1898 South Australian Federation Referendum', in A. W. Martin (ed.), *Essays in Australian Federation*, Melbourne University Press, 1969.

Norris, R., *The Emergent Commonwealth*, Melbourne University Press, 1975.

Oldfield, Audrey, *Woman Suffrage in Australia*, Cambridge University Press, 1992.

Palmer, Vance, *The Legend of the Nineties*, Melbourne University Press, 1963.

Parker, R. S., 'Australian Federation: The Influence of Economic Interests and Political Pressures', *Historical Studies*, vol. 4, no. 13, 1949.

Pearce, Vicki, ' "A Few Viragos on a Stump": The Womanhood Suffrage Campaign in Tasmania, 1880–1920', *Tasmanian Historical Research Association*, vol. 32, no. 4, December 1985.

Pettman, Janet, 'The Australian Natives' Association and Federation in South Australia', in A. W. Martin (ed.), *Essays in Australian Federation*, Melbourne University Press, 1969.

Price, C. A., *The Great White Walls Are Built: Restrictive Immigration to North America and Australia, 1830–1888*, Canberra: ANU Press, 1974.

Pringle, Rosemary, 'The 1897 Convention Elections in New South Wales: A Milestone?' *Journal of the Royal Australian Historical Society*, vol. 58, pt 3, 1972.

Pringle, Rosemary, 'Public Opinion in the Federal Referendum Campaigns in New South Wales, 1898–1899', *Journal of the Royal Australian Historical Society*, vol. 65, pt 4, 1979.

Quartly, Marian, 'Mothers and Fathers and Brothers and Sisters: The AWA and the ANA and Gendered Citizenship', in Renate Howe (ed.), *Women and the State: Australian Perspectives*, Melbourne: La Trobe University Press, 1993.

Reynolds, Henry, *Dispossession*, Sydney: Allen & Unwin, 1989.

Reynolds, John, *Edmund Barton*, Sydney: Angus & Robertson, 1948.

Reynolds, John, 'A. I. Clark's American Sympathies and His Influence on Australian Federation', *Australian Law Journal*, vol. 32, July 1958.

Rickard, John, *Australia: A Cultural History*, London: Longman, 1988.

Roberts, Jan, *Maybanke Anderson: Sex, Suffrage and Social Reform*, Sydney: Hale & Iremonger, 1993.

Roe, Jill, *Beyond Belief*, Kensington: University of New South Wales Press, 1986.

Said, Edward, *Orientalism*, London: Routledge & Kegan Paul, 1978.

252 Select Bibliography

Sawer, Geoffrey, 'The Australian Constitution and the Australian Aborigine', *Federal Law Review*, vol. 2, no. 17, 1966.

Sawer, Geoffrey, *Australian Federalism in the Courts*, Melbourne University Press, 1967.

Scott, Ernest, *A Short History of Australia*, Melbourne: Oxford University Press, 1916.

Scott, Ernest (ed.), *Australia*, vol. VII, part I, of the *Cambridge History of the British Empire*, Cambridge University Press, reprint 1988.

Serle, Geoffrey, *From Deserts the Prophets Come*, Melbourne: Heinemann, 1973.

Shaw, A. G. L., *The Story of Australia*, London: Faber & Faber, 1954.

Shortus, Stephen P., ' "Colonial Nationalism": New South Wales Identity in the mid-1880s', *Journal of the Royal Australian Historical Society*, vol. 59, pt 1, 1973.

Sinclair, Keith, 'Why New Zealanders Are Not Australians: New Zealand and the Australian Federation Movement, 1881–1901', in Keith Sinclair (ed.), *Tasman Relations: New Zealand and Australia, 1788–1988*, Auckland University Press, 1988.

Souter, Gavin, *A Peculiar People*, Sydney: Angus & Robertson, 1968.

Souter, Gavin, *Acts of Parliament*, Melbourne University Press, 1988.

Souter, Gavin, *Lion and Kangaroo: The Initiation of Australia*, Sydney: Sun Australia, 1992.

Stokes, Geoff (ed.), *Australian Political Ideas*, Kensington: University of New South Wales Press, 1994.

Stokes, Michael, 'Is the Constitution a Social Contract?', *Adelaide Law Review*, vol. 12, no. 3, 1990.

Swinfen, David B., *Imperial Appeal: The Debate on the Appeal to the Privy Council, 1833–1986*, Manchester University Press, 1987.

Thorpe, William, 'Archibald Meston and Aboriginal Legislation in Colonial Queensland', *Historical Studies*, vol. 21, no. 82, 1984.

Trainor, Luke, *British Imperialism and Australian Nationalism*, Cambridge University Press, 1994.

Wallace-Crabbe, Chris (ed.), *The Australian Nationalists*, Melbourne: Oxford University Press, 1971.

Ward, John M., 'The "Germ of Federation" in Australia', *Historical Studies*, vol. 4, no. 15, 1950.

Ward, Russel, *The Australian Legend*, 2nd edn, Melbourne, Oxford University Press, 1966.

White, Richard, *Inventing Australia*, Sydney: Allen & Unwin, 1981.

Willard, Myra, *The White Australia Policy*, Melbourne University Press, 1923.

Wood, F. L. W., 'Why did New Zealand Not Join the Australian Commonwealth in 1900–1901?', *New Zealand Journal of History*, vol. II, October 1968.

Wright, D. I., 'The Australasian Federation League in the Federal Movement in New South Wales, 1893–1899', *Journal of the Royal Australian Historical Society*, vol. 57, pt 1, 1971.

Wright, D. I., 'River Murray—A Continuing Debate', *Journal of the Royal Australian Historical Society*, vol. 61, pt 3, 1975.

Yarwood, A. T., and Knowling, M. J., *Race Relations in Australia: A History*, Sydney: Methuen Australia, 1982.

Index

Abbott, Joseph, 65, 87
Aborigines, 6, 11, 15–16, 96, 111–14, 116, 120, 124, 127–8
Ackerman, Jessie, 104, 106, 174
Adelaide Advertiser, 197, 198
Age, 13, 29, 53
Agnew, James, 32
America
  Civil War, 63, 69–70, 110, 146, 181, 183, 199, 201, 203
  Constitution, 58, 68, 69, 71, 74, 75, 86, 92, 95, 96, 157, 162, 167, 169, 198
  culture, 69, 71, 72, 75, 123, 163, 167, 219
  War of Independence, 37, 63, 69, 205
Americans, 12
Anderson, Benedict, 28
Anti-Billites, 5, 7, 45, 50, 100, 126, 197, 200, 219
  and Commonwealth Inauguration, 8, 16
  labour and socialist, 141, 147, 148, 165
  women, 28, 182, 184, 185, 187, 190
Archer, Edward, 90
Archibald, J. F., 19
Argus, 9, 10, 138, 208
art and Federation, 34–5, 131
Astley, William (Price Warung), 34, 41
Australian character, 35, 38, 72, 215
Australian Federalist, 132, 173, 186
Australian Natives' Association, 88, 91, 132, 134, 135, 145, 176
  'constitution' of 1890, 49
  and Federation, 124–7
Australian Star, 184
Australian 'type', 15, 72, 119–24, 131–3
Australian Woman, 176
Australische Zeitung, 12

Baker, Richard Chaffey, 65
Barlow, Andrew, 139
Barnett, Herbert, 136

Barton, Edmund, 5, 22, 27, 32, 57, 66, 77, 95, 106, 116, 146, 158, 161, 162, 186, 187, 189, 190, 198, 205
Barton, G. B., 142
Barton, Mrs (Jean), 187, 189, 190
Bathurst People's Federal Convention, 4, 28, 34, 66, 88, 108, 125, 126, 144–7, 152, 185
Bellamy, Edward, 39, 212
Bennett, Scott, 31
Bentham, Jeremy, 215
Besant, Annie, 122, 174
Bingara, 185
Bird, Bolton, 87
Black, George, 48–9
Blackmore, Edwin, 21
Blainey, Geoffrey, 214
Boer War, 10, 204
Boomerang, 41
'Braddon Blot', 165
Braddon, Edward, 59, 89, 168
Brisbane Courier, 44, 52, 141
Britain
  Colonial Office, 47, 50, 54, 83, 102, 203, 205–6
  constitution, 73, 75, 123, 132, 162, 204
  investment, 36, 205
  parliament, 203, 204, 206, 207, 209
  trade, 49, 115
British North America Act *see* Canada, Constitution
British 'type', 72–3, 101, 104
Broken Hill, 14
Brunker, James, 179
Bryce, James, 76, 122
Bulletin, 8, 9, 18, 20, 29, 33, 34, 35, 52, 109, 132, 147, 172, 188, 208
Byrnes, Thomas, 90, 140

Caldwell, George, 206–7
Cameron, Mary, 176
Canada, 12, 30, 63, 66
  Constitution (British North America

253

254   *Index*

Canada *cont.*
  Act), 47, 52, 64, 65, 66, 68, 69, 92,
    95, 96, 157, 205, 210
Carrington, Lord, 3, 140
Carruthers, Joseph, 93, 94, 161, 217
Chamberlain, 49, 115, 205
Champion, 163, 172, 178
Chinese
  in Australia, 12–13, 105, 117, 156, 157,
    164
  and citizenship, 156–7, 159, 162, 180
  Commissioners, 106
  immigration, 100–11
  labour, 104–5, 111, 118
Chinese Australian Herald, 12, 118
Churches, 20–1, 103, 166–7
citizenship, 13, 14, 15, 97, 126, 127
  and Aborigines, 112, 114, 116
  Convention debate, 156–70
  and race, 106–7, 108, 116, 117, 118,
    156–7, 159, 162, 180
  and women, 179, 180
civil aviation, 98
Clark, Andrew Inglis, 29, 70–1, 86, 89,
    103, 107, 110, 133
  draft constitution, 50, 51, 148
Clarke, J. W. R., 57, 98, 128–30
Clemens, Samuel (Mark Twain), 120
Clifford, John, 120
Clipper, 68
Cockburn, John, 64, 75, 83, 113, 152,
    162, 200, 217
Cole, E. W., 105
Collins, Hugh, 215
Colonial Laws Validity Act, 50, 97, 204,
    210
Commonwealth, 34
Commonwealth, name of, 32, 40, 76–8
Constitutional Commission 1985, 218
Consitutional Convention 1998, 218–19
Constitution Bill (1891), 66, 77, 134, 137,
    141, 148, 160, 179, 206
  compared to later Bill, 53–5, 68, 71,
    166, 192, 199, 202
  discussed at Bathurst, 126, 145
  discussed in Federal Council, 90, 91,
    139
  labour criticism of, 147
Corowa Conference, 4, 66, 125, 134–6,
    164
Corowa Free Press, 136
Corowa Plan, 135–8, 139–41, 144, 148,
    152
Courrier Australien, 9–10, 12, 17, 18, 21,
    22, 60
Cowan, Edith, 173
Crisp, L. F., 153
Crossley, Ada, 35

Cultural nationalism, 35, 40
Curtin Labor government, 217

Daily Telegraph, 45, 184
Dale, R. W., 48
Darley, Frederick, 21
Darville, Jane, 183
Dawn, 173
Deakin, Alfred, 7, 26, 30–1, 34, 61, 97,
    116, 144, 169, 170, 200, 219
  at 1890 Conference, 28, 75
  and Corowa Plan, 136, 138, 139
  and Federal Council, 82, 86, 88, 91, 132
  Federal Story, 136, 205
  at Inauguration, 21, 22, 23, 24
  Member of London delegation, 205–6
  and name of Commonwealth, 76, 77
  and women's suffrage, 148, 178
Deas Thomson, Edward, 2
de Brosse, Charles, 37
defence, 3, 59, 65, 79, 82–3, 85, 108,
    203, 204
de Foigny, Gabriel, 36
Depression (1890s), 36, 52
Derby, Lord, 35
Dibbs, George, 7, 32, 51–3, 66
Dickson, James, 22, 23, 88
divorce powers, 69, 92, 169
Dobson, Henry, 89, 95, 154, 159
Douglas, Adye, 89, 90, 178, 181
Douglas, Mary, 118
Downer, John, 68, 77, 93, 96, 150, 151,
    155
Drake, James, 88
Du Faur, Edward, 11
Dugdale, Henrietta, 38
Duke and Duchess of York, 10, 15, 118,
    204
dystopianism, 40–1, 57, 110

education, 122, 172
environmentalism, 57, 98, 125–31
Evans, James Essex, 58
Evening News, 185

Farnell, Frank, 129, 131
federal capital, 8, 55, 59–60
Federal Council of Australasia, 2, 3, 4,
    47, 82, 84–91, 95, 132, 139–41, 142
Federal Parliament (opening), 10, 204
Federation Conference (1890), 4, 27, 43,
    61–6, 70–2, 75, 79, 80, 82, 83, 86,
    103, 110, 112, 140
Federation Convention (1891), 4, 43, 47,
    49, 50, 51, 53, 71, 122, 148, 171,
    176, 199–200
Federation Convention (1897–98), 4, 39,
    43, 50, 53, 59, 67, 68, 69, 92, 94, 96,

113, 116, 130, 148–52, 158–61, 164,
166, 169, 171, 178, 179, 207
elections for, 177–8
Federation leagues, 134, 136, 138, 139,
140, 144, 145, 173, 185, 186, 187–8,
198
Fiji, 32, 85
fin de siècle, 36, 45, 172, 212
First World War, 81, 156, 165
foreign consuls, 13, 21, 23
Forrest, John, 22, 60, 77, 90, 95–6, 100,
141, 158–9, 208, 237, n71
Foundation Day, 126
France, 37
government, 91
franchise law, 97, 113, 127, 149, 180,
182
Fraser, John Foster, 121
Fraser, Simon, 178, 181
French community, 12, 21, 114
French, Major–General (George), 82
Froude, J. A., 39–40, 48, 120
Fysh, Philip, 102

Garran, Robert, 25, 34, 135–7, 146, 217
George, Henry, 39, 40, 106
Germans, 12, 67, 114
Germany, 35, 108, 115
constitution, 67, 95
Gillies, Duncan, 40, 148, 199
Glynn, Patrick, 69, 98, 151–2, 217
goldfields, 32, 69, 105, 106, 142, 164,
191, 197–8
Golding, Annie, 171, 183
Golding, Belle, 183, 185, 187, 188
Goldstein, Vida, 119, 174, 184
Gordon, John, 94
Governor–General (office), 54, 74, 83,
143
Grant, Charles, 181
Grey, Earl, 2
Grey, George, 77, 200
Griffith, Samuel, 22, 29, 34, 50, 51, 63,
71, 83–4, 87, 141, 169, 206

Hackett, John, 139
Hebrew Standard, 21
Henning, Andrew, 217
Henry, Juliette, 34, 185
Hickman, May, 183
Higgins, Henry, 96, 97, 116, 149, 155,
160, 162, 167, 168, 217
High Court, 46, 97, 160, 163, 205, 206,
213, 216
Holder, Frederick, 149, 178, 181
'Hopetoun Blunder', 5
Hopetoun, Lord, 5, 20, 21, 22, 23
Howard, John, 218

Howe, James, 68, 95
Hughes, W. M. (Billy), 145
Hummer, 78
Hutton, Major–General (Edward), 82

immigration
Act (1901), 80, 108, 115
acts, 108, 109, 156
policy, 82, 110, 115, 117
powers, 80, 114–15, 116
Imperial Federation, 29, 40, 83, 86, 87,
136–7
Inauguration of Commonwealth, 6–14,
28, 125, 127, 134, 162, 163, 194, 211
industrial arbitration powers, 51, 81,
95–6, 165, 169
intercolonial conferences, 88–9
1867, 2
1883, 3
1888, 101–2, 108
1896, 108
International Council of Women, 173
Irish community, 21
Isaacs, Isaac, 116, 150–1, 152, 155, 159,
162, 217
Italian community, 12

James, Walter, 184, 217
Japan, 12–13, 108, 110
Anglo–Japanese treaty, 108, 161
Jewish Community, 21
Joint Parliamentary Committee 1956, 218

Kalgoorlie Miner, 191
Kingston, Charles, 22, 89, 100, 117, 139,
149, 155, 159, 160, 178, 205
draft constitution, 50, 51, 96, 148
Knight, E. K., 9, 10
Knutsford, Lord, 101

Labor Party, 1, 33, 116, 143, 165, 213–14
labour
Council, 16, 18
and Federation, 54–5, 143, 147,
213–15
movement, 13, 16, 54, 104, 118, 145,
213–14
La Nauze, J. A., 76, 162
land settlement schemes, 42
Lane, William, 41–2, 110, 176, 202
'New Australia', 42–3, 61
Lang, John Dunmore, 49
Lawson, Henry, 48
Lawson, Louisa, 48, 173
Lecky, William, 76
Lee Steere, James, 89
Levvy, Frances, 185
Lewis, Neil, 22, 148, 217

256 *Index*

Lister Lister, William, 19
London delegation (1900), 5, 205
Long, Sidney, 19
Lowe, Annie, 38
Lucinda, 51, 53, 71
Lyne, William, 5, 16, 21, 22, 59, 88, 126, 146

McCubbin, Frederick, 34
Machattie, Thomas, 66, 145
Macintyre, Stuart, 138
Mackay, Kenneth, 110
MacLaurin, H. N., 16
McMillan, William, 65
McMinn, W. G., 35, 85, 153
Maiden, Joseph, 131
Markus, Andrew, 114
Marmion, William, 77
Martel, Nellie, 184
Maxwell, George, 179
Melba, Nellie, 35
Meston, Archibald, 16, 127
Métin, Albert, 122
Mill, John Stuart, 168, 215
Miller, Anna, 188
Moran, Cardinal, 20–1, 146
Mordike, John, 83
Munro, James, 76
Murray, David Christie, 48, 49, 58
Muskett, Philip, 123

National Council of Women, 173
National Defence League, 179
naturalisation law, 102, 107, 117, 156–8
Nelson, Hugh, 90, 141
New South Wales
    government, 109, 110, 134, 145, 204
    Native Flora Protection Bill, 129–31
    referendums, 152–3
New Zealand, 7, 30, 32, 43, 66–7, 82, 85, 96, 112–13, 121, 181, 202, 207
Nicholls, Elizabeth, 171, 174, 175, 194
Nordern, 12
Norris, R., 100
Northern Territory, 112, 113, 201, 216
Norton, John, 146

O'Connor, Richard, 94, 159, 160, 161
O'Malley, King, 157
Onslow, Madeleine, 194
O'Rell, Max, 120

Palmer, Vance, 33
Parker, R. S., 214
Parkes, Henry, 2, 3, 4, 27, 28, 34, 40, 50, 51, 98, 101, 103, 115, 124, 138–9, 140, 200

and Federal Council, 85, 86, 87, 88
Federation Conference, 1890, 61, 63, 64, 72, 75, 76
'Tenterfield Oration', 4, 48
Parsons, Langdon, 172
Patterson, James, 52, 66, 140, 164
Peacock, Alexander, 217
People and Collectivist, 188
petitions to Federal Convention, 56, 117, 128, 164, 166, 167, 179, 182
Philp, James, 118
Piddington, A. B., 69–70
Playford, Thomas, 28, 62, 63, 77, 86, 87
Portus, John, 11, 19
postal and telegraphic services, 81
    conferences, 82, 88
Preamble, 53, 55, 58, 166–7, 196, 201, 202, 204, 210
Premiers' Conference, Hobart, 1895, 4, 32, 82, 89, 137, 139–40, 144, 177
Premiers' 'Secret' Conference, 1899, 4, 46, 59, 141, 196
Privy Council, 26, 40, 50, 51, 56, 86, 115, 203, 205, 206
protectionism, 80, 126, 165

Queensland, 35, 42, 56, 67, 82, 107, 108, 141–2, 153, 201
    Aboriginals Protection Act, 127
Quick, John, 34, 44, 116, 135–9, 146, 158, 159, 160, 161, 163, 179, 209, 217
Quick and Garran, 92, 97, 135, 136, 137, 161, 166, 177, 200, 202–3, 209
Quong Tart, 105–7, 110, 117, 172

race power, 115–17
railways, 98, 201
Reeves, William Pember, 60
referendum, 4, 51, 68, 141, 148–52, 154, 155, 199, 200, 203, 210, 214
    1898, 59, 65, 69, 152–3, 154, 173, 185, 196, 206, 207
    1899, 67, 118, 142, 153, 154, 187, 188, 189, 190, 196
    1900, 5, 142, 153, 184, 190–1, 196
    1946, 93, 214
referendum questions, 218–19
Reid, George, 22–3, 82, 89, 117, 118, 138, 139, 143, 146, 182
Reid, Mrs (Flora), 187
religion and Federation, 55, 56, 92, 165–8
republicanism, 40, 42, 49, 54, 75–6, 208, 218
republicans, 33, 41, 48, 146, 207
Review of Reviews, 19, 153
Reynolds, Henry, 127

rights, debates about, 97, 102, 117, 127, 159–60, 162–8, 180, 183
Riverina, 134, 188, 189
rivers, 82, 98, 164
Roberts, Tom, 34
Robertson, Nugent, 40–1
Rosa, S. A., 41, 202
Ross, Andrew, 56–7, 130, 131
Royal Commission 1927, 216, 217
Russell, William, 66, 82, 112–13

Sandhurst, Lady, 177
Sawer, Geoffrey, 46
Scandinavian community, 12, 114
Scott, Rose, 28, 43, 61, 94, 175, 182–5, 187, 198, 201–2
Senate, design of, 70, 142, 147, 183, 202, 212
'Separation for Federation', 142, 191, 197
Service, James, 48, 80, 134
Sinclair, Keith, 67
Soudan, 204
Souter, Gavin, 6
South Australia, 94, 96, 98, 101, 113, 120, 145, 148, 156–7, 214
    women's suffrage, 149, 172, 174, 176, 177, 180
Spence, Catherine Helen, 38, 174, 177–8, 192
Sport, 35, 125
Stephens, James Brunton, 58
Streeton, Arthur, 34
Stroud's *Judicial Dictionary*, 161
suffrage (*see also* franchise law)
    campaigns, 93–4, 127–8, 158, 175, 176, 178–80, 181–2, 186, 194
    societies, 38, 93, 171–4, 179, 180, 182, 184–5, 186
Switzerland, 68
    constitution, 51, 68, 154
Sydney Mail, 10
Sydney Morning Herald, 8, 52, 106, 143, 163
Symon, Josiah, 60, 149, 159, 160, 169, 217

tariffs, 57, 80, 84, 118, 164–5, 201
Tasmania, 102, 129, 202, 173, 179
Taylor, Henry D'Esterre, 136–7
temperance (*see also* Woman's Christian Temperance Union) 59, 109, 142, 179, 201
Thynne, Andrew, 243
Tillett, Ben, 148
Tocsin, 55
Town and Country Journal, 19, 106
transportation, 37
treaties power, 54, 97, 98

Trenwith, William, 97, 116, 143, 149, 150, 182
Turner, George, 22, 60, 140

United Australia, 192–3
utilitarianism, 43, 168, 199, 215
Utopianism, 37–46, 49, 59, 61, 98, 110, 212–15

Vernon, Walter, 19
Victoria, 42, 53, 145, 162, 180, 188
    Melbourne Cup, 88
Victoria, Queen, 22, 23, 48, 77, 171, 180, 204, 207
    Golden Jubilee, 48, 208
    Diamond Jubilee, 8–9, 10, 49, 182, 207, 208

Walker, James Backhouse, 88, 202
Walker, James Thomas, 117
Wallace–Crabbe, Chris, 33
Ward, Elizabeth, 171
Ward, Russel, 33
Watson, J. C. (Chris), 130, 147
Way, Samuel, 45
Webb, Beatrice, 121–3, 174–5
Webb, Sidney, 121–3
welfare powers, 67, 93–5, 169, 183, 214
Wentworth, William, 2
West Australian, 65, 67, 83, 200, 207, 208
West, John, 178
Western Australia, 98, 141–2, 172, 190, 201, 203, 208
    secession movement, 209–10
White Australia, 36, 74, 100–18, 169, 215
Windeyer, Margaret, 173
Wise, Bernhard, 43, 150, 152, 181
Wise, Mrs Bernhard, 187
Wise, Walter, 50
Wolstenholme, Maybanke, 31, 173, 174, 186–7, 188, 189, 190, 198
Woman's Christian Temperance Union, 171–3, 177–8, 179, 184, 188, 191
Woman's Voice, 186–7
women, 93, 109, 121, 160
    and Federation, 145, 148–9, 165, 171–95
    journals, 173
    'New Woman', 172, 175
    organisations, 171–2, 173, 174, 194
Women's Federal Leagues
    Hay, 187–90
    Sydney, 185–7, 189
    Western Australia, 191
Worker, 60, 65, 69, 95, 166
Wright, John, 77

Zeal, William, 60, 151

For EU product safety concerns, contact us at Calle de José Abascal, 56–1º,
28003 Madrid, Spain or eugpsr@cambridge.org.

www.ingramcontent.com/pod-product-compliance
Ingram Content Group UK Ltd.
Pitfield, Milton Keynes, MK11 3LW, UK
UKHW020153060825
461487UK00017B/1388